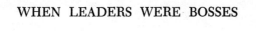

WHEN LEADERS WERE BOSSES

★★★ When Leaders Were Bosses

An Inside Look at
Political Machines and Politics

★★★ NOAL SOLOMON

EXPOSITION PRESS
HICKSVILLE, NEW YORK

To My Parents

Contents

Contents

Introduction

Most political bosses have faded into history, but the Democratic boss in Albany, New York, Daniel P. O'Connell, is still left. The late Speaker of the United States House of Representatives, Sam Rayburn, once said that "Albany is the citadel of democracy." Rayburn was referring to the powerful O'Connell machine. While the O'Connell machine may not be as well known as Tammany Hall, the power of Dan O'Connell has lasted longer than any one of the several Tammany leaders. The late Thomas E. Dewey, who served as a Republican Governor of New York and later ran for President, once compared Tammany Hall and the O'Connell machine. Dewey said "The Tammany braves are pikers by comparison with this [O'Connell] machine." Even so, no political machine could go on for more than fifty years unless the people approved it. As O'Connell said, the machine will go on for a long time as long as "the people are a part of it."

Dan O'Connell has survived through three generations, longer than any political boss ever to hold power. One faithful Democrat in Albany might say that "Uncle Dan has been good to my father and grandfather and now he's good to me." Today Dan O'Connell, or "Uncle Dan" as he is called by his friends, is old in age only. He has young ideas, a good sense of humor, a warm heart, and a good personality. While he is financially well off, he lives modestly and likes helping people. It is through helping people that he has been able to be in power for so many years. After all, he had to be doing something right. By serving himself, Dan O'Connell and other political bosses served the public good.

The rise of the welfare state has hurt machines. Unemployment insurance, Social Security, and welfare checks are doing what the ward leaders use to do. Today the buckets of coal and turkeys aren't appreciated very much. Civil service reform also cut down on patronage. The passage of time has seen the decline of political machines. And it seems that the once-powerful machines that are left, such as in Chicago and in Albany, won't last much longer, at the most maybe another ten years. As with other institutions, they have served their purpose. The era of bossism, as it was known, is coming to an end, and the time when political leaders were bosses will be over.

This book has not been an easy effort to complete. Much time and work were required for completion. It represents a comprehensive study of political machines and politics. Much of the information in the chapter on the O'Connell machine was obtained from numerous personal interviews with Uncle Dan himself. It was Dan O'Connell who suggested, about five years ago, that I write this book. The O'Connell machine is used as a basis for this book largely because of the writer's knowledge of Albany politics and his friendship with Dan O'Connell. The history of Tammany Hall is examined in detail because it represents the most well-known political machine in the United States, although the power of Tammany Hall, which made the machine famous, ended more than fifty years ago. Chapters on other political bosses, including Richard Daley and Huey Long, and others, are included to give a wider perspective to the reader and enhance his knowledge of politics and our governmental system.

Personal thanks are in order to the following individuals: Dan O'Connell, who has given me much valuable information about himself and others in the political arena; Dr. Robert L. Bock, a Professor of Government at Western New England College, who has read the manuscript and has offered his thoughtful suggestions; and Mrs. Clara Malone, my father's secretary, who typed the final draft of the manuscript.

I hope that the readers of this book will learn a great deal about political machines and politics. The material presented is something every American should be familiar with. Political machines have played an important part in the history of our country and have affected the lives of Americans since the Civil War. I hope you enjoy reading *When Leaders Were Bosses.*

WHEN LEADERS WERE BOSSES

★ 1 ★

The O'Connell Machine
of Albany

The prince must be a lion, but he must also know how to play the fox.

NICCOLÒ MACHIAVELLI

They "beat a pathway" to O'Connell's door. As Emerson said, men would beat a pathway to the door of the man who could make a better mousetrap than his neighbors. Only, Dan O'Connell and other political bosses dealt not in mousetraps but in politics. No matter where Dan O'Connell is, at his home in the city of Albany, New York, or at his summer home twenty minutes away in the country, his regular visitors and candidates seeking his support all come to him. Candidates for local, state, and national offices have come to see the Albany boss and are still coming. Robert Kennedy, Hugh Carey, Howard Samuels, Franklin D. Roosevelt, Jr., Frank O'Connor, Arthur Goldberg, George McGovern, Teddy Kennedy, Joe Kennedy, Robert Wagner, and many others. Those who can't pay a personal visit called him on the telephone.

They come for his support and help because the boss is the person who can get them elected or solve just about whatever problem they have. He can cut bureaucratic red tape, get someone a job or a government contract. In more ways than one, his power closely parallels that of a Mafia chieftain. The boss's organization is called a machine because it has the capability of performing as such in a contriving and semiautomatic manner. The secret of any successful political machine, like Tammany Hall and the O'Connell machines, is that the bosses know how to get power, hold on to it and exploit it for their own personal gain.

The rise of political machines across the country took place after the Civil War. Many voting restrictions, such as landownership, literacy tests, poll taxes, and residency and citizenship requirements, were eased, permitting more people to vote. It wasn't until 1920, when the Nineteenth Amendment to the Constitution was ratified, that women had the right to vote. William Barnes, the Republican boss who controlled Albany for more than twenty years until the O'Connells took over, was against women's suffrage, while the O'Connells and their ticket were for giving women the right to vote. Because of this, after women got the right to vote, most women voted Democratic.

Mass immigration was an important factor in the bosses' obtaining power. Dan O'Connell's grandparents came to Albany in 1850 from Ireland, just as many of the other Irish did. This was just after the

3

potato famine in Ireland (1845-1847). Hundreds of thousands of Irish came to America as a result of that famine. Because of the unsuccessful revolution of 1848 in Germany large numbers of Germans also came to America. Between 1850 and 1930, the time when most of the immigrants came to the United States, about 35 million people immigrated to this country. They came to the United States to improve their living conditions, to get better-paying jobs, and to escape religious persecution.

The immigrants settled mainly in large cities. They didn't have much money when they came to the United States. Many immigrants used up what little money they had in coming to America by ship in steerage class. After arriving in the United States the immigrants usually settled in areas with other immigrants from their previous country. They found that it wasn't easy to start life over again in a new country. They had difficulties adjusting to the different language, customs, and life-style in America. The cities soon became overpopulated and faced problems involving housing, sanitation, and the standard of living. Luckily for the immigrants, political machines got their start around the time of the Civil War and the ward leaders were able to help them during hard times. After the Civil War cities expanded rapidly, leaving more opportunities for corruption. Schools and hospitals were built, streets repaired, sewage systems put in, and other improvements were made. More government jobs were available for patronage.

Boss O'Connell once said the best patronage he ever had was to the old people, men who are retired. A job gives them independence and they live longer. They appreciate it and their family appreciates it. Many elderly men are employed in the park department. They mow lawns, rake leaves, weed the flower gardens, plant flowers, and sometimes just sit in the capitol park. "It costs the taxpayers less than welfare grants and it gives them dignity," says O'Connell.

As soon as the immigrant came to America the party (Tammany Hall in New York, the O'Connells in Albany, and others) helped him and his family get situated. The immigrant didn't know where to turn for help, so the party workers helped him and he was obligated to them. Even though there was public welfare for the needy, the immigrants and the other poor people didn't know this. Besides, local welfare departments have been operating only for the past fifty years. The immigrants thought the party was giving them help from their pockets like philanthropists. In many instances this was true. But even after welfare departments were in existence, it was as if the party were providing the assistance, because the caseworkers were mostly Democratic. The party did often go out of its way to help partisans in return for their vote. They made the immigrant feel he was important. Once in a while an immigrant was given an important position in the government through patronage. This was appreciated by the large families. The party helped the immigrants to get jobs, get their naturalization papers, and register to vote, and especially reminded them to vote on election day.

The organization, as a machine is called, distributed clothing, fuel, money, and food baskets among the needy. This was appreciated especially during hard times. When there was a fire, and if a family was burned out, the party would get them a place to stay, and get them clothes, food and whatever else they needed to get started again. So, by being charitable to the poor the Democratic Party became known as the party of the masses. The depressions of 1873, 1893, and 1929 were easily blamed on Republican presidential administrations, and the people voted the Democratic ticket, hoping for better times. The Democrats distributed food baskets and coal for the needy. In those days, you got a lot of food for your money. All this cost the organization money but it was well worth every penny. If you lived during the depression years you would feel the same way.

In New York during the turn of the century, three out of every four residents were either immigrants or the children of immigrants. The same is true for Albany. If an Italian ran for public office all the Italians would vote for him. Most people voted for their own kind. Many American-born children of immigrant parents were made ward leaders and committeemen to make them feel important and bring out the vote of their ethnic groups. They were hard workers also. They knew that if the vote went Democratic they would be rewarded. The ward leaders were a symbol of power to the immigrants. They were in a position to help the immigrant families in a time when they needed help. The families showed their gratitude by supporting the party, year after year without question, on election day. Thus, balanced tickets on ethnic and religious lines have helped the O'Connell organization to some degree in recent years. The candidates, for the most part, have been socially acceptable, qualified, well-educated candidates for major offices.

Most of the leaders of Tammany Hall, as well as the O'Connells, came from average, middle-class families. They worked hard helping, O'Connell says, "the rank and file of New York—the poor people." They helped the immigrants who were coming in a hundred thousand at a time. If someone needed help in New York City he went to one of the clubhouses operated by Tammany Hall. The party workers were at the clubhouses to help the residents of the neighborhood. Albany never had a Democratic clubhouse or hangout where the people went for help. In the neighborhoods the ward leaders did favors for the residents. Some people went directly to Democratic headquarters (now located at 75 State Street in the State Bank of Albany building) to get favors.

O'Connell says, "We had leaders in every district and every ward" to help the people. He adds, "A smaller city is closer together," so clubs were never needed in Albany.

Mr. O'Connell says the ward leaders "did anything that they could. If someone needed anything they got it for them if they could." There have been accusations that votes are sometimes bought for five dollars by Democratic workers. But grand juries, even under a Republican district attorney, have never brought an indictment. Nothing has ever been proven that the Democrats in Albany had bought votes or stuffed ballot boxes. (There used to be ballot boxes instead of voting machines, as are now common, and election fraud was easier then.) "I never bought votes," O'Connell says. "All I did was help people during the year." The party workers "were always supplied with money for that purpose."

Because of the high voter turnout, there has been speculation that the Albany Democrats stuffed ballot boxes. Charges have also been made that absentee ballots, if written in pencil, were changed. O'Connell denies that such illegal tactics ever took place. The voter turnout in Albany has been high because of the party organization. The ward workers see to it that voters register and cast their ballot on election day. If they can't walk or drive to the polls themselves, a ward worker will pick them up at their homes so that they can vote.

The Albany Democratic organization consists of around five hundred party workers, who come from all walks of life and whose principal duty is to bring out the Democratic vote on election day. These workers, committeemen and ward leaders, volunteer their services to the party with the hope of being rewarded in the future. The committeemen are the largest part of a political organization. It is their responsibility to register the voters in their district, get to know them, remind them to vote, and work at the polls on election day. Postcards are often sent to voters reminding them to vote and whom to vote for. On election day, party workers offer rides to those voters who don't have a car and can't walk to the polling place. At the polling places, committeemen offer candy and cigars to voters. Committeemen are at the bottom of the political ladder but they play an important part. Someone who wants to become involved in politics will most likely first become a committeeman.

It is the responsibility of the ward leaders to organize and direct the activities of the committeemen. There are only about thirty ward leaders in Albany, compared with around four hundred committeemen. A hard-working committeeman might be promoted to a ward leader if a vacancy existed. Neither committeemen nor ward leaders are paid, full-time positions. Naturally, a ward leader has more influence than a committeeman. While the committeemen report to the ward leaders, the ward leaders report to the executive secretary of the party. The executive secretary in Albany, now Jimmy Ryan, is the person who is in charge of Democratic headquarters. His position is a full-time one, although it is not uncommon for the executive secretary to have outside business interests. The executive secretary is normally in headquarters, Monday through Friday, from about 9:30 A.M. to 12:30 P.M. In the afternoon, he usually meets with Dan O'Connell for an hour or two. The executive secretary does most of the legwork for O'Connell. He makes most necessary calls to get someone a job, get a ticket fixed, get someone's taxes reduced. He gives patronage to the ward leaders, who in turn give patronage to committeemen, and the committeemen in turn to the voters. If a voter wants a favor from the party, protocol is for him to turn to his committeeman. However, many people go directly to party headquarters. Albany's Democratic headquarters has a better record of finding jobs for people than most professional employment services, and accordingly many people go to "headquarters" to get jobs. If a voter wants a favor from a committeeman, the committeeman will go up the ladder to handle the situation, unless the matter is one that the committeeman can handle himself. Everyone in the organization knows his responsibility. Because the political organization runs smoothly, it is labeled a machine. And like other machines, political machines have been known to break down. The O'Connell machine, like the Daley machine, is composed of a tightly knit organization. Tammany Hall used to be the same way.

Every Saturday night O'Connell walked from the Elks Club on State Street to Fourth Avenue and Pearl Street. On the way, people would buttonhole him. They would stop Dan and ask him for five or ten dollars or more. They usually never paid him back his money, but Dan didn't mind, because they voted Democratic. Dan has been charitable all his life. He has given a lot of money to the churches in Albany. Dan has always been a friendly person with a sympathetic ear. If he doesn't like someone, which is rare, he will most likely keep his thoughts to himself. Anyone who wants to see him can do so without much difficulty. He has made himself available and welcomed people he never met before. While some political leaders today are independent and are difficult to see, this is not the case with Dan O'Connell. One of the things the O'Connells provided Albany with was a municipal golf course where golfers could play at a low cost. In fact, the greens fee is probably less than any place in the United States, only $1 on a week day or $20 for a season's pass. Golfers, young and old, beginners and advanced, enjoy the course. Even though it is somewhat hilly and the fairways and greens are not as plush as one might find at a country club, for the golfer it's a bargain. There was even a bookie on the premises for a long time. For many years, you could even place a bet in the state capitol building as well.

Most of the political bosses didn't have much of an education. They were rugged individuals who worked hard to obtain their leadership position. Politics was a way of life for the bosses. It was all they usually knew. But they were professionals at what they did for a living. This is one reason why reformers usually never succeeded in politics. Reformers are only amateurs. O'Connell calls reformers "busybodies." George Washington Plunkitt referred to reformers as "morning glories." They "looked lovely in the morning and withered up in a short time, while the regular machines went on flourishing forever, like fine old oaks." Plunkitt said, "Politics is as much a regular business as the grocery or the drug business." He added, "If you're not trained, you're sure to fail."[1]

Most bosses try to avoid publicity. They usually never make public speeches. The bosses don't usually give away the secrets of their trade. Boss O'Connell has never liked to be interviewed because he thinks this is bad business. It ruined Kansas City boss Thomas Pendergast and Memphis boss Ed Crump. No publicity is good publicity for the bosses. An interview requires the boss to put himself on record as saying something, unless, of course, he is evasive or refuses comment. The boss does not usually like to commit himself to a candidate until the last moment. Such a position gives the boss the flexibility he desires.

DANIEL PETER O'CONNELL

Daniel Peter O'Connell was one of the five children of John and Margaret O'Connell. Dan was born on November 13, 1885, on O'Connell Street and Second Avenue in Albany, New York. He had three brothers and one sister: John J. ("Solly"), Patrick H. ("Packy"), Edward J., and Maude. Dan's grandfather, John O'Connell, Sr., came to Albany in 1850 from the southwest part of Ireland, and went into farming around O'Connell Street and Second Avenue. "Old Red John," Dan's grandfather, "had a lot of money and went broke." He, Maude, and Packy had red hair. Dan's grandfather died in 1896. His grandmother, Margaret Dempsey O'Connell, died ten years later in 1906.

Both Dan's father and grandfather were Republicans. Dan's father ran for coroner on the Republican ticket in the year Dan was born, but he lost. It was the only time he ever ran for public office. Dan says his father was never a Democrat but he wasn't angry when Dan became a Democrat: "He never mentioned it to me." Dan's father supported him when he ran for assessor in 1919. Originally Dan's father was a Democrat, but "there was some fellow (a Democrat) beat for mayor that they thought was robbed and that's what made them Republicans," Dan says. He notes, "At that time there would be three or four Democrats running for everything." Dan admired his parents. He says his mother and father were always very agreeable and pleasant.

Dan's father was a farmer. He sold land but later went broke. About forty streets near O'Connell Street were named by Dan's father. There used to be much farmland in Albany around O'Connell Street in the South End and the residential neighborhood of what is now uptown Albany (off New Scotland Avenue). It is hard to imagine that there was so much farmland because today there are few vacant lots available in the city to build on. Dan says he liked farming, and if it wasn't for politics he might be a farmer today.

Dan's father went into the saloon business at 379 South Pearl Street after he got married. They lived over the saloon. He had to do so in order to support his family. "I always believed he should never have gotten into the saloon business," Dan says. Dan first helped out in his father's tavern when he was about eighteen, and he tended bar for several years until he went into the navy. In doing this Dan got to know all the people in the neighborhood. His associations helped him when he got control of the party. There were many German families living in the South End, where Dan lived. Mary Marcy's family was one of them. Dan later made her vice-chairman of the party. Mary is the same age as Dan. Before she moved to Albany she lived in Troy, where she worked in a saloon and met her husband, Will, there.

Both Dan and his father learned to speak German. Dan's father "spoke German as fluently as anybody in Albany." Dan once said his parents had a housekeeper who "couldn't speak a word of English and my mother was the only one in the house who couldn't understand her." He laughed after he said that. Dan used to speak German, but, he says, "you forget it after you're away from it for a while." They spoke German in Dan's father's saloon.

Dan says there never was a woman in his father's saloon. It wasn't common for women to visit bars then. As Dan remarks, "You wouldn't see a woman in any saloon outside of some whore." The saloons were where party workers and leaders would meet, drink, and swap stories. In Albany, where there weren't any political clubhouses, the saloons were a popular meeting place and a place to recruit party members. The bosses were able to meet in the back rooms of the saloons when they needed to discuss politics privately. When the Eighteenth Amendment was ratified the saloons were put out of business, and, in many places clubhouses were established as a replacement. But clubhouses weren't needed in Albany, which has a smaller population than New York City.

Doyle was Dan's mother's name. Her father, Patty Doyle, was a policeman. Dan's mother and father were neighbors on Second Avenue before they were married. Dan never really liked school. Although he used to miss his classes sometimes, Dan says old Pete Hagerdorne, the truant officer, never bothered him. Dan left school after the sixth grade.

Dan says, "Dave Cook married Annie O'Connell and they had a bakery in Watervliet and Troy. I wanted to get out of school so I went to work in their bakery shop." It was Dan's first job. He says he was paid about four or five dollars a week then. Dan also worked in the baking business of John W. Hard, a former sheriff, in Watervliet.

Although Dan didn't have much of a formal education, he is an avid reader of English literature and American history. He likes the Dickens and Thackeray stories, especially Thackeray's *Vanity Fair*. He is an expert on the Civil War. Dan became interested in the Civil War because, he says, "you are always interested in your own wars" and the Civil War was fought on American territory. Dan says Grant was a great soldier. He mentions that "the South made a hell of a fight with what they had down there." But as with other Northerners Dan is on the side of the Union Army.

Dan says his brothers "were very close with one another. Ed and I were very close together. We were together most of the time. Solly was always on his own." His sister Maude was "very busy" as a school teacher. Dan says she liked teaching. She never married. Dan's brother Ed was his only brother to go to college, although his parents could afford to send all of their children. Dan's sister went to a teacher's school. Dan says his family was "very, very close." All the O'Connells were tall men, very handsome, blue eyes with an Irish twinkle and a coy smile. Ed was a lawyer. Solly ran a saloon and restaurant on Broadway. He was a sportsman and tried to open a gambling house. Solly was always a Republican and was the Republican district leader in the same district where Dan was a Democratic district leader. Dan says he wasn't much of a rival because "he was just looking out for himself." Solly was later indicted, never convicted, because, as Dan says, "he was a common gambler." Solly naturally voted Democratic after the O'Connells took control. He was very popular with the "sporting element" and was gracious with his favors to them.

Patrick H. O'Connell, one of Dan's other brothers, was clerk of the State Senate. He served as clerk only for about six months, because he died suddenly, at age fifty-four, on June 22, 1933, after he suffered a stroke while driving to his summer home in the Helderbergs after playing a round of golf at Wolfert Roost Country Club, the country club that Dan still belongs to. Packy was president of the first ward in Albany. He was married and had one daughter.

Dan had a "very happy childhood." He was never bored. To keep active Dan "did what any other kid did." He used to hunt and fish mostly. While a youngster he used to play pitch. In the summer he went swimming in the Normanskill Creek. He played football for about twelve years and his team was never beaten. Dan played any position he wanted to because "I was the boss," he proudly says. He was the team's captain, and was very popular.

Dan liked cockfights (chicken-fighting). He says, "I beat a fellow out of $65,000 one night fighting chickens." At one time Dan had about a hundred cocks. Dan took care of his chickens over in the parking lot at First Avenue and Pearl Street in Albany. He had some fine game-cocks and he would fight them as far south as Florida for big money. He got interested in chickens when his father had a farm. Dan used to go to Florida about four or five times a year to fight his chickens. Chicken-fighting used to be a big sport in Albany but because of its cruelty to animals it was outlawed. Dan says there is chicken-fighting in Mississippi today. He never cared for gambling on horse races or investing in the stock market. He had some opportunities to make some money through stock but passed them up.

Dan was twenty-seven when his father died at age sixty-three. His mother had died, age fifty-nine, from cancer the year before, in 1913. Dan has always lived modestly. He was born on O'Connell Street and Second Avenue, Albany. Today Dan has two homes: one in the city on the corner of Holmes Court and Whitehall Road, where he has lived since 1927, and one in the Helderbergs on Beaver Dam Road in the town of New Scotland, which he built in the same year. Dan moves to the "country," in the Helderberg Mountains, in early June and moves back to the city around election day. It is nice at his country home in the summer. When it is hot in the city, it is usually comfortable and cool because of the mountain breezes. He has a swimming pool at his home in the mountains. He built the pool for fire protection. Dan can look out of his back window, in his Helderberg Mountain home, and see all of Albany and miles around because of the elevation. It certainly is a magnificent sight.

Dan never went out much when he was single. He never had any steady girl friends other than his wife, the former Leta Burnside. She didn't mind Dan being in politics. Dan says, "She never knew nothing else. She was a young kid when I started going with her." He says she never gave him any advice on politics. She didn't mind so many people visiting Dan, unlike Bess Truman, who disapproved of people visiting the President. Dan was a good husband. He was neat and clean, and wasn't difficult to please. He had known his wife "ever since she was a kid." She was six years younger than Dan. He married her on December 5, 1927. They had a small wedding. Dan said that his brother Ed didn't even know when he was getting married. Marie Lynch, the former Marie Burnside, who is Dan's niece through marriage, was raised by Dan and Mrs. O'Connell. Marie, or "Tootsie" as she was called by Dan, went on the honeymoon. He says he thought nothing about having her along. The future Mrs. O'Connell lived next door to Dan on Broad Street before they got married. She died in 1963, age seventy, from cancer. The O'Connells have a family burial plot at St. Agnes Cemetery.

When Dan isn't reading or talking to visitors, he watches his color television. He likes to watch the ball games, especially baseball. In the afternoon he usually takes a ride with Jimmy Ryan, a leader in the party, for about an hour or so. They drive near the waterworks and other favorite spots. Dan used to have a big black Cadillac and a chauffeur. Mayor Corning visits Dan about two or three times a week. Dan's barber, who was arrested for bookmaking a few years ago, comes to his home once a week to give him a shave and haircut. Dan hasn't eaten in a restaurant, except when he went to Florida, in more than forty years. He always has dinner at home. There are some people who visit Dan at a regular time every week, including the writer's family. Many others visit on a more infrequent basis. Dan owned a furniture storage company on the corner of South Pearl Street and Fourth Avenue for about twenty years (around 1925-1945). His partner was John Barry, an undertaker in Albany. For a while, Democratic headquarters was also located in that building. Dan made most of his money from owning Hederick's Brewery. He bought Hederick's because the people who owned the brewery went broke from Prohibition. The owner was a bookie. Dan loaned him money and took over the brewery. Hederick's flourished when Prohibition was repealed. Those taverns that sold Hederick's didn't have to worry about curfews. Hederick was the one beer to have in Albany. Dan ran Hederick's for thirty-five years. There wasn't a bar or store in Albany that didn't sell his beer. When he sold the brewery about ten years ago he made a lot of money.

As with most political bosses, Dan O'Connell's wealth could not easily be tabulated. It is likely that, at one time, he was worth at least a couple of million dollars. However, he gave much of it away to relatives, charities, and others. Uncle Dan never spent much on himself, and always lived modestly. He admits giving relatives, including nieces and nephews, cars and large amounts of cash, but most of this wasn't appreciated afterwards. Dan doesn't see too much of his nieces and nephews, except the two Lynch daughters. He said he gave one of his relatives $20,000 to buy a house a few years ago.

In the early part of this century, Albany was considered a wide-open city on gambling. Slot machines were all over and horse rooms flourished. But Dan did not share in the "take." This was strictly for the ward leaders and party loyalists who made a lot of money this way. Dan says Paul Carrol, a friend of his, owned slot machines in Albany. Dan admits that there were slot machines all around Albany, and that they produced much revenue. However, Dan says, "I never got a quarter from them. I never wanted to." Today Carrol has parking lots in Albany that he got for very little money. Dan says Carrol "always liked to make money." Who doesn't?

In December, 1971, Dan fell in his home on Whitehall Road and broke his hip. He was admitted to St. Peters Hospital, where he stayed for a few weeks. For a while he didn't look too good because he developed a respiratory disease but later he recuperated. However, he still uses a walker to get around his home by himself. Someone fixes his meals and cleans the house. He has a special chair, and when he touches a button the seat moves up and down. He was a heavy smoker of cigarettes and cigars but quit smoking after he got sick. He never wanted to smoke again, and he didn't for a couple of years, but he started to at a more moderate pace. When he was sick he had private nurses around the clock while in the hospital and at home. It cost him a lot of money in salaries and they took plenty from him. One of his nurses asked him for a down payment for a house. He gave it to her. He got rid of the nurses after almost a year and a half because of the financial drain, but now has a maid with him during the daytime.

Dan's mother went to mass every morning at St. Ann's Roman Catholic Church at Fourth Avenue and Franklin Street, just two blocks from where they used to live. Dan's parents were married at St. Ann's, and Father Doran baptized Dan there. Dan always went to church every Sunday but since he broke his hip and can't get around too well he hasn't been attending services. Also, he hasn't been attending the biannual meetings of the party since he broke his hip, because he doesn't like to be seen in public in his condition.

The biannual meetings of the Democratic organization are short and without opposition and argument. The meetings usually last no longer than ten minutes or so. All the committeemen, judges, party faithfuls, and leaders of the party attend the meeting. People from all walks of life get together and participate in the democratic process of nominating their party's candidates for election and taking care of regular party business. The meeting is called to order by the chairman (at the recent meetings the mayor has assumed that role). Then the secretary calls the role of the committee members. Because the list is so long someone usually makes a motion to do away with calling the roll. In 1964 there were 510 committeemen. The nominations are made next. A preselected person in the room nominates the candidates. "I nominate Erastus Corning for Mayor." The chair asks for someone to second the nomination according to Roberts' Rules of Order. Several people usually yell loudly "second." The chair says the motion was duly made and seconded. The chair then asks for all those in favor of nominating the candidate for the office. Knowing that the name presented for nomination has been approved by Uncle Dan, everyone respectfully yells "yea." The chair then dutifully announces that the motion has passed. A nonpartisan observer might notice that the chair forgot to ask if anyone was opposed to the nomination. Tammany's Boss Tweed also used to forget to call for the negative vote when he wished to have something determined in his favor. Even if the chair asked if anyone was opposed the room would most likely be so quiet that you could hear a pin drop. No one would dare ever think of opposing the boss. In recent years there have been a couple of times when some of the younger Democrats would raise a question. In going against the grain these people were cutting their own throats. All the candidates are selected prior to the nominating meetings by Uncle Dan and other higher-ups in the party.

At the meetings Dan always stood in the rear of the room. He rarely sat down to listen to the proceedings. He didn't have to because he knew before the meeting what would be said. In that spot, year after year, party faithfuls would greet their leader. As the television cameras would focus on Dan, those nearby would get close to Dan so that they would be seen on television near the most important person in Albany for more than fifty years. Next to being invited to a presidential inaugural ball, it was quite an honor. Many of the people who attended the meetings rarely saw Dan except when he would go to church or the party meetings. Not everybody had the privilege to be welcomed into Dan's house, so at the meetings they all made it their business to greet Dan to let him know that they still existed and that they were faithful Democrats. It was clear at all meetings that the center of attraction wasn't the party's business proceedings but Dan O'Connell himself.

In the winter Dan use to drive down to Miami Beach but he hasn't done that in the past four years because of his difficulty walking. He never went to Ireland and didn't do much traveling because his wife never liked to travel. O'Connell went to Miami Beach because the climate was good. While there he stayed at the Colonial Inn Motel. Dan says, "I'd rather be with the people I knew" than travel.

Why do people work for the party? They hope to be rewarded with jobs, handouts, friendship, and status, and be remembered in wills. Sometimes it takes many years of dedication to get even a "nominal" reward. Others may wait a lifetime without getting what they want. It's a matter of luck and being around at the right time to get what you want. Up until about five years ago in Albany you didn't have to worry about being elected because all Democrats on the ballot won. Sometimes you have to wait until someone dies or retires for you to fill their position. If your name was "O'Connell" or "O'Rourke," "Devine," or any other Irish name, your chances of getting what you want were greater than if you came from another ethnic group.

Sol Reubenstein, George Meyers, Sam Jacobs, Sam Rosenstock, Harold Segal, and Dave Wanger were Jewish City Court judges. Outside of those patronizing minor judgeships there have been few other Jews to hold high city or county offices in Albany in the last fifty or more years. It's the luck of the Irish. In the past few years Dan O'Connell has felt that a Jew is the best candidate. The reason he feels this way is that Arnold Proskin, a Republican and also Jewish, was elected district attorney in 1968. However, he won not because he was Jewish but because the people in Albany were tired of the machine candidates and wanted a change.

The Negro voters in Albany were among the most loyal Democrats. In exchange for a job and favors now and then the black voters vote the straight Democratic ticket. The lower income wards in Albany are more heavily Democratic than the higher income, upper-middle-class wards. One patronizing county legislator's job went to Homer Perkins, a black man. It was for appearance' sake more than anything else. One well-known politician in Albany said, "We even have a nigger on the slate" because of the reform rules in selecting delegates to the 1972 Democratic National Convention. The role of the black person in politics has been limited, just like any other minority group. In 1974, two highly respected members of Albany's black community, one a priest and the other a funeral home director, wanted to run for the school board, but the Albany Democratic machine did not support them, and they lost the election. While about 35 percent of the student body in Albany public schools is black, there is not one black person on the seven-member school board.

A few years ago when Albany firemen wanted to unionize and get a pay increase, O'Connell publicly called the firemen's chaplain, an Italian Catholic priest, a "Dago son of a bitch." That remark irritated many Italians and Catholics in Albany. Albany police and firemen were able to form unions within the past few years despite opposition from the Albany Democratic organization. Until recent years, anyone could be hired in the police and fire departments at the say-so of Democratic headquarters; the same was true for promotions. Some firemen and policemen were told if they were against unionization, they would be promoted.

Among the things a person first learns in politics are that "you fill your own pockets first," "you get what you can when you can get it because you might not have another opportunity," and "one hand washes the other." The faster you learn in politics, the better off you'll be, because mistakes are often costly. When Dan O'Connell was campaigning for assessor in 1919, and in the first few years after he got control, the Democrats had several large ads in the local newspapers prior to election day. The newspapers attacked the Barnes machine in 1919 and supported the Democratic ticket after O'Connell got control. Times have changed since then. There have been accusations of vote fraud and corrupt government. In the past ten years the newspapers have been supporting Republican candidates in an effort to help get rid of the O'Connell machine. The machine that was once supported in the newspapers is now criticized. Understandably, O'Connell doesn't like the local newspapers.

Would things be better if there was a change in party in power?

Not likely. In all reality things might be worse, especially considering the Republicans who would take over.

WILLIAM BARNES

William F. Barnes, Jr., was the Republican boss who controlled Albany for about twenty years until the O'Connells got power in 1919. Barnes was as strong in his day as Dan O'Connell was in his. Barnes once boasted of a letter from a Republican President asking him if it was all right for him to run for a second term. Boss Barnes was the grandson of Thurlow Weed (1797-1882), a newspaper editor and politician who was active in New York and national politics first with the Whig Party and then as a founder of the Republican Party. Both Barnes and Weed were shrewd and distinguished politicians, but they were unscrupulous in their political dealings. They both believed that to the victor goes the spoils.

William Barnes was born on November 17, 1866, in Albany. After he graduated from Harvard College in 1888 he became the owner and editor of the *Albany Evening Journal,* the forerunner of the *Albany Knickerbocker News,* which had been founded by his grandfather. The newspaper helped Barnes get power. While the *Times Union* attacked Barnes, the *Albany Evening Journal* praised Barnes and his efforts. The editor and publisher of the *Times Union* during the Barnes era and the early years of the O'Connell takeover was Martin H. Glynn. Glynn was a Democratic congressman, state comptroller, lieutenant governor, and governor. The newspapers then were biased and supported their partisan goals throughout the papers, not only on the editorial pages.

In 1892 Barnes became a member of the Republican State Committee. He got control of the Republican Party because the Republicans were unorganized and divided; and because the Democrats were split between McCabe and Herrick, Barnes was able to get control of the city. Barnes's power grew stronger year after year. Because he wasn't even twenty-five years old when he got power, Barnes was called "the boy leader." Like his grandfather, he was a president-maker and a governor-maker. At the Republican National Convention in 1912 Barnes helped Taft get renominated and was against the nomination of Theodore Roosevelt. That defeat drove Roosevelt from the Republican Party, and he started the Bull Moose party, which led to the election of Woodrow Wilson, a Democrat, as President. During the campaign of 1912, Roosevelt spoke of "Boss Barnes of Albany," as "a corrupt boss." Barnes brought suit for libel, and although no damages were awarded to Barnes, Roosevelt was required to pay the court costs. No one said the courts are perfect and they don't make mistakes! Barnes was divorced from his first wife, Grace Davis, of Cincinnati, in 1922 and the following year he was married to Maude Fiero Battershall. His second wife died a year before he died.

Barnes was a United States surveyor of customs from 1899 to 1911. He was Republican state chairman from 1911 to 1914, and a national committeeman from 1912 to 1916. He never bought any votes, according to Dan O'Connell. O'Connell says, "That was a lot of talk. I was in the poorest district in Albany for thirty years and I never saw a vote bought." He was liberal with money for rent and coal. O'Connell adds, "He was quite a fellow—everybody liked him."

The Bayne Legislative Investigating Committee described Boss Barnes in the following manner: "He testified before us that he had taken an active part in politics from early life, and that he had entered upon this career 'for the purpose of obtaining honest elections in Albany and elevating politics.' We regret to say that the evidence before us showed that Mr. Barnes's efforts in these particulars had resulted in dismal failure. Elections are not honest in Albany, and politics are not elevated. The most conspicuous beneficiary of graft, public extravagance and raiding the municipal treasury, we find from the evidence, to be Mr. William Barnes, Jr., himself, as the owner of the majority of the stock of the Journal Company."[2]

Boss Barnes broke with the Chief Justice Charles Evans Hughes shortly after Hughes was elected governor. Barnes criticized Hughes for his appointments and called him "the representative of an effete oligarchy." Barnes also broke with former Governor Charles S. Whitman after Whitman was elected, although Barnes got him the nomination in 1914. Barnes helped get James W. Wadsworth, Jr., elected United States Senator. In 1920 he was one of the little group of men who sat in a Chicago hotel room and got Warren G. Harding the presidential nomination. In the same year, however, after Dan O'Connell was elected assessor, which was a sign that Barnes's power was slipping, Barnes failed to get State Senator Henry M. Sage of Albany nominated for governor.

In February, 1925, Barnes sold the *Albany Evening Journal* to the *Evening News,* which had been started in 1922 and was controlled by Stephen Clark of Cooperstown, a son of Corning Clark, who made a fortune in the manufacture of the Singer sewing machine. After Barnes relinquished control in Albany, younger Republicans took over the party, and "the old guard" dropped into the background. George W. Greene was county chairman for a while, until Barnes's followers backed Judge Isadore Bookstein, a Barnes man. After Barnes sold his newspaper, he retired to Mount Kisco, in Westchester County, where he died on June 25, 1930, of pneumonia at age sixty-four. In an article following Barnes's death, on July 3, 1930, the *New York Times* said that "the fortune which Barnes was believed to have amassed during his years in political power is not revealed in papers filed here with the will today." The newspaper added that "over $5,000" was the noncommittal value placed on the estate in the petition for probate. Barnes's two sons and three grandsons shared the bulk of the estate, which consisted of personal property that was auctioned.

Barnes himself never made much money through politics, according to Dan O'Connell. It was his friends and political associates who made plenty. Before O'Connell was elected assessor there was a coal scandal in Albany, and Barnes was accused by the newspapers of stealing coal. O'Connell says that Barnes was falsely accused of his part in the scandal. Dan says that he loaned Barnes $10,000 after Barnes lost power. He said Barnes paid the money back to him. Charges of corruption, a coal scandal, Barnes being against Prohibition, the women getting the right to vote, and Dan O'Connell all led to the decline of William Barnes.

FROM THE BEGINNING

"When McCabe and Herrick got quarreling over the Democratic Party," according to Dan O'Connell, "McCabe made an agreement with Barnes and they agreed to elect a bipartisan mayor and split the patronage for six years. Two years after, McCabe thought he could win it all, so he broke the agreement. He had Emasa Parker run for mayor but he lost, and there wasn't a Democrat elected" until O'Connell won in 1919. Parker, a lawyer, was Mayor Corning's uncle. O'Connell said he used to ride a horse every day and he was popular.

Judge D-Cady Herrick was the Democratic leader in Albany before McCabe. Judge Herrick was a well-known lawyer. While at Albany Law School, he was a classmate of William McKinley. In 1880 Herrick was elected district attorney of Albany County, and was reelected in 1883. In 1885 he resigned as district attorney to accept the appointment of corporation counsel of the city of Albany. He was elected justice of the Supreme Court in 1891. In 1895 Judge Herrick was designated an associate justice of the appellate division of the Supreme Court. He ran for governor on the Democratic ticket in 1904 but was defeated by Frank W. Higgins. In 1885 he became a state committeeman and Democratic county leader. Judge Herrick had an accident when he was four years old that left him a cripple for life. He died on February 21, 1926, at the age of eighty. He was the father of former district attorney Charles J. Herrick.

Patrick E. ("Packy") McCabe was appointed deputy county treasurer in 1891. He served as deputy treasurer until January 1, 1897, and in the fall of the following year he was elected county clerk. He was the last Democrat to hold that office until 1922. When McCabe was county clerk, a group of younger Democrats under his leadership started to rebel against Judge D-Cady Herrick, who was the Democratic leader at the time. In 1899 the McCabe group demanded the mayoralty nomination for James Rooney. But the Herrick wing renominated Mayor Van Alstyne. Mayor Van Alstyne was beaten for reelection that fall and was the last Democrat to hold that office until Hackett won in 1921. Herrick's followers blamed the defeat on the McCabe faction because they didn't support Van Alstyne.

McCabe was elected to the state Democratic committee in 1900. The following year McCabe became county chairman after a struggle with Herrick. McCabe was instrumental in the election of Martin H. Glynn as lieutenant governor, from which office Glynn stepped into the governorship through the impeachment of William Sulzer. In 1910 McCabe was appointed clerk of the Senate. McCabe brought about an investigation of the Barnes machine by a special committee of the Senate in 1912. The probe caused no overthrow of the Barnes machine, although they recommended that Mayor James B. McEwan, a Republican, be removed from office, but he wasn't. They also recommended that the commissioner of police, Edward B. Cantine, and the chief of police, James L. Hyatt, be removed from office, but they weren't. Boss Barnes was listed in the report as a "contumacious" witness.

THE O'CONNELLS TAKE OVER

The present power of the Albany Democratic organization goes back to 1919, when Dan O'Connell ran for assessor and won. "I got control when I went out and ran for assessor, then I got control of the party," O'Connell proudly said. "The next year I beat the Barnes machine and got them all out." He had a right to be proud, because there wasn't a Democrat elected for about twenty years until Dan took over. "There wasn't a Democrat in Albany when I ran for assessor," he said. "Nobody was paying any attention to the Democrats then. I took Franey, the former assessor, on and beat him."

O'Connell returned to Albany in the fall of 1919, after serving in the navy during the First World War, and he and his brother Ed decided to strengthen the then divided Democratic Party. They lived above their father's tavern on South Pearl Street. That November Dan ran for assessor, while still wearing his sailor suit, and was elected. He united the Democratic Party, gained the support of the voters at the polls, and within two years was the beginning of what would be one of the most powerful and longest-lasting political machines in the country. It was the only elected office Dan ever held. He served only one term as assessor because he was the leader.

Dan says that "nobody" influenced him into going into politics. "I just drifted in. I was a district leader [at nineteen] before I was of age." As a young man, Dan was always interested in politics. He dreamed of being a district leader when he was only ten years old. The election of 1892, when Grover Cleveland, a former governor of New York, was elected to his second term as President, is the first presidential election Dan can remember. Cleveland was the first Democratic President elected after the Civil War and was the only President who served two terms that did not directly follow each other. He was first elected in 1884, but lost to Benjamin Harrison four years later when Cleveland won the popular vote but lost in the electoral college. This was the second time in twelve years that this happened to a Democratic candidate. However, Cleveland beat Harrison in 1892. O'Connell says Cleveland was a good President.

Dan remembers everybody being excited over William Jennings Bryan when he ran for President (three times from 1896 to 1908, losing every time) because "he was a great orator." He didn't get elected because "he wasn't the right kind of guy for the people of the country at that time" due to his stand on gold and silver. He was a "radical." Bryan, who wanted to unite the masses, said at the 1896 Democratic National Convention, when he delivered his famous "Cross of Gold" speech, "The sympathies of the Democratic Party, as shown by the platform, are on the side of the struggling masses who have ever been the foundation of the Democratic Party. There are two ideas of government. There are those who believe that if you will only legislate to make the well-to-do prosperous, their prosperity will leak through on those below. The Democratic idea, however, has been that if you make the masses prosperous, their prosperity will find its way up through every class which rests upon them." He went on: "Having behind us the producing masses of this nation and the world, supported by commercial interests, the laboring interests and the toilers everywhere, we will answer their demand for a gold standard saying to them: You shall not press down upon the brow of labor this crown of thorns; you shall not crucify mankind upon a cross of gold." Bryan lost in 1896 and in 1900 against the big money men who spent millions of dollars against the Democrats' few hundred thousand to elect William McKinley, author of the highest tariff in history. Bryan was for the common man.

At the Democratic convention in 1912 a candidate was not nominated until the forty-sixth ballot because of the two-thirds majority then needed. On this late ballot Woodrow Wilson, a former governor of New Jersey, got the nomination and was elected in 1912 and 1916. As with other third parties, the Progressive Party brought up many good ideas, but on Election Day they didn't receive the winning votes. The Democrats and Republicans borrowed ideas from third parties. The third party is usually a temporary party because they don't have a broad base. After Theodore Roosevelt had been President he defected from the Republican Party. He ran as a Progressive candidate in 1912 but lost.

When asked if in 1919 Dan O'Connell thought he would be so powerful and successful in politics, Dan modestly said, "I didn't know I was ever powerful." When asked if in 1919 he thought he would be the Democratic county chairman, Dan said, "No, I just did what I had to." Uncle Dan never admitted having any major obstacles to overcome. He said he never regretted doing anything in his life. Dan said he was always happy in politics.

He wanted to enlist in the Marines when World War I came, but they wouldn't take him because he was then thirty years old. He was disappointed when they wouldn't take him. His uncle, Kim O'Connell, whom Dan liked very much, died in the Marines. So Dan entered the navy in 1917. Pat, one of Dan's brothers, ran the saloon while Dan was in the navy. He served on the *Prairie* as a baker. The *Prairie*, the ship that fired the first and last shots on Vera Cruz, was one of the four old battleships docked in Philadelphia (the *Prairie*, the *Panther*, the *Dixie*, and the *Buffalo*). While in the navy Dan was a popular sailor. He went to the Azores and Bermuda, and did patrol duty along the Atlantic coast. Dan never went to Europe on the ship. When he ran for assessor in 1919 his shipmates on the *Prairie* sent a letter from the ship, addressed to the "Citizens of Albany." In the letter, which appeared in the *Times Union*, Dan's shipmates urged Albanians, "to vote for and stand by" him. While on the *Prairie* Dan arranged boxing matches for the crew.

The leaders of the Barnes organization were old. A trolley strike, a series of municipal contract scandals, and a split in the Republican organization over a judicial nomination set the stage for the Democratic victory in 1921. In 1919 the O'Connell brothers (Edward J. and Daniel P.) led the younger Democrats against the McCabe leadership because McCabe had failed to record a success against the Republicans for twenty years. When Dan was elected assessor their power was enhanced. In February, 1920, McCabe gave up as chairman, and Edward J. O'Connell took over. Dan says Ed was county chairman instead of him because Ed was a lawyer and "better qualified and had more time for it than I did." McCabe wasn't bitter over the O'Connells taking over. And his nephew, John J. McCabe, was later elected city treasurer. McCabe died on November 3, 1931, at the age of seventy, as the result of a stroke.

Edwin Corning, the present mayor's father, his brother Parker Corning (a banker who was later elected to Congress), and Robert Whalen (an attorney) helped the O'Connell brothers obtain power. Dan says that Edwin Corning "wasn't particularly interested in politics but he'd do anything that I wanted him to do. He was a good fellow and a close friend." Edwin Corning served as lieutenant governor from

1926 to 1928. He was chairman of the executive committee of the Democratic General Committee in Albany. He also served as chairman of the State Democratic Committee. Edwin was the father of Mayor Erastus Corning II. During the first Wilson administration he was chairman of the Democratic county committee. In December, 1912, he resigned as chairman. At one time while he was lieutenant governor he was mentioned as a possible candidate for governor. He was born in Albany on September 30, 1883, and died while at his summer home in Bar Harbor, Maine, at the age of fifty, on August 7, 1934. About a year before his death he had one leg amputated. After Edwin graduated from Yale University in 1906 he went to work for the Ludlum Steel Company and was elected president in 1910. At that time the company was the largest manufacturer of high grade tools in the United States.

When Dan ran for assessor in 1919 the people were disgusted with the Barnes machine. They had a right to want a change. Albanians had been swindled by the corrupt Republicans for twenty years. In the days prior to election day in 1919 the Democrats had several large ads in the local newspapers. The *Times Union* (Albany's morning newspaper) attacked the Barnes machine throughout the paper. A cartoon entitled "Smash This Machine" was on page one of the November 3, 1921 issue. It had a picture of a slot machine and the caption said that "this [Barnes] machine has been taking for twenty-one years."

When Dan campaigned for assessor he promised to lower real estate taxes, to assess property at its fair value, to keep politics out of the Board of Assessors, and to assess corporations on the value of their property without regard to the political influence of the corporation. After he was elected, he kept his promise to lower taxes. As far as the other promises go, well that's another story.

Dan said that the high tax rate, before he took over, was caused by the great number of people on the city payroll. In addition, the business of the city wasn't conducted efficiently. He said that under the Barnes machine corporations were "assessed in accordance with the size of the campaign contribution it made to the Republican organization. The larger the contribution, the lower the assessment." There have been charges that the O'Connells also maintained political control by controlling assessments of property. While it has never been proven in a court of law, if you ask your ward leader to see that your assessment be lowered, he could probably help you if you are a registered Democrat. To be on the safe side, many voters in Albany register Democratic just so their taxes won't be raised—an important reason for continued success at the polls. After one recent election, a Democrat who had publicly supported a Republican candidate had his assessment raised. Because he couldn't afford the increase he was told that if he paid some money to a certain Democratic lawyer his assessment would be lowered. Sure enough, he paid the money and his assessment was lowered.

Because Dan had just gotten out of the navy, he wore his sailor suit while he campaigned for assessor. The following is an exerpt from a letter that appeared in the *Times Union* on October 30, 1919, from Dan's shipmates on the U.S.S. *Prairie:* "For two years Dan served on board this ship and during that time we have come to know him as a man of sterling qualities, a good sailor and fighter, an honest man and a firm friend of every man with whom he came in contact." Dan says that some of his friends "did more for me to get elected than I did for myself." He was elected assessor over Republican John Franey, a former county clerk, with a plurality of 163 votes. Dan was the only Democrat elected in 1919. It was a blow to the Barnes machine. A look at the title of a newspaper article well describes the election. It is "Election Earthquake Rocks G.O.P. Machine."

Captain Reynolds King Townsend, the Democratic candidate for mayor in 1919, lost by only 1,546 votes to Mayor James R. Watt. The *Times Union* wrongly predicted that Townsend would win. However, they weren't too far off, because Mayor Watt's reelection margin was sharply cut from 10,324 votes just two years before. Townsend carried eleven of the nineteen wards in Albany. When Townsend ran for mayor in 1919 he was only 35. He was the grandson of an earlier mayor and was a military secretary to Governor Glynn. The election of 1920 was reassuring to Albany Democrats because they elected Peter E. Ten Eyck to Congress and John J. Merrigan to the New York State Assembly. It was a further blow to the Republican machine. The Democrats were able to wipe out Republican majorities in what the Barnes machine had considered their strongholds.

HACKETT ELECTED MAYOR

The return of the Democrats to Albany after more than twenty-two years of Republican domination welcomely occurred in 1921, when all the Democratic candidates in both the city and county were elected. After the Democrats won in 1921, Dan said "it was all easy sailing." William Stormont Hackett, a Democrat, was elected mayor with a plurality of 7,153 votes. Some of the other Democrats elected were: Thomas Fitzgerald for comptroller, John Boyd Thacher for city treasurer, and Frank S. Harris for president of the Common Council.

Dan says, "I didn't know Hackett when he was elected." He notes that Hackett was selected to be mayor because he was well known in Albany, being president of the Albany City Savings Bank. He was born on December 7, 1868, on South Ferry Street in Albany's South End. He received his education in the public schools. When he graduated from

the Albany High School in 1884 he decided to enter the legal profession. He joined the law offices of Parker and Countryman. He was
admitted to the bar in 1889 but he never practiced. Hackett decided
to join the Albany City Savings Bank, where he went from bookkeeper
in 1887 to president in 1916. He was then the youngest savings bank
president in Albany. He was still the bank's president at the time of
his death. Mayor Hackett was reelected in 1923 with an unprecedented
plurality of 15,218 votes. He carried every city ward. The other Democratic candidates were also elected.

The Albany Democratic organization scored a notable victory in
the election of 1922. They won every office, with the exception of
assemblyman in the first district. Parker Corning was elected to Congress, and, among others elected, Charles Herrick, son of the former
leader of the Albany Democratic organization, was elected district
attorney. Corning represented Albany in Congress for fourteen years.
He was chairman of the board of the Albany Felt Company and served
as vice-president of the Ludlum Steel Company while his brother Edwin
was its president. Parker was born in Albany on January 24, 1874, and
died at the age of sixty-nine on May 24, 1943. Like his brother Edwin
and his nephew Erastus, he attended Yale.

Dan says that the Alleghany-Ludlum Steel Works in North Albany,
owned by the Cornings, and the Port of Albany brought roughly two-
thirds of the black population to Albany. They came from the South
in the 1920s when cotton picking in the South began to decline as a
means of livelihood; also welfare programs were better in the North
than in the South.

Although the Democrats lost two out of three assembly seats in
1924 they elected their other candidates. The small loss for the Democrats was due to the Republican Coolidge landslide for President. In
1924 in New York City the Democrats had the longest national convention in history. It lasted for fourteen days before nominating, on
the 103rd ballot, a compromise candidate, John W. Davis, a New York
lawyer who had been Wilson's solicitor general. Davis lost to Coolidge
and gave the Democrats their lowest popular percentage in history—
28.8.

The election of 1925 was a Democratic landslide in the city and
county of Albany. Mayor Hackett was reelected with a plurality of
more than 15,000 votes. John McCabe, nephew of the former county
chairman, was elected city treasurer, and John Boyd Thacher was
elected president of the Common Council, among other Democratic
candidates elected. One day before the election of 1925 Dan said to
Thacher, the son of a banker and car wheel manufacturer, "You ought
to get out of that city treasurer if you want to be mayor. It looks like
Hackett will go to the State Capitol. You better run for president of
the Common Council," which was a stepping-stone for the mayoralty.

Thacher was a member of an old Albany family. In an article on page one of the November 4, 1925 issue, the *Times Union* said that the Democratic victory in the election "marks Edwin Corning, Edward J. O'Connell and Daniel P. O'Connell as among the greatest political leaders in the country."

Dan grew up with Leo Doody, and made him the commissioner of charities (now the welfare department). Dan says that although Doody was older than he was "we were very friendly." As with Doody, most of the people who helped Dan lived in his neighborhood but didn't go to school with him. Doody helped the O'Connells a lot when they first got started. He owned the *Telegram* in Albany. Dan says it was a scandal newspaper.

Mayor Hackett left Albany on February 9, 1926 for a three-week vacation in Cuba. He was accompanied by Frederick M. Lamb, assistant treasurer of the mayor's bank and his closest personal friend. After Hackett died, Lamb became president of the bank, but later went to jail for about two years for fraud with the accounts. Dan says Freddie Lamb was "a nice fellow." At nine o'clock on the night of February 16 the mayor was returning to his hotel, accompanied by Mr. Lamb and Joseph Brennan of New York. The automobile was driven by a Cuban racing driver. The accident occurred when the car struck a hole in the pavement on the Avenue Almendarex in the Miramar section of Havana. The swerve threw the mayor, who was said to have been drunk at the time, against the door, which sprang open, precipitating him into the street. He struck on his head and was unconscious for six hours. It was said that the accident was the result of careless driving (February 18, 1926, the *Times Union*). Hackett was taken to the hospital and had X-rays that showed no fracture of the skull, while the mayor had a brain concussion. A couple of days after the accident there was hope that the mayor would recover, but after an operation on February 23 he fell into a coma. He seemed to be getting better but got worse. On March 3, it was reported in the *Times Union* that the mayor could not live more than a day or two. He was totally unconscious and was unable to swallow. The next day, March 4, 1926, Mayor Hackett died at 4:35 P.M. in Havana. The city lost a great mayor, and the state lost a future governor and the nation a possible president. His death ended his short-lived but admirable political career, which began in 1921 when he was elected mayor.

THACHER IS THE NEXT MAYOR

John Boyd Thacher II, president of the Common Council became the sixty-eighth mayor of Albany, as provided by law. He was the third member of his family to become mayor of Albany. His grandfather, George H. Thacher, was four times mayor, and his uncle, John Boyd

Thacher, was twice mayor of Albany. Thacher was born in Leadville, Colorado, on October 28, 1882. He attended the Albany Boys Academy, Princeton University, and graduated from the Albany Law School in 1906. He was elected city treasurer in 1921 and reelected in 1923. In 1925 he was elected president of the Common Council. He was elected mayor with a plurality of more than 21,000 votes in 1926. Elected along with him were the other Democratic candidates in the county. Parker Corning was easily reelected to Congress with a 20,176-vote margin.

The election of 1927 was another landslide for the Albany Democrats, with higher pluralities than ever before. Surrogate Gilbert V. Schenck had a plurality of 18,905. He was the father of former County Judge Martin Schenck. In the presidential election of 1928 former governor of New York Alfred E. Smith, a Democrat, carried Albany County by 13,829 over Herbert Hoover. But while Smith was not elected president, all the Democrats in Albany County were elected. Smith lost because he was a Roman Catholic. Under Hoover's administration the nation suffered the Great Depression of 1929.

Mayor Thacher was relected by over 22,000 votes in 1929 along with the other Democrats in Albany. The county helped reelect Governor Franklin Delano Roosevelt by giving him a plurality of 33,509 votes in 1930. He was not the only Democrat to win in Albany County because, as in every election since 1921, the Democrats won in 1930. The election of 1931 was no different, because all the Democratic candidates were elected. In 1932 John McCooey from Brooklyn and John Kelly, the Tammany leader, and Al Smith wanted Thacher to run for governor, but they ended up nominating Herbert Lehman instead. On the eve of the nomination, just about every delegate wore a "Thacher for Governor" button. But while the session began the word was out that Roosevelt wanted Herbert H. Lehman as the candidate, and everyone but O'Connell voted for Lehman. Thacher was given an ovation when he said he was withdrawing in the interest of party unity.

Dan O'Connell says "we won" in Albany County "no matter" who the gubernatorial candidate was. Herbert Lehman was elected governor, and Franklin Roosevelt gave up the governorship to be elected President in 1932. Lehman had a winning plurality of 35,376 votes in Albany County. Judge Gilbert Schenck was elected to the Supreme Court. Parker Corning was reelected to Congress. The other Democrats elected were two coroners, a county treasurer, and a state senator. What could please the Democrats more than a winning ticket year after year?

Because of the period of economic crisis during the Republican Presidential administration, Franklin Roosevelt was elected with the most decisive Democratic victory since Andrew Jackson's in 1832. Roosevelt was the only President who was elected four times. He was a great leader. The New Deal, as FDR's administration was known, made progress in social, economic, and world issues and helped rebuild the country and the Democratic Party. He made the Democratic Party "the voice of the forgotten masses" again.

The only national convention Dan O'Connell ever attended was in 1932 in Chicago when Roosevelt was nominated. Dan says that FDR hated Tammany Hall. Dan never went to a state convention. However, he always sent someone in his place to cast his vote. Usually the mayors represented Dan at the conventions. At the 1932 Democratic National Convention, the Albany machine and Tammany Hall wanted Al Smith to get the nomination for President but FDR was given the nomination on the sixth ballot. While Dan O'Connell supported Roosevelt on election day, he wasn't fond of the President. Dan said FDR didn't like poor people, and has referred to him as a son of a bitch. An example of Roosevelt's contempt for Tammany Hall came when he forced New York's Mayor Jimmy Walker to resign. If Walker hadn't resigned, Roosevelt as the governor would probably have removed him from office because of a scandal Walker was allegedly involved in.

"We never went out of Albany County for anything," Dan says. "I was satisfied with Albany County." He says, "We did all right . . . We can't kick." But nevertheless his support at the state conventions means a lot to the candidates. Joe Kennedy sought O'Connell's support for his son John shortly before the younger Kennedy ran for President in 1960. O'Connell has always been more interested in electing the local ticket than the state or national ticket. However, the state and national ticket usually did well in Albany anyway because most people voted Democratic. Dan proudly admits that he has always voted the straight Democratic ticket. He declares, "You got to have good thick skin to be a Democrat and I wouldn't be anything else."

Mayor Thacher was reelected by almost 25,000 votes in 1933. Thacher ran against Captain Townsend, who ran on the Fusion ticket. Townsend ran for mayor as a Democrat in 1919 but lost. Dan says Townsend "wasn't a sound fellow." According to him, Townsend ran against Thacher because Townsend thought he wasn't used right. "He was a bug." Democrats were reelected to fill the offices of sheriff, comptroller, city court judge, police court judge, city treasurer, surrogate, coroner, and president of the Common Council.

Governor Lehman received a reelection plurality of 46,544 votes in Albany County in 1934. Dan says he liked Lehman: "Lehman was a high-class fellow." Congressman Parker Corning was reelected with 43,733 more votes than his opponent. As usual the other Democrats in the county were elected. Erastus Corning II was elected to the State Assembly in 1935. He was later to be mayor. The Democrats did it again. The next year, 1936, Assemblyman Corning was elected to the State Senate. Former State Senator William T. Byrne was elected to Congress to replace Parker Corning. Democratic candidates continued to be victorious in the county. The Democratic convention compromise of 1936 eliminated the two-thirds majority requirements for nomination, so that nomination would require only a simple majority, as is needed today. A delegate apportionment formula was developed that would reflect a state's Democratic vote-producing strength in the previous election.

The Democrats had another election celebration in 1937 as their candidates were swept into office again. Mayor Thacher was reelected to a fourth term with a record plurality of 48,867. The mayor received 61,029 votes over the Republican candidate, William J. Walker, who received 12,162 votes. They did it again in 1938. Erastus Corning II was reelected to the State Senate with a plurality of more than 30,000 votes.

Daniel P. O'Connell and his brother Ed turned the Democratic Party into a powerful organization. But on June 6, 1939, the two brothers were separated because Edward J. O'Connell died at the age of fifty-one from a heart attack. Not only did Dan lose a close brother, Ed's friends lost a good friend. Ed O'Connell took over as county chairman from McCabe in February, 1920, and held the position at the time of his death. Edward J. O'Connell was born in 1887, two years after Dan. He was president of his class when he graduated from the Albany High School. He graduated from Union College and, in 1914, from Albany Law School. While a young attorney he became an expert in the financing of public service corporations. Ed held public office only once and that was as county attorney in 1922. He helped M. William Bray, a law school classmate of his, get the nomination for lieutenant governor in 1932, a post he held for three terms.

In 1933 a nephew of Dan and Ed O'Connell was kidnapped from his home and held captive for twenty-three days, being blindfolded and handcuffed by four local hoodlums until his uncles paid $40,000 ransom. The kidnapping received national attention in the news. The gang was later caught and all were sentenced to long prison terms. One committed suicide. None of the ransom was ever recovered. Although they made a lot of money through politics, Dan says it was a hard job raising that kind of money in the depression years. He says of the gang that kidnapped his nephew, "They were just a gang around here trying to make money. The beer business went out and they went out with it. They were a lot of bums. A few New Yorkers mixed up in it." Dan says he knew who they were: "I was riding with two of them everyday almost," while they had his nephew. Dan says the O'Connell family was scared, worried, and terrified, but "for all I knew he was all right. I knew I would have killed those two [kidnappers] anyway" if anything happened to the boy who was kidnapped. Like Harry Truman, Dan never scared easily. There was once a kidnap attempt on Truman's daughter, and Truman's life was threatened, but he didn't scare or change his intentions. The victim of the kidnapping,

John J. O'Connell, age thirty, was elected county chairman on August 4, 1939, to succeed his Uncle Ed. John, Dan's brother, was the father of "Young John," as the new chairman was known.

Just because there was a new county chairman didn't stop the Democrats from obtaining another victory in the election of 1939. The vote for the Supreme Court Justice in Albany County that year was as follows: Russell (Rep.) 35,940; Russell (Dem.) 76,369; Russell (ALP) 2,925. As you may notice, no matter what the results were he couldn't lose because he was endorsed by all three parties. This was occasionally done in the past, but it isn't usually done now because the parties want all they can get. In 1974 Arthur Levitt, New York State's Comptroller, and Congressman Samuel Stratton, Albany's representative in Congress, were both offered the Republican nominations as well as their regular renomination on the Democratic ticket. However, they both turned down the Republican offer because they were guaranteed to be elected anyway, and having their name on the Republican side of the ballot would have helped other Republican candidates. In addition to Russell being elected in 1939, the other Democrats were elected as usual.

Mayor Thacher decided to run for Children's Court Judge in 1940. He was elected to the judgeship with a plurality of more than 38,000 votes. Dan says the judgeship "paid two or three times as much money" as being mayor did. Dan says Thacher didn't have much money. "John Boyd," Dan remembers, "was a good fellow." The president of the Common Council and deputy state tax commissioner, Frank Harris, who was then seventy-two, served as acting mayor until the next election. Harris, who also served as Democratic city chairman, was "a nice fellow." He used to be in the hat business. He was about twenty years older than Dan. Senator Erastus Corning was mentioned as a possible successor to Mayor Thacher. Senator Corning was reelected along with the other Democrats in 1940.

CORNING ELECTED MAYOR

And then came the election of 1941. Erastus Corning II, the present mayor of Albany, was elected the next mayor with an outstanding plurality of more than 46,000 votes. Corning was replaced in the State Senate by fellow-Democrat Julian Erway. The pluralities received by the other Democratic candidates were about the same as the new mayor received.

Mayor Corning's father, Edwin Corning, was lieutenant governor and one of the builders of the O'Connell machine. The youngest mayor in the history of the city was elected at the age of thirty-two. How many people knew then that Erastus Corning II would be in office for so many years, longer than any mayor in the country? His uncle,

Parker Corning, had been congressman from Albany. Corning's great-grandfather and namesake was mayor of the city from 1834 to 1836, and one of the founders of the New York Central Railroad. The young future mayor attended Groton Prep School and Yale University, where he graduated as a Phi Beta Kappa scholar. He was later elected to the state assembly and then to the state senate before being elected mayor. Dan knew the Corning family well. They were "a prominent family in the South End." The Cornings owned a felt mill and a steel mill.

The Democrats were far from having any problems electing their candidates in 1942, 1943, and 1944. State Senator Julian B. Erway was elected district attorney in 1944 over Republican Ernest B. Morris, president of Saratoga Raceway. Before the election Morris was appointed district attorney by Governor Dewey and served about seven months. O'Connell says Morris "never knew what a horse was until his father-in-law bought them for him." Dan didn't like Morris.

Around this time we were fighting World War II, and like other able American young men Mayor Corning was classified 1-A and drafted into the army in April, 1944. Mayor Corning appointed Frank S. Harris, former state treasurer, as temporary mayor while the mayor served in Europe. He won several battle stars and the infantryman's combat badge. While in the service, he was renominated for mayor and returned in September, 1945, with an honorable discharge (private, first class) to resume his duties as mayor.

On at least one occasion Mayor Corning was reported to be in high spirits, although he is by no means an alcoholic. Shortly before midnight on October 28, 1967, Corning was arrested in Colonie, a town that neighbors Albany, by the state police for driving while intoxicated. The charges were later dismissed. There was even an article about his arrest in the *New York Daily News* on November 7, 1967, entitled "Albany Mayor Nabbed as Tipsy." But despite his moralities he is well educated and is very capable. He could have been governor if he wanted to. Corning is married, although his wife rarely, if ever, attends any public functions with him. Their married son and daughter have long since left Albany.

On April 12, 1945, the President of the United States, Franklin Delano Roosevelt, died. His Vice-President, Harry S. Truman, took over the Presidency. The night after Roosevelt's death the Albany Democrats elected a new county chairman. The new chairman, John J. Murphy, replaced John J. O'Connell, Jr., who resigned because of illness. Dan says his nephew John wasn't interested in politics. "He had no patience for it. He was a nice boy." Before O'Connell resigned, he underwent an operation for removal of a cyst to make himself eligible for military service. Murphy was the only person outside of the O'Connell family to be county chairman since 1920. Jack Murphy was charged, before his election as county chairman, with stealing money from Democratic headquarters while he was executive secretary of the party, and with income tax evasion. Dan didn't believe the charges were true and he made Murphy county chairman and treasurer of the party. Murphy gave Dan a grandfather clock. It is still in Dan's home on Whitehall Road.

Murphy's political career stems from his early friendship with Edward O'Connell. When the O'Connell brothers got control of Albany, Dan suggested that a party office be established with a full-time executive secretary for political party management instead of using City Hall, as was done in the Barnes era. Dan's brother Ed recommended Murphy for the job. He held the position when he died, at fifty-two on October 16, 1945.

DAN O'CONNELL ELECTED CHAIRMAN

The last of the old-time big city bosses, Daniel Peter O'Connell, was elected county chairman on October 29, 1945. He succeeded John Murphy. Although Dan did not become "chairman" until 1945 he had been the leader—the man who made it all happen for so many years— since 1919.

Charles W. Ryan was elected treasurer at the same meeting in which Dan was first elected county chairman. The meeting was held at the Odd Fellows Hall. Other meetings of the party were held in the Ten Eyck Hotel, Knights of Pythias Hall, and most recently the Polish Hall. Dan was nominated by former Sheriff Joseph Henchey. Ryan was the leader of the eleventh district of the eighteenth ward and was general manager of a tobacco company in Cohoes. His parents, Mame and Jim Ryan, were from Chicago. Dan was friendly with the elder Jim Ryan, whom he met in New York City. After he died the rest of the family moved to Albany and son Charlie went to work with a vending machine company and also sold office furniture to the state. Today, they own a very successful vending-machine business in Albany. They made much money through politics. James A. Ryan, now executive secretary of the party and the person who is in charge at Democratic headquarters and gives out patronage, served as Superintendent of County Buildings in Albany from 1944 to October, 1954. From October, 1954, until about 1963 he was Albany County Purchasing Agent at a salary of $5,000 per annum. He was appointed to that position by the County Board of Supervisors. He said he obtained that position through the efforts of his father-in-law, Frank O'Brien, now deceased, who was at that time the leader of the thirteenth ward in Albany. Charlie is treasurer of the party and an Albany County elections commissioner. Mrs. Mary Marcy was vice-chairman of the county committee when Dan was elected chairman. Dan was previously president of the second ward.

In 1945, when Mayor Corning got out of the army, he was reelected along with the other Democrats in that off-year election. In 1946 the mayor unsuccessfully ran for lieutenant governor, the office that his father once had, on the Democratic ticket with United States Senator James M. Meade of Buffalo. Dan says Corning ran because "Meade had done some favors for me." Meade wanted Corning to run for United States Senator, but Corning wouldn't; he ran for lieutenant governor instead. As Dan says, "it was mostly an accident" that Corning ran.

Needless to say, both Corning and Meade carried Albany but lost statewide. There were the usual victories in 1946 except that the pluralities were smaller because of. Republican Governor Dewey's coattails. Former Mayor Thacher left the Children's Court and lost the election for the Supreme Court in 1946 against Isadore Bookstein. Until recent years it was a usual practice to make a deal with the other party and decide which party would elect a Supreme Court judge that year. When a deal took place both parties would endorse the same candidate. Albany is in the third judicial district, which is composed of Albany, Rensselaer, Columbia, Sullivan, Greene, Schoharie, and Ulster counties. Most of these counties were as heavily Republican, or more so, as Albany was Democratic. Sometimes a deal was not acceptable. Such happened in 1946 when Bookstein beat Thacher. Also in 1946 Donald Lynch, Dan's nephew through marriage, was first elected county clerk. Dan says, "Donald's a millionaire." Lynch made more money through his political connections than perhaps any person in Albany. Peter Dalessandro, who is now the receptionist in Democratic headquarters, was first elected state senator in 1946. Dalessandro, a Congressional Medal of Honor winner, served five terms as State Senator.

Thomas Dewey, a Republican, was elected governor in 1942 and reelected in 1946. Dan says that "when Dewey was elected governor we had been in here for twenty years. He thought he had something. He started out with an investigation. He investigated every department for twenty-two months—*me* particularly, and when he got done he didn't get a goddam thing. It was a flat failure." Dan adds, "We never did anything crooked around here in politics. I never took anything and wouldn't let anyone else. It was always square and it always will be."

Dewey, in his autobiography, *Twenty Against the Underworld*, said some things about the O'Connell machine as it was more than thirty years ago, such as "When a tavern keeper puts in Hederick's beer, 100 per cent, the sky's the limit." At that time O'Connells owned the brewery. The assessment on Hederick's, $250,000 in 1937, was cut to $125,000 in 1938. "A handsome two-and-one-half story dwelling, gable, and with a three-car garage at 50 Rensselaer Avenue," Dewey said was assessed at only $1,800, because the owner's brother was an office-holder in Albany. He added, "On the other hand look at this little shingled house, up close to the street on a tiny lot. Its owner is Elmer Ludlum, who made the mistake of registering as a Republican, and his assessment is $7,500, almost four times as much."

Dewey told about some of the people of the O'Connell machine. One, Sammy Magliocca, "a self-confessed gun toter and a confessed burglar . . . but now he is one of the boys. For years Sammy had a place on Dongan Avenue. . . . In 1935 there were 78 persons registered as voters from Sammy's tavern. Sammy had an explanation. There were only 22 beds in the place, but his flock of voters slept in three eight-hour shifts."

The former Republican governor said a grand jury that was to investigate charges of election frauds in 1935 in Albany "had 19 registered Democrats out of its 23 members. The foreman of that grand jury was a man whose company had done $36,000 worth of coal business with the city of Albany. The secretary was a former Democratic supervisor."[3]

Not too long ago Dan said that he thought his telephone was tapped. A friend of his, who is a judge, confirmed that his phone was tapped. About thirty years before, Dan's phone was also tapped when Governor Dewey tried to find something on the O'Connells. Mayor Corning said he was certain his phone was also tapped during the Dewey investigation.

On November 11, 1944, George P. Monaghan, Dewey's special prosecutor, made public some of the tapes of conversation over Dan's phone. Four of the five Supreme Court justices of the judicial district that included Albany were accused by Monaghan as having "flouted the well recognized concepts of comity and judicial propriety." The justices he was referring to were Gilbert V. Schenck, Francis Bergan, Harry E. Schirick, and William H. Murray of Troy. Dan O'Connell made Bergan a State Supreme Court justice at the early age of thirty-two. Bergan was later elected to the Court of Appeals, the state's highest court. The special prosecutor also said that Dan, Jack Murphy, and Robert E. Whalen "have so conducted themselves in their relations with certain Supreme Court justices in this judicial district as to bring the administration of justice into serious disrepute." Robert Whalen was a lawyer who Dan says he did a lot of business with. Dan said Whalen was "very much interested in politics." Whalen was married to one of the Herrick women but never had any children. At this time Murphy was treasurer of the party and was indicted for stealing $85,000 from Democratic headquarters. Dan showed his confidence in Murphy and made him the county chairman. Murphy's case was never tried because he soon became ill and died of cancer.

Mr. Monaghan wanted a change in venue in the Murphy case because, not only were the judges close to Dan, the juries were packed with Democrats, and Albanians who were afraid of opposing the machine even in a court of law. Monaghan charged that Albany jury lists are "packed with henchmen and friends of the machine." Timothy J. O'Sullivan, who was executive officer of the Albany County Alcoholic Beverage Control Board, stated in an affidavit that he had observed Commissioner of Jurors Elizabeth F. Pinckney marking "REP" or "DEM" after some names as she prepared jury lists. He also stated he overheard Mrs. Pinckney telephoning Democratic headquarters, mention the names of prospective jurors, and ask whether they were "OK."

Judge Schenck was tapped telling Dan over the phone about his difficulty in getting another judge to go along with the organization. Schenck said, "I would have had three votes tonight, except your little boy out in Schoharie—even when I got in his own room, and tried to pin him down, he wouldn't go with me." Dan interrupted Schenck because he knew his phone was tapped and said, "You got to be careful with the phones." Schenck said, "Yeah, I know. I'll do the best I can. One fellow's all right—I'm all right—but it takes three to do it." Because it is improper for a judge to show favoritism to a political party, the American Bar Association recommended Schenck be removed from the bench. He was not removed, although he was censured by the State Assembly. Gilbert "Gil" Schenck came from Rensselaer, across the river from Albany, and "we made a Supreme Court judge of him." Dan adds, "We made a County Court judge of his son who was a stiff."

Dan O'Connell proudly said he made more than a hundred judges. One was John Clyne, who was county attorney before he was elected a County Court judge in 1972. After Dan made Clyne a judge, Dan was sorry because Clyne gave out big sentences. In 1973, when New York State's stiff drug law went into effect, all convicted pushers were sentenced to life in prison. Dan felt that only murderers and people who commit serious crimes of violence (and Republicans) should receive long prison sentences. The first time Judge John Clyne helped the Democratic organization in Albany was some two years after he became a county judge. It was in June, 1974, when he refused to make public a grand jury report of their investigation of the Albany police department involving corruption and police brutality. Because the report was not made public, no indictments against policemen were secured, and the policemen who should have been punished went free. With the high cost to the taxpayers it was a waste of money to give long prison sentences, especially considering that most of the criminals released from prison are arrested for subsequent crimes. The cost of keeping a prisoner in a New York State institution is $9,024 per year. Yet when they get out, 70 percent of all inmates will commit another crime. Also, the Democratic lawyers hoped for lesser sentences for their clients. Because Judge Michael Tepedino gave out stiff sentences while he was Police Court Justice of Albany, Albany lawyers were glad when he went to the Family Court. Before the county clerk and sheriff received an annual salary in the late 1930s, they collected fees for everything that they did. The fees were enormous and the office-holders received a cut. The rest of the money was given to Dan by means of contributions to the party.

George P. Monaghan, appointed by Governor Dewey as a special prosecutor in 1943, investigated political corruption by the O'Connell machine in Albany. Although Dewey had pledged that the investigation would "end the despotic rule of Dan O'Connell," the twenty-two-month probe resulted in only five minor indictments and no convictions. He had Dan's and others' phones tapped. Monaghan served as Police Commissioner of New York City from 1951 through 1953, after seven months as Fire Commissioner. In 1959 Monaghan resigned from the State Harness Racing Commission in the midst of charges of corruption by the State Investigation Commission. His troubles did not end that year, however, because in 1974 he was charged in an indictment as serving as attorney to at least one of four loan-shark operators and being an active participant in a loan-sharking scheme in which one victim was threatened with being defenestrated from the eighteenth floor of a hotel. Specifically, the indictment charged Monaghan with six counts of perjury in connection with a grand jury investigation into loan-shark-ing operations. Three other men who allegedly participated in the loan-sharking operation were known Chicago underworld figures. What is ironic about the situation is that Monaghan tried to get Dan and a few years later he was in trouble himself. Dan says, "They all had bad luck when they fooled around with me."

In 1948 some Democrats wanted to dump Harry Truman as President because they did not feel he could beat Tom Dewey. Dan said, "They are like a bunch of rats deserting a sinking ship." Dan supported Truman and gained his friendship. Dan says, "I was for Truman when there was nobody in the state for him." Franklin Roosevelt had spoken well of Truman to Dan. Dan declares, "Truman was a great man." After Truman was elected President he showed his appreciation of Dan's support. Truman was quoted as saying after the '48 election, "Whatever that guy [O'Connell] wants up in Albany he can have." Oscar Ewing, a friend of Dan's, distributed patronage for Truman. Dan supported Ewing for the Democratic Presidential nomination in 1952, but Adlai Stevenson got the nomination. Ewing, from the Bronx, was "a fine fellow." Dan says, "He and I were very friendly. I'd be for him for anything."

O'Connell says Truman was a great person and a great scholar. He agreed with Truman when Truman said Eisenhower and Nixon didn't give a damn about the welfare of the people. Dan says, "Eisenhower was nothing and Nixon certainly wasn't anything." Dan agrees with the late President Truman when he said, referring to Nixon, "I don't think the son of a bitch knows the difference between telling the truth and lying." Dan says, "I think he's right."

In 1948 President Truman made the United States the first country to recognize the State of Israel and he helped Israel gain admittance into the United Nations. This is one reason why the Jewish people have supported the Democrats. Truman was also the first President to make civil rights a major issue, and this almost cost him the election of 1948. In fact, voters went to bed on election day thinking that the Republican candidate, Thomas E. Dewey, had won. But as it turned out on the next day Truman was elected.

The Albany Democrats easily won the elections in 1947, 1948, 1950, and 1951. Leo Quinn was first elected county treasurer in 1947. Mayor Corning was reelected in 1949 with a plurality of almost 44,000 votes. Martin Schenck was first elected to the County Court bench in 1950. So, for the most part, the O'Connell machine didn't have much opposition from the Republicans in Albany until recent years. The Republicans found that any efforts against the machine were fruitless. Albanians, for years, were afraid of registering Republican and were even afraid that the machine knew how they voted on election day. It was not unusual for a Democratic poll worker to come into the voting booth with a voter. Although there are two Republicans on the County Board of Elections, until Joe Frangella became the Albany County Republican chairman in 1966, these two Republicans, who were appointed by the machine-controlled county legislature, were Republicans in name only. The machine would have some loyalists register Republican for purposes like this.

In 1948, when there was opposition from the American Labor Party (ALP) the machine had some Democrats register ALP. What happened was that there were more real Democrats registered ALP than the ALP had before. At the primary that year, the ALP-Democrats wrote in the names of the machines candidates and won over the ALP choices.

Albanians feared that their taxes would be raised, and worried about other acts of retaliation if they didn't vote Democratic. Besides most voters in Albany preferred the Democrats. Most voters who registered Republican, especially the businessmen, were Republicans in name only. They realized they had to work with the Democratic machine in order to survive. Some Republicans even contributed money to the O'Connell machine. Since the O'Connells got control in 1919, the Democratic party in Albany has been virtually free of dissension. While in recent years there have been more unhappy Democrats than in the past, those who aren't satisfied find it best to keep their thoughts to themselves. Any attempt to overthrow the O'Connell leadership would be fruitless and cause problems for the dissidents.

In recent years the voter's fear of the machine hasn't been as great.

Although most voters are still registered Democratic, they split their votes and don't always vote the straight Democratic ticket as they once did. Thus, in 1952 the Eisenhower-Nixon presidential ticket scored a political upset in Albany County when the Republicans won by more than 7,000 votes over the Stevenson ticket. In 1952 Republican Senators Joseph McCarthy of Wisconsin and Richard Nixon of California insinuated that the Communists were associated with the Truman administration. This bad publicity, even though it may not have been true, cost the Democrats the election in 1952, except in Albany.

The same Eisenhower ticket carried Albany County again in 1956 over the Stevenson ticket, this time with a plurality of almost 20,000 votes. Eisenhower was the only Republican presidential candidate ever to carry the county since 1920. But while Eisenhower carried the county he lost both times in the city. The Eisenhower coattails were noticeable in both 1952 and 1956, but they weren't strong enough to fight the O'Connell machine because the other Democratic candidates won in the city and county during both elections. For example, in 1952 Leo O'Brien, a former political reporter for the *Times Union,* was elected to Congress. After being elected he supposedly called Democratic headquarters in Albany from Washington and asked, "How do you want me to vote?" They replied, "Vote the way you want to." As long as Albany wasn't concerned, Dan never cared how his congressmen and legislators voted.

Mayor Corning was reelected to office again in 1953, along with the other Democratic candidates. Averell Harriman, a Democrat, was elected governor in 1954. Dan says that Harriman wasn't a good governor. He "was a dope and did nothing. He had $200 million and couldn't make a living." In that same election Mayor Corning's brother, Edwin Corning, was elected to the State Assembly. Edwin Corning was vice-president of Albany Associates, Inc., the insurance firm of which his brother, Mayor Corning, is president. Like his brother, Edwin was educated at the Albany Academy, Groton School, and Yale College.

In the election of 1955 the Democratic candidates for city office carried the city by about 47,000 votes, and the Democrats for county office carried the county by about 43,000 votes. In 1957 Mayor Corning was reelected with a plurality of almost 48,000 votes. Julian Erway left as district attorney and returned to the State Senate that year. Harold Koreman, now a Supreme Court justice, was elected surrogate of Albany County in 1957.

Former Mayor John Boyd Thacher II died on April 26, 1957, age seventy-four, from progressive asthma and bronchitis. After Thacher retired from the bench, on January 1, 1947, he was elected president of the City and County Savings Bank on November 15, 1949. He served as bank president until he died. The same day Thacher died John

Curry, who was leader of Tammany Hall from 1929 to 1934, died at age eight-four from a heart attack.

Although Governor Harriman carried Albany County in 1958 he was defeated in his reelection attempt by Nelson Rockefeller, who was governor until December, 1973. The greatest weakness of the Republican Party in Albany has been their weak tickets. In Albany while Rockefeller and Wilson were governor the Republicans had a lot of patronage with the state. There is more patronage with the state in Albany than there is in the city or county government level. Now, with a Republican-controlled State Senate, the Albany Republicans get jobs there.

Before 1883, the year when the Pendleton Act for civil service reform was passed, government employees were hired on a spoils basis. Congressman George H. Pendleton of Ohio introduced the bill in order to reduce patronage. Today 85 percent of federal employees are hired through the civil service or merit system. Because there are ways of getting around the civil service, the percentage in Albany County is not nearly as high as on the federal level. Only 16.4 percent of 4,174 local government employees in Albany County under civil service classification held their jobs in 1973 as a result of passing an examination (see the annual report of the Albany County Civil Service Commission). In 1971 the State Civil Service Commission noted that Albany County had the highest percentage of provisional employees of any local civil service agency in the state. A provisional employee is one who hasn't passed a civil service exam.

Albany has had the largest municipal work force for a city its size in the nation, and one of the lowest paid, but at least there was plenty of patronage to maintain a degree of content. The Bureau of Streets in Albany, it was disclosed at State Investigation Commission hearings in 1972, as a matter of general policy pays some of its 40-hour-a-week workers for working a 48-hour week to compensate for low hourly wages.

Albany County employs 175 men and women as custodial workers for the county courthouse, even though the county budget permits only 72 workers. Salaries for the 175 workers total $375,026 annually, while the budget provides for $155,220. Nearly all of the custodial workers in the four-story courthouse are retired. Their salaries range from $548 a year to $3,800. While even seventy-two custodial workers would be more than necessary, the additional workers are hired to spread out the patronage—patronage controlled entirely by the Democratic machine. The machine controls three thousand-plus jobs. While the wages are low, the jobs are sought after. And because the city and county employees aren't being paid much, they don't, as you'd probably expect, break their backs at work. In addition to much patronage at the county courthouse, in the streets and parks department, and other municipal departments, there is a lot of patronage at the county jail, the sheriff's department, and the police department.

A July 9, 1974, editorial in the *Knickerbocker News,* Albany's evening newspaper, said, "For the most part, operations of the jail have been placed in the hands of unqualified and incompetent political hacks chosen by Democratic boss Dan O'Connell and the jail staff has consisted chiefly of political hangers-on hired more on the basis of how they voted than for any abilities they possessed." In 1974 an Albany County grand jury reported that unsanitary conditions and poor personnel practices existed at the county jail. The grand jury found the jail "generally infested" with cockroaches, particularily in the living, kitchen, and dining areas. A former sheriff and jail warden were held by another Albany County grand jury directly responsible for the county jailbreak by a dozen prisoners in October, 1972. Also in recent years there were charges that employees at the jail stole turkeys, hams, bacon, milk, and bread from the jail. There were also allegations that some guards smuggled liquor and drugs to prisoners.

Many government employees, primarily on the city and county level, don't work very hard, and there are a number of "no-show" and "seldom-show" jobs. An example of "no-show" jobs came up in Albany in 1962 when the State Investigation Commission disclosed, among other things, that John Dawson, the brother of a local political figure, had a no-show job as an assistant purchasing agent of Albany County at $4,000 a year from 1959 to 1962. When Dawson was asked at the hearings what his working hours were and what he had done since being hired, he replied, "I refuse to answer that question on the grounds that it might tend to incriminate me."[4] He resigned shortly after he had testified.

Occasionally after no-show and seldom-show jobs receive notoriety in the newspapers some "no-showers" and "seldom-showers" get the word to do eight hours' work a day for eight hours' pay. But the trouble is frequently that while at work they have trouble finding things to do. When they do work, what they do is often not necessary. They just do it to look busy. Frequently one worker could do the work that two or even three people are getting paid for. But because their jobs are patronage jobs, their positions are rarely eliminated. Those who have no-show and seldom-show jobs usually just show up one day every other week to pick their check up. Some just work in the mornings, four or five days a week, for a few hours a day. When the races are at Saratoga in August, many government employees work in the morning and go to the races in the afternoon.

The Democratic candidates in Albany County won again in 1958 and 1959. In 1959 John Garry was elected district attorney and Eugene Devine was elected county treasurer. In 1960 John Fitzgerald Kennedy fought a close race with Richard Nixon across the country, but it wasn't close in Albany because Kennedy received a plurality of 30,737. Kennedy became the first Roman Catholic and the youngest person, at age thirty-six, to be elected President.

Before John Kennedy announced that he was running for President in 1960, his father, Joe Kennedy, came to Albany to see Dan about his candidacy. Sure enough, Dan promised to support the younger Kennedy, and Dan O'Connell was the first delegate Kennedy had. By the way, O'Connell was the first politician outside the state of Massachusetts whom Joe Kennedy saw about his son's candidacy. When John Kennedy was campaigning in Albany in 1960 he called Dan on the phone. When Joe Kennedy suffered his stroke, President Kennedy wanted to send a presidential plane to Albany to take O'Connell to Palm Beach to visit his father. Dan didn't go because he "wanted to wait to see how he was first. When I found out he couldn't talk I wasn't going to go there." Dan said he was invited several times to the Kennedy Compound in Hyannisport but he never went. Dan says that he wished he had visited Joe Kennedy when he was invited. He didn't visit the Kennedy patriarch because Kennedy was very rich. Dan says, "If he didn't have a dime I would have visited him." Dan likes to associate with ordinary people. He speaks with Rose Kennedy from time to time. According to O'Connell, she had more of an interest in politics than her husband. After all, she is the daughter of a former mayor of Boston, the wife of an ambassador, the mother of nine children, including a President and three U.S. Senators.

CORRUPTION IN ALBANY

Corruption in Albany is perhaps not greater than in any other American city. However, just because corruption exists elsewhere does not provide the excuse for corruption and inefficient government in Albany. The Commission of Investigation of the State of New York has conducted investigations in the city and county of Albany on four different occasions within the past twelve years. What follows are some examples of times when government in Albany wasn't at its best.

An editorial in the December 29, 1972, issue of the *New York Times* expressed an opinion on the accomplishments of the SIC, as the Commission is more popularly known: "The State Commission of Investigation has been a diligent crusader for clean government in the fourteen years since its creation. It added to that record of accomplishment this week with a devastating report on the fleecing of the city of Albany as a result of the suffocating grip maintained by the local Democratic political machine on every aspect of municipal government." Previously mentioned in this book was an SIC investigation in 1912 which recommended that the mayor, commissioner of police, and chief of police be removed from office, but they weren't.

Although the conditions may continue after the SIC issues its report, at least the public knows the way things are. In more recent years there have been investigations into real estate tax delinquencies in Albany County, purchasing practices and procedures of Albany County, and city, and alleged police corruption in the city of Albany. In 1960 the SIC looked into the accumulation of delinquent real estate taxes and wasteful tax compromise practices and policies in Albany County.

In the summer of 1959, the Comptroller of the State of New York released an official report stating that real estate tax delinquency in Albany County had accumulated to more than seven million dollars. This delinquency, the report indicated, was steadily increasing each year because the available means to collect delinquent taxes "have, except in a few instances, not been employed."[5]

The Commission's public hearings in December, 1960, brought to light (a) ineffective tax billing, (b) absence of collection followup, (c) many compromises of tax delinquencies which were unjustifiably lenient, and (d) advantages gained by "insiders." The Commission noted that "one of the consequences of permitting such a situation to exist was the shifting of the necessary burden of taxes from the delinquent property owner to the law abiding taxpayer."[6]

With regard to ineffective billing of tax bills, in Albany County the report noted that there were then thousands of tax bills each year that never reached the owners of the property taxed. If the property owner doesn't receive his tax bill there is the likelihood that his taxes will become delinquent. This may be due to incorrect records of the names and addresses of all property owners in Albany County. The report also mentioned "the indifference of local and County officials towards the condition of those records."[7] One local Albany newspaper quoted the city treasurer as saying that "about 90 percent of the tax bills that bounce back are returned because the property involved has changed hands" and the new owner is not known. Unless property owners receive their tax bills, even though they know they must pay annual taxes on their properties, they don't usually go and inquire about where their bill is. Donald Lynch, who was county clerk when the hearings were being conducted, testified that the county clerk records the transfers of property but that there was no system for notifying the Bureau of Tax Delinquencies of changes in ownership of real estate in Albany County.

If a tax bill is returned there is rarely any further attempt to contact or locate the taxpayer. The Albany County officials' rationalization for this practice was that for the purposes of foreclosure in the County, the bill or notice need not actually reach the taxpayer before the County may proceed to foreclose. The SIC said that "with the exception of a few perfunctory foreclosure complaints signed during the very week of the public hearings, the County has had no policy for foreclosing on property to collect delinquent taxes."[8] If there were a followup system the County would collect a significant amount of taxes that might have gone unpaid under the system of collection before the SIC investigation.

There was an absence of pressure to pay the taxes. A taxpayer may actually profit from his failure to pay taxes, and at worst he will lose nothing by accumulating delinquencies on his properties. This is due to the lenient compromises of tax delinquencies, whereas, if the property owner paid his taxes when due, he would pay 100 percent of the tax bill. But if he waited a few years or more he might have to pay as little as 20 percent of his original tax bill. This amounts to quite a saving. The SIC report said that "in several instances, the opinion was expressed to Commission agents that it was necessary to retain particular local attorneys in order to obtain such tax savings."[9]

The O'Connell organization has believed in the "live and let live" policy that has sustained its power: Do whatever you have to in order to keep the people happy. Taxes in Albany have been low, until the past few years, although low taxes have prevented many needed improvements. The people usually vote their pocketbook. For example, in France, where there are two elections to determine the winner, in the first election, the impulsive French voters choose their candidates based upon their emotions and a sense of liberalism and reformism. But in the second and final election they become reflective and usually vote their pocketbooks.

Another SIC investigation took place in 1963. This time the Commission looked into Albany County's purchasing practices. Six indictments resulted but they were later dismissed. The indictments involved larceny in a transaction with the Ann Lee Home for the Aged (a county facility), and with presenting false claims to the County of Albany.[10]

After a delay, caused by county officials who did not want the investigation to proceed, hearings were held, and the evidence "uncovered serious irregularities, deficiencies, laxities and incompetence in the administration and operation of the office of the Purchasing Agent and certain other County unities; it also revealed improper practices, such as short deliveries, deliveries of goods not conforming to bid specifications and gross overcharging. All of this, for the period under consideration, resulted in a very substantial loss of public funds."[11]

One of the functions of our cities and counties is the purchase of goods, supplies, and equipment for public agencies and institutions. One would assume that, to obtain the most for the money provided through taxes, the city and county purchasing agents would use taxpayers' funds prudently and wisely as a housewife would for her family. However, this is not always the case in local, state, or even national government. This is because of the vast profits made by the suppliers. Because a substantial amount of money is spent by the city and county every year the profits made by any one of a number of suppliers can amount to thousands of dollars. Naturally, a supplier is not expected to go broke in order to supply the city or county; however, when it is possible to obtain the same or a comparable product at less cost, then the less expensive product should be obtained if it's needed.

The SIC learned that meat deliveries to the Ann Lee Home for the Aged were made on Tuesdays and Wednesdays of each week. On one Tuesday in 1961 they made an unannounced visit to the home in order to check the quality of meats delivered against the specifications, and the quantity of the deliveries against delivery receipts. The SIC hired a meat grader to compare the meat delivered to the home with the County specifications. Of fifteen different fresh meat items evaluated, only six were in conformity with the official specifications. The home was receiving "standard" grade of meat, while the specifications called for a better quality, "top choice." The home was receiving hind saddles of veal containing two ribs instead of one. The inclusion of two ribs resulted in the County paying for more bone than meat. The condition of the ribs received by the home was described in the SIC report as "either sticky or slimy" and "dangerous to serve in that condition."

Colony Markets, owned by a Democratic committeeman, was the largest single vendor of fresh meats to Albany County institutions from 1958 to 1962, and did over $100,000 business with Albany County annually. From July through October, 1961, according to the SIC, "the claims paid to Colony for alleged deliveries of hind saddles of veal amounted to 7,676 pounds. In this same period the total available hind saddles as measured by Colony's purchases was 4,949 pounds, resulting in a minimum shortage during this period of 2,727 pounds. At an average price of 88¾¢ per pound the loss to the County during this representative period amounted to $2,420.21. The projected loss for the contract year 1961-1962 was $7,260.63."

The SIC revealed there were considerable shortages in the deliveries to the County Jail by the George F. Mahar Company, which had been selling fresh produce to the County Jail for at least twenty years, and more recently to the Ann Lee Home as well. According to the SIC report, "a comparison of the information contained in the County Jail receiving records with the paid claims on file in the County Treasurer's office disclosed that Mahar charged, and was paid, the sum of $11,687.75 in the year 1960 for fresh produce that was never delivered." The SIC made a similar comparison for the year 1961 and they "disclosed that Mahar charged, and was paid, the sum of $9,569.00 for fresh produce that was never delivered."

The Commission also found that the prices charged for fresh produce were "exorbitant and substantially above prevailing market rates." As an example, the SIC report noted that on May 22, 1961, the County was billed for 60 crates of cabbage at $8.75 per crate. On the same day, a well-known restaurant purchased one crate of cabbage and paid Mahar $3.75.

The SIC also uncovered shortages in deliveries of toilet tissue, paper towels and canned goods. They discovered collusive practices for drugs, and milk bidding. In addition, the SIC looked into the Albany County Highway Department and found that the largest single vendor of equipment and automotive supplies to the Highway Department from 1956 to 1961 was the Beatty Supply Company. During that period that company did approximately one million dollars worth of business with Albany County. The company would negotiate purchases from authorized distributors for items requested by the County. They maintained little or no inventory, according to the SIC. The results of an investigation, the SIC said, "disclosed gross irregularities, fraudulent billings and unconscionably high prices." An SIC investigation in December, 1972, disclosed some of the same deficiencies in connection with the purchasing of goods and services for the city of Albany, which the Commission previously found with respect to the county of Albany, among other things. One other revelation was that the city of Albany had turned over to Albany County Democratic headquarters each year since 1942 a list of city vendors and the volume of their city business so that they could be assessed political contributions.

The report contained testimony from City Purchasing Agent Mary Dollard, who said that she was instructed to keep the records for the party by her predecessor, the late Francis W. Grady, and Donald L. Lynch, former secretary of the County Democratic Committee. She said the practice ended last year when the SIC investigated her office. An SIC counsel asked her if "they wanted to know because the company would then be hit with a percentage of that amount that they would have to contribute in order to continue in business." Mrs. Dollard replied that "I never wanted to know the answer." After the attorney asked her again she said, "I imagine it is the same as the state. I mean, if you do business with the city or state or anything like that, you are supposed to give a contribution and a little thank you."[12]

Summaries of SIC findings involving major city vendors are as follows:

North End Contracting Corp. It was revealed that the North End overcharged the city by at least $450,000 for operation and development of the city landfill between August, 1969 and December, 1971. North End was allowed a 25% markup on the landfill, and a 15% markup of the cost of supplies and equipment for all other city work. However, its books showed a net profit of 43%. The SIC said Albany could save $100,000 of the $170,000 it spends annually to clean catch basins if it did the job itself, instead of hiring a private contractor.

The firm's president, who is a city Democratic ward leader, William

Carey, refunded almost $89,000 to the city after the SIC began auditing its books. An additional $370,000 was refunded to the city later on. Mr. Carey invoked the Fifth and Fourteenth amendments seven times when asked by the SIC if he had kicked back a large amount of money to Democratic headquarters or city officials in October, 1969, 1970, and 1971. Because he refused to answer, he forfeited his right to city work for five years.

Carey said that his company had paid Mayor Corning's insurance firm, Albany Associates, Inc., a total of $81,000 in premiums during the period it ran the landfill. The County Attorney said that Albany County purchase a substantial portion of its insurance from Albany Associates, with premiums totaling approximately $200,000 per year.

Albany Supply & Equipment Co., Inc. It was disclosed that the president of Albany Supply, William Graulty, had a "little black book" (a small looseleaf notebook) in which he listed names of city officials and employees along with coded notations of cash amounts and other gifts such as hams or turkeys. The company did about 95% of its business with the city of Albany by acting as a middleman. Phone orders were received from city officials and then goods were ordered from other wholesalers. In the fiscal year 1970 Albany Supply did $450,000 worth of business. The company made a profit of up to 60% on the goods delivered to the city.[13] Mrs. Marvele Gaul, vice-president of Albany Supply, testified that the firm's president had instructed her to keep all of the city bills under $500, the maximum non-bid contract allowed by law.

Buying gifts for city employees was also done in New York City. Broadway Maintenance Company had serviced New York City's traffic light, parking meters, and air raid sirens for many years. The SIC issued charges of "extensive irregularities, inadequate performance, and excessive profits "against Broadway Maintenance in 1961 when it had more than $5.7 million in city contracts." The SIC also reported that the company allocated $50,000 a year to the purchase of Christmas gifts, such as television sets and "fancy smoked turkeys," for city officials and employees.[14]

Municipal Sales & Service Corp. Municipal Sales was described by the SIC as a "corporate shell" with capital of only $3,000 when it was granted a city sweeping contract that grossed the company $1.65 million from 1969 to 1971. Municipal Sales was able to get equipment to perform the contract by a lease arrangement with Heartland Leasing Corp., passing finance costs of $111,307 along to the city. The SIC said Heartland is owned and controlled by the officers and directors of National Commercial Bank & Trust Co., of which Mayor Corning is a director. It said further that Municipal Sales purchased about half of its equipment from its sister firm, William H. Clark Municipal Equipment Inc., and in the process "frequently" passed a 119% markup along

to the city. The report showed that another city got 1,200 miles out
of one of its sweeping brooms, while Municipal Sales got only 360 miles.

Albany Dodge, Inc. Until May, 1970, the city bought almost all of
its vehicles from Albany Dodge without public bidding. When state
bidding laws were tightened at that time, the city got around the
stricter law by writing specifications that were tailored to Dodges, or
possibly Plymouths. The police sergeant who ran the police garage said
the specifications were taken directly from a Dodge sales flyer.

The SIC said an analysis of repairs to police vehicles "revealed that
certain cars appeared to have sustained unusually high repair costs."
One car underwent repairs costing $2,265 in a seven-month period, and
another sustained repairs costing $1,637 in five months. The cost of
a new cruiser at the time was about $3,000. Albany Dodge billed the
city $52 for 16 tappets for car no. 9 on May 10, 1971. On a bill dated
the following day, the company billed the city for 16 more tappets for
the same car. The car has only 16 tappets.

The police officer who ran the police garage said he had bought
three Dodge vehicles from Albany Dodge since 1969. In August, 1972,
he purchased a new 1972 Dodge pickup. The sticker price of the
vehicle was $3,935. He said that he paid $1,560 in cash, and the balance
due of $2,375 was satisfied by a trade-in allowance for his pickup truck
purchased in 1969 at a cost of $2,107. Albany Dodge thus granted him
a trade-in allowance that was approximately $200 greater than the
original cost of the vehicle purchased three years earlier. The SIC
said "one can reasonably doubt whether their relationship served the
best interests of the city of Albany."[15]

Hudson River Construction Co., Inc. Hudson River, according to
the SIC, farmed out a city contract for cleaning catch basins to a
subsidiary, Alascon Inc., and charged the city $154,000 between 1969
and 1971 to rent a piece of equipment that cost $36,000. The city
could have saved much money had it done the job instead of paying
Hudson River to do it.

North End Cleaning Service. On July 23, 1971, Albany received
$74,249 from the State of New York for an ecological project. Two
months later it paid $73,914 to North End Cleaning, which was given
the job without bid by John Phelan of the Albany Department of
Public Works. The SIC claimed that the job cost Paul Leonard, owner
of North End Cleaning, only $26,206. Leonard claimed it cost about
$40,000 or $45,000. Either way the profit was very substantial.

John P. Martin Plumbing & Heating Corp. The SIC noted that
John P. Martin, president, has been an Albany County Democratic committeeman for twenty-four years, and thirteenth ward leader for seven
years. The company, according to the SIC, did about $300,000 worth of
work for the city in 1970 and 1971, all without public bid and all paid
in claims lower than the $500 no-bid maximum. Martin contributed

$11,000 to the Albany County Democratic Committee between 1969 and 1972, in the months of October and November. The contributions were made by corporate check, according to the SIC, a misdemeanor under the state election law. The SIC said Martin placed 90% of his insurance with the firm owned by Mayor Corning, Albany Associates.[16] Most of the contractors mentioned had large amounts of unexplained cash disbursements, according to the SIC, during October and November of each year. The SIC insinuated that the cash was given to the Albany County Democratic Committee as a "thank you."

Mayor Corning testified before the SIC, and the Commission said, "The mayor's testimony was, to some extent, characterized by indefinite and evasive answers and at times was contradictory. It appears to indicate a personal lack of knowledge of city operations. This was particularly unusual in view of his thirty-year tenure as mayor."[17] An example of the mayor's elusive testimony came when the SIC asked him about Mr. James Ryan, an individual whom the mayor has known well for more than thirty years and who has been executive secretary of the Democratic party.

Q. Mr. Mayor, do you know Mr. James Ryan?
A. James Bryan?
Q. Ryan, Mr. Mayor.
A. Yes, James Ryan, yes I do.
Q. How long have you known James Ryan, Mr. Mayor.
A. Well, I should say perhaps twenty years, perhaps twenty-five.
Q. What does Mr. Ryan do for a living, Mr. Mayor?
A. I don't know.
Q. You have known this man for twenty years, Mr. Mayor, and you are not aware of what he does for a living and/or livelihood.
A. That is correct.
Q. Is he in any way associated with the Democratic Albany County Democratic Committee?
A. I believe he is, yes.
Q. I am asking you, Mr. Mayor, if you know for a fact that this gentleman is associated with that Committee?
A. All I know is that he is in Democratic Headquarters from time to time.

In recent years, the Ryans didn't particularly like Corning, and a deepening split between them occurred after the mayor pretended to the SIC that he didn't know Jimmy Ryan well. Nonetheless, the Ryans, being the faithful Democrats that they are, always supported the mayor and other Democrats on election day. Jimmy Ryan visits Dan O'Connell almost every day, and is O'Connell's closest friend. Today, Jimmy is the only person Dan will let drive him. Until a few years ago O'Connell had a chauffeur. O'Connell's trust and confidence in Jimmy Ryan are overwhelming. If Mayor Corning does not succeed Uncle Dan as county chairman, his successor will most likely be one of the Ryans.

Shortly after the SIC completed its investigation of the purchasing practices in Albany, it began an investigation of alleged police corruption in the city. On October 4, 1973, the acting chairman of the SIC, Edward S. Silver, after completing an eight-day public hearing, said, "We believe that it was a comprehensive hearing at which startling facts were unfolded before the eyes of the people of Albany." Silver added, "This was a very difficult investigation. It is well known that in investigations of alleged official misconduct or corruption, witnesses do not come forth voluntarily to furnish essential information; nor are they willing to tell all they know, or anything they know, even when testifying under a subpoena. The usual results of such self-protective circumstances is that the police corruption that exists continues and grows greater, bolder and more oppressive as time goes on." Silver said that "it would appear from the evidence that such a sordid condition has existed in Albany."[18]

The evidence presented at the SIC's hearings shows that members of the Albany Police Department, over a period of years, engaged in such acts of misconduct and corruption as (1) burglaries of business establishments, (2) larcenies in taking moneys from parking meters, (3) receiving, on a regular basis, payoffs from persons involved in narcotics and prostitution, (4) permitting after-hours "joints" to operate openly where liquor was sold illegally and patronized at the same time by police officers, pimps, prostitutes and narcotic addicts and sellers, and (5) paying inadequate attention to illegal gambling operations so that it often became necessary for other law enforcement agencies to move in and make raids and arrests.

Bars in Albany have long been permitted to stay open after hours. And even though the police have been aware of such violations, the number of arrests for ABC violations has been practically zero. An examination of the annual reports of the Albany Police Department shows that the number of arrests for ABC violations during the five-year period 1968 through 1972, inclusive, is as follows: 1968—0; 1969—1; 1970—0; 1971—0; and 1972—2. The department's record of gambling arrests was also very poor, and often the state police or other outside law enforcement agencies had to step in to fill the void. Following are the gambling arrest figures by the Albany police over the five-year period 1968 through 1972, inclusive: 1968—0; 1969—7; 1970—29; 1971—0; and 1972—65.

On August 26, 1971, the New York State Organized Crime Task Force conducted a series of gambling raids and arrested 24 persons in the Albany area. On September 1, of the same year, 7 additional arrests were made, bringing to a total of 31 the number of persons arrested for gambling by this outside law enforcement agency. One of those arrested was connected with organized crime, according to the Organized Crime Task Force, with their annual gambling gross estimated at between $4 and $6 million in layoff action. It is interesting to note that the Albany police failed to make a single gambling arrest during that year. But even when an occasional arrest was made for gambling offenses, those arrested would be let off with a light fine and be in business again the same day.

With respect to burglaries, a former member of the Albany Police Department testified that he and other police officers, including a sergeant who has since been promoted to lieutenant, burglarized business establishments, from small stores to the A&P and J. C. Penney. On occasion, when a call was received to investigate a burglary the police officers first on the scene would help themselves to whatever they wanted. According to the SIC, "Officers developed their own special talents in the methods of breaking into closed business establishments. Some, crude in their methods, were known as 'crashers.' Others developed more sophisticated techniques and attempted to avoid any evidence of a forced entry. This also obviated the need for reporting a burglary."[19]

Albany police officers both as individuals and as groups stole various kinds of merchandise from area stores. The goods included tires, television sets, bicycles, clothes, hams, cigarettes, appliances, and furniture. Officers committed these crimes on a regular basis, often while in uniform and on duty. Patrol cars were often used to transport the stolen merchandise. At the SIC hearings, some police officers confessed that they committed burglaries with fellow officers because of peer pressure. One officer said that in order to remain in good standing in the squad he had to tell them that he was stealing more than he actually did. Even officers who didn't want to be involved did so because of fear of bad assignments and intimidation. Officers above the rank of patrolman were involved in the illegal activities. One police sergeant "instigated" and was the leader of the group of officers who participated in these larcenies.[20] The wife of a former Albany police officer testified that on occasions when her husband worked the midnight to eight A.M. tour, she awoke in the morning and found merchandise, including a television set, which had not been there the previous night.[21]

Another kind of alleged corruption mentioned in the report was the taking of money and other gifts by policemen from firms doing business with the city. Some officers were given free meals or meals at a discount at local restaurants. While this practice has been criticized on occasion, it is minor compared with the larcenies and burglaries committed by policemen. With respect to parking meter collections, according to the testimony of several former police officers, this was a "very desirable and much sought-after assignment." One former police officer said that he recalled taking home as much as $250 to $280 as his share from just one day's parking meter collections. Quite a fringe benefit!

The SIC deposited chemically-treated coins into parking meters scheduled for collection. The chemical was a dye that was invisible to the naked eye but luminous under ultraviolet light. A specific number of coins, e.g., 100, were deposited in certain meters. These meters were then under constant observation until they were collected, by a police officer in the Traffic Division, and deposited in the bank. The bags of coins were opened at the bank under SIC supervision, and the coins were put under an ultraviolet light. On one occasion when 100 chemically-treated dimes were deposited in parking meters, only 23 such dimes were turned in to the bank. On another occasion, only 48 of the 100 coins were deposited. These results substantiated allegations of thefts of parking meter revenue by members of the Albany Police Department.[22]

Metered parking in Albany is charged at the rate of ten cents an hour. In 1971, the New York State Department of Audit and Control said that "on the basis of the approximately 1400 meters operated by the city of Albany in the 1969-70 year, the average yield was less than seven cents a day per meter."[23]

Witnesses testified before the SIC that prostitution was quite open and that the police knew this. There was testimony that a detective had a prostitute working for him. The detective said he knew and saw this girl, on and off, on a weekly average over about three years; he visited her at her home; went with her to after-hour liquor "joints," and received gifts of clothing and jewelry from her; but he didn't know what work she did for a living. He said he thought she was someone's mistress. Other police officers and persons in Albany knew differently.

A well-known procurer, who was considered one of the big traffickers in narcotics in Albany, testified that he ran several houses of prostitution and that the police knew this. In order to continue his business, he had to pay about $240 to $245 to police officers each week. He stated that these payoffs were so costly that he had to seek other sources of income to keep going. And that is how he decided to go into narcotics. His narcotics operations were known by the police. Another witness before the SIC testified that her house of prostitution made payments to police of about $500 to $600 per week.

Former Detective Sergeant Robert Byers testified that while he was in charge of the Narcotics Enforcement Unit in the Albany Police Department he realized that narcotics was a serious problem in Albany. He felt that some police officers were tipping off narcotics dealers, thus frustrating police investigations.[24]

New York State Commission of Investigation was critical of the judiciary in the city and county of Albany because the judges continually quashed Commission subpoenas, despite being consistently overturned by higher courts. The SIC said, "Motions attacking Commission subpoenas were signed by and returnable before several Justices of the Supreme Court, Albany County, and were argued not only in Albany but in Troy and Monticello as well. . . . The Commission found it necessary to formally move in court that two Supreme Court Justices who were scheduled to hear matters involving the Commission, disqualify themselves on the grounds of alleged prejudice against the Commission. Both Judges denied these motions, both subsequently rendered decisions against the Commission, and both were unanimously reversed by the Appellate Division, which reversals were unanimously affirmed by the Court of Appeals."[25] Such favoritism toward the Albany County Democratic machine by area judges and "the disruption it caused upon the orderly administration of justice" led the Commission to ask, "in a most unusual application" for a special judge to hear and determine all matters involving the Commission's investigation.

After the SIC's 1973 investigation of the Albany Police Department, the Commission filed with the Chief Judge of the New York State Court of Appeals a formal complaint alleging judicial misconduct on the part of Supreme Court Justice John H. Pennock. Justice Pennock was one of two Supreme Court Justices whom the Commission had asked to disqualify themselves on the grounds of alleged bias against the Commission. The State Committee on Judicial Conduct disapproved of the conduct of Justice Pennock and said that his actions "violate the high standards of propriety expected of judicial officers."[26]

Albany County Judge John Clyne, a Democrat who has been publicly criticized by Dan O'Connell for giving such harsh sentences, ordered sealed a grand jury report on its investigation of the Albany Police Department. Clyne's decision, although one that the Albany Democratic machine liked, was not one that did justice for the citizens of Albany. In an editorial entitled "Let's Get Courts Out of Politics" the *Times Union* wrote: "The obstructionist tactics granted by area Supreme Court judges in the SIC investigations of Albany purchasing practices, police activity and other areas of city management have by now made a mockery of the judicial process." The editorial continued: "The local Democratic organization, faced with a continuing SIC probe of its municipal operations, apparently has found a series of willing accomplices to delay, obstruct, confuse and disrupt the SIC attempts to get all the facts it wants and needs in its Albany investigations."[27]

Politics has played a significant role in the Albany Police Department. According to testimony by present and former Albany police officers at the 1973 SIC investigation, many police officers joined the force through the help of their ward leaders. They also turned to politicians for assistance in getting favorable assignments or promotions.

In appreciation, the police officers would annually contribute to the party an amount of money directly related to their positions. A patrolman gave about $30 annually, before the election. A look at testimony by Albany police officers before the SIC is as follows:

Q. How did you get on the Albany Police Department? How did you go about doing that?

A. I approached the ward leader and asked him if I could be assigned to the Albany Police Department.

Q. Why did you do it that way?

A. Because I was told from various City agencies and members of the Department at the time that was the procedure.

Q. Were any references required?

A. Yes.

Q. What type of references were you advised to get for your application?

A. Influential people in the City, preferably politically influential.[28]

Another police officer testified: that, before he was hired, he was looking for a job and a ward leader told him if he wanted to he could either go on the police or the fire department.[29] One police officer said he made his contribution to the party, in uniform, to a stranger in the back room of a local downtown hotel. He said after he gave a man thirty dollars, the man crossed off his name on a roster of police officers.[30]

One witness, a former detective sergeant, testified that "although he did not make contributions, he recalled a command officer showing members of the Detective Division a card which bore the name of the place to which contributions were to be brought; the hours and days to do it; and the man to see." The detective was asked about one conversation he had had with the Chief of Police concerning this subject:

Q. Did any officer with rank of either Deputy or Chief of Police make any comment to you ever about your failure to make contributions?

A. Yes, sir.

Q. Can you relate that?

A. Yes. This is only a rumor that there was a list of violators that were not contributing and that I seemed to be one of the top violators. And the present Chief of Police, Edward McArdle, stated that I should square up with 75 State Street just in case some time I might need a favor.

Q. What did 75 State Street mean?

A. That's Democratic Headquarters, I believe.[31]

One prostitute testified that she "was in jail one time and they [the Albany police] told me before election time that if I would vote, go down and vote Democratic, they would let me out of jail. They took me down in the paddy wagon down Hudson Avenue where the fire station is, and that is how I got out of jail." The fire station was a polling place.[32] Other persons involved in prostitution gave similar testimony concerning the "requirement" that girls vote Democratic if they wanted to remain in business.[33]

RECENT POLITICAL DEVELOPMENTS

In 1961, Donald Lynch gave the county clerk's office to Gilmartin, William Rice was elected sheriff, Richard Conners was elected president of the Common Council, Larry Ehrhardt was elected comptroller (Ehrhardt was first elected to that position in 1945), and Erastus Corning was reelected as mayor by 33,483 votes. Rockefeller was reelected governor in 1962 and he lost the county by only 3,202 votes against Robert Morgenthau. However, Rockefeller lost in the city by about 20,000 votes. The other Democrats won again in 1962 and 1963. John Bartlett was elected county clerk in 1963 and John McCall was elected surrogate. President Lyndon Baines Johnson carried Albany County by more than 82,000 votes in 1964. Congressman Leo O'Brien carried the county by more than 75,000 votes. The other Democrats also came in with huge margins because of President Johnson's coattails.

The election of Robert Kennedy, John Kennedy's brother, campaign manager, and attorney general, in 1964 to the United States Senate brought inspiration to New York State politics. Just like Jack Kennedy, Bobby had much charisma. Although Massachusetts was the state brothers Jack and Teddy represented in the Senate, Bobby ran for election in New York State. While Bobby was younger he also lived in New York. I can remember seeing Robert Kennedy, during the campaign and after he was elected, and would remind him to call Dan O'Connell. I would say, "Bobby, don't forget to call Uncle Dan." He once confusedly replied, knowing my last name was Solomon, "Is he your uncle?" To that I responded, "He's everybody's uncle."

Although O'Connell liked John Kennedy and Teddy he didn't care for Bobby. However, Bobby seemed to like Dan. Dave Powers, an aide to President Kennedy and author of the best-selling book *Johnnie, We Hardly Knew Ye*, was in Albany in 1973 and said that Bobby Kennedy took Dan seriously. Robert Kennedy was different from his two older brothers. He was ruthless and had a love of power. After President John F. Kennedy was assassinated it was up to Robert to take over because he was the next oldest. That's the way Joe Kennedy would have wanted it.

The New York Sheraton Hotel was where Bobby waited while the returns were coming in on election day. After he was assured victory and made his speech, he acted as if he did it alone. Before then, however, he was more congenial. Power sometimes goes to people's heads. Perhaps that is what Dan didn't like about him. Success never went to Dan O'Connell's head although he was among the most successful of political bosses. The true politico is always prepared for the next election and realizes that the support of the voters and bosses is needed in order to be reelected.

That November, Bobby ran against Kenneth Keating, the Republican incumbent. President Johnson helped campaign for Bobby in New York State. President Johnson, in his autobiography *The Vantage Point*, said he had to disappoint his friend Adlai Stevenson, who also wanted the New York senatorial nomination. The late President said Stevenson "abandoned the idea when I told him that I felt I must support Bobby" because of the loyalty Johnson felt to President Kennedy. Johnson added that "Stevenson was hurt, and my inability to encourage him constituted one of my deepest regrets about the New York campaign."[34]

Mayor Corning was reelected by a majority of 34,000 along with the other Democrats in 1965. Then, when the voters went to the polls on Tuesday, November 8, 1966, and the results were tabulated, it was announced that Albany had elected a Republican Congressman. Leo O'Brien did not run for office again, so the president of the Common Council, Richard Conners, ran against newspaper editor Dan Button, a Republican. What a surprise! Button won by about 16,500 votes. This was the first time in Albany since 1921 that a Republican had been elected to an important office. Leo O'Brien never visited Dan after he declined to run for reelection in 1966. Dan was angry because he wanted O'Brien to run for Congress again because he knew he could have been reelected. O'Connell said O'Brien was ungrateful.

Also in 1966 Governor Rockefeller carried Albany County by about 3,000 votes over New York City Council president Frank O'Connor, now a federal judge. But O'Connor won in the city by about 14,000 votes. That year Franklin D. Roosevelt, Jr., son of the late President, also ran for governor but only on the Liberal ticket. He received only 1,206 votes in the city, compared with O'Connor's 35,454. It's a shame that Roosevelt, an Under Secretary of Commerce under LBJ, did not wait until the next gubernatorial election because he most likely would have gotten the nomination had O'Connor lost in 1966. Even though Button was elected and Rockefeller carried the county, the other Democratic candidates won.

There was a weakness in the Democratic party in Albany. Edward Fischer was elected sheriff in 1967 by 9,126. In the same year County Clerk John Bartlett won by only 3,612. While the Democrats for county office had challenging races, the Democrats for city office had easy victories. Segal was elected City Court Judge by 29,529 votes. Button was reelected to Congress with 9,128 votes over Jacob Herzog in 1968. Sadly for the Democrats, Button was not the only Republican to be elected. State Senator Julian Erway was defeated by Walter Langley, a Republican. Assemblyman Harvey Lifset was defeated by Republican Fred Field, Jr. Democratic Assemblyman Frank Cox was defeated by Raymond Skuse, another Republican. But the worst news was yet to come. A Republican, Arnold Proskin, was elected district attorney over Joseph Scully by about 8,000 votes. John Garry did not seek reelection as district attorney, and Scully was nominated instead. The loss of the district attorney's office was the worst loss of all that year. The Democrats did elect two coroners, and county treasurer Gene Devine won, but by only 8,334 votes. The trend could not continue if the Democrats were to remain in power. The Humphrey-Muskie Democratic ticket carried Albany County by 25,944 votes over Nixon and Agnew that year.

In Chicago at the 1968 Democratic National Convention, the Albany O'Connell delegation voted the Humphrey side on all issues. For example, while 116 New York delegates supported the dovish Vietnam plank which called for an end to the war in Vietnam, the Albany delegation was among the 24 delegates from New York State who supported the Humphrey plank, which largely followed President Johnson's policies. (For additional information on the 1968 Democratic National Convention see the chapter on Mayor Richard Daley.) Johnson's administration was known as the "Great Society," and many important pieces of social and economic legislation were passed by Congress. Medicare was established, and much progress was made in civil rights. The Twenty-fourth Amendment, ratified in 1964, abolished poll taxes in federal elections.

The Vietnam War cost the United States many lives and much money. And although our involvement in Southeast Asia can be traced to the Eisenhower administration, it was during the Johnson years that the war came to a peak. The war made it look as though Johnson's Great Society had been more trouble than good. We often forget the good things and remember the bad. Because Humphrey was Johnson's Vice-President, he was associated with the Johnson administration and the Vietnam War. The trouble in Chicago during the Democratic convention also hurt Humphrey's chances. Nevertheless the election was very close, and the Republican candidate, Richard Nixon, won by only about 500,000 votes. Nixon was a minority President because he didn't get more than half of the votes cast (43.4%). George Wallace, governor of Alabama, ran as a third-party candidate of the American Independent Party and received 13.5% of the votes. Wallace received a respectable showing, considering that he was a third-party candidate.

The Democrats needed a rest and the off-year election of 1969 let them rest a little. At least there weren't any county offices at stake in Albany. Mayor Corning was reelected with 22,663 votes along with his fellow Democrats for city office. Then former Supreme Court Justice Arthur Goldberg and State Senator Basil Paterson, a black, were defeated for governor and lieutenant governor by the Rockefeller ticket in 1970. Rockefeller lost in the city of Albany by about 1,500 votes, but he carried the county by about 25,000 votes.

Governor Rockefeller's South Mall project, now called the Empire State Plaza, chased about 6,000 families out of Albany's South End, and they couldn't buy new homes for $6,000 or $7,000. Dan O'Connell said the place was worse than Longfellow's Acadia. Acadia, a district in Nova Scotia, was a bone of contention in the wars between France and England. In 1775 about 6,500 residents were forcibly deported by the British because of the imminence of war with France and because their neutrality was questioned. O'Connell says that when the South Mall project is completed it will be like Wall Street on Sunday. Blocks and blocks of big buildings but no one there.

O'Connell noted that "there was a shift of the population." About 30,000 people left Albany because of that project. He says "it was very bad for the city. Mayor Corning raised hell about it but it didn't do any good." That area was heavily Democratic, and many good votes were lost by the machine as residences were torn down to make way for the expensive state office buildings. Many businesses in downtown Albany were forced to close because of the construction. The mall cost more than $1 billion. While it looks beautiful with all the Vermont marble, the cost certainly was tremendous both for the taxpayers in New York State and for the O'Connell machine. The mall is supposed to be completed in 1976, and 11,000 state employees will be working there.

In recent years the City of Albany has purchased much real estate in downtown Albany in an attempt to renovate the downtown area, which currently doesn't say too much for the city. Those who owned buildings and property that were sold to the city made a nice profit. And many property owners in downtown Albany are patiently waiting for the city to purchase their property because if they tried to sell it to a private individual they couldn't get nearly what the city would give them; real estate in the downtown area isn't worth very much. While it is expected that many of the city-owned buildings will be torn down in the future (maybe another three to five years), so that new buildings can be put up, many businessmen who are tenants to the city continue to pay low rents, particularly if they are Democrats. It is not unusual for businessmen who previously paid $750 rent per month to pay half that amount, provided the Democratic machine goes along. Also, some tenants of the city have skipped paying rent for one or two months at a time.

In 1970 Congressman Daniel Button of Albany was defeated by Congressman Sam Stratton of Amsterdam by almost 27,000 votes. The congressional district for Albany was changed, thus permitting Stratton to run against Button. The Albany Democrats regained their seat in Congress after four years. Republican State Senator Walter Langley was reelected to a second term by about 3,000 votes over former sheriff Rice. Democrat Ed Fischer was reelected sheriff by only about 6,000 votes. Republican District Attorney Arnold Proskin was reelected by about 12,000 votes over Tom Keegan, who is now police court justice in the city. The Democrats elected a city court judge, recorder of the Traffic Court, and two county coroners that year.

Also in 1971 it looked as if the Democrats had lost the county treasurer's office the day after the election, but a recount showed that the Democrats would have at least another three years in that office. O'Connell says that if the Democrats ever lost the county treasurer's office they could always move the records over to the county attorney's office. The county attorney is appointed by the Democratic-controlled county legislature.

The Albany county treasurer (salary is $10,000 a year), as the title signifies, has the responsibility to pay all county bills; so he is privy to all county transactions. O'Connell said if there were a Republican county treasurer in Albany with a Democratic county legislature, much of the treasurer's power could be transferred to the county attorney. However, the treasurer could still be able to make any bad or illegal contract or bad purchasing procedure a public issue in the news media. In November, 1973, there was a referendum to establish a county executive. O'Connell was against the move but gave in because it won't make much difference; most important things the county executive will do must be approved by the county legislature, now controlled by the Democrats.

Richard Nixon carried Albany County in 1972 by about 16,000 votes over Senator George McGovern (Nixon lost the county by about 26,000 votes in 1968, so apparently not too many people liked McGovern). In his campaign of 1968 Nixon promised to end the war, but as of the campaign of 1972 we were still in Vietnam. Before the Democratic convention was held many people thought anyone could beat Nixon because of the war and the poor economy. At the convention in July, 1972, the Democrats nominated Senator George McGovern of South Dakota for president and Senator Thomas Eagleton of Missouri. Many labor leaders and old-time politicians did not like McGovern, who was very liberal and viewed as almost radical by some. Mayor Richard Daley and his delegation from Chicago were not seated at the convention. Daley helped Humphrey get the nomination in 1968 instead of Senator Eugene McCarthy, also of Minnesota. Many of the people who helped institute the new Democratic reforms promised that Daley would get his day. It happened in Miami Beach.

The Democrats should have been able to do some serious campaigning because their convention was held early in July, but shortly after

their convention was over with it was disclosed that their vice-presidential candidate, Eagleton, has a history of mental illness. Eagleton was
forced to leave the ticket, and Sargent Shriver, former head of the
Peace Corps and a brother-in-law of the famous Kennedy family, took
his place. Eagleton's disclosure hurt the ticket. But many Democrats
did not like their party's nominee, so a "Democrats for Nixon" committee was established for disenchanted Democrats. There were many
alienated Democrats and voters in this election. Few people voted,
and Nixon won by a wide margin. Many voters did not want Nixon
or McGovern, so they did not vote. This was the first presidential
election when eighteen-year-olds were allowed to vote as a result of
the Twenty-sixth Amendment. Not as many young people voted as were
expected, and as McGovern had hoped.

At the 1972 Democratic National Convention in Miami Beach the
power of the O'Connell machine was definitely noticeable in that
Albany's eight delegates were for Hubert Humphrey, later Henry
"Scoop" Jackson, while the rest of New York's delegates (264) were
for George McGovern. The O'Connell delegation had voted consistently
against the McGovern forces in caucus and floor votes. The Twenty-
eighth Congressional District, which Albany is in, was the only one in
New York State where Senator McGovern was shut out in the June 28,
1972, primary as the O'Connell organization carried in all eight of its
uncommitted delegates. Had Humphrey decided to run in the New
York primary, the O'Connell slate would have committed itself to him.

At the top of the list of delegates on the primary ballot in Albany
was the name of Daniel P. O'Connell. When the voters in Albany saw
his name on the ballot they knew which slate to vote for. It was the
only time his name had appeared on an election ballot since 1919,
when he was elected assessor. O'Connell never intended to go to the
convention, but his name was used to give the slate an identity. The
McGovern slate didn't have a chance. By running as a delegate O'Connell put his reputation on the line. He won easily. McGovern workers
in Albany said the O'Connell organization was the best operation they
had come up against in months of primary campaigning for McGovern
across the country.

O'Connell always sent Albany's mayor to represent him at state and
national Democratic conventions, so Mayor Corning led the delegation
from Albany in 1972. Corning was named by the state committee as
a delegate at large. This was his seventh national convention. Mary
Marcy was elected as a delegate but she didn't attend the convention.
Charles Ryan, Albany County Democratic party treasurer, attended the
convention. Also one black man from Albany attended, only for appearance' sake due to the reformed delegate selection rules. After
Humphrey dropped out of the nomination while the convention was
in session, the Albany delegation supported "Scoop" Jackson. Only

after Senator McGovern's total mounted over the necessary 1,509 mark did the Albany delegation switch their votes to McGovern to get on the bandwagon.

When George McGovern was in Albany campaigning after he got the nomination, an aide of his offered to send a limousine to pick up O'Connell and take him to the airport to meet McGovern. Little did he know that Dan O'Connell never went to meet any candidate. Big or small, they all came to see him. O'Connell didn't like McGovern. He said he was a radical. However, Dan still voted for McGovern because Dan always voted a straight Democratic ticket.

Even the powerful Richard J. Daley of Chicago was not elected a delegate in the 1972 primary. Daley, the man who controlled the 1968 convention, which was held in his home city, was thrown out of the 1972 convention. It was a very rude ouster. Daley had supported Humphrey. The O'Connell delegation voted to seat Daley and his delegation, but they weren't successful. The McGovern group was surely in control in Miami Beach, just as Daley had controlled the Chicago convention four years earlier. In addition to party leaders who weren't seated at the convention as delegates, many party members were alienated against the party, because it was extremely difficult to obtain credentials to get into the convention center. This happened in 1968 and 1972. Many delegates brought their wives to the convention, but found that they could not get them into the convention hall because a very limited number of passes was available.

Many new convention rules for the 1972 Democratic National Convention were brought about because of the turmoil and disorder of the 1968 convention. Also, many liberals who supported Senator Gene McCarthy of Minnesota in 1968 felt that their voices had gone unheard because of the old-time politics. Not since Andrew Jackson had the Democratic Party undergone so much reorganization as in 1972. Party reform has opened the doors for many more people and has strengthened the two-party system. As Thomas Jefferson said, "Laws and institutions must go hand in hand with the progress of the human mind. As that becomes more developed, more enlightened, as new discoveries are made, new truths disclosed, and manners and opinions change with the change of circumstances, institutions must advance also, and keep pace with the times." The Democratic Party must change with the times too.

The new guidelines on the selection of delegates required states to select their delegations in a way that gave "full opportunity for participation by all Democrats," including women, young people, and minorities. The guidelines were proposed by the Commission on Party Structure and Delegate Selection under its two chairmen (first, Senator George McGovern of South Dakota, and later, Representative Donald M. Fraser of Minnesota). All delegates had to be chosen openly during the year of the convention, at least three-fourths of them by popular election. In 1972 as a result of reform there were Democratic primaries in a record twenty-three states, seven more than in 1968. Another reform enacted at the Democratic National Convention was the abolition of the unit rule, under which the entire vote of a state delegation was cast as the majority of the delegation had voted. The Republican National Convention does not permit the unit rule, but many state conventions still follow it.

Sam Stratton was reelected to Congress in 1972, carrying the city of Albany by about 39,000 votes and the county by about 78,000 votes. Stratton has been the strongest Democrat vote-drawer at the polls in Albany in the past few years. Before World War II, he worked in Congress as an aide. When the war started, he joined the navy because he realized that a veteran would have a better chance in politics than a nonveteran. In his campaigns, he could say that he was a war hero. After leaving the navy, wanting to enter politics, Stratton thought it would be best to get his start where he had roots—where he lived. He was born in Schenectady, and his father was a minister there until his family moved to Rochester, where he attended school. Thus his roots were in two places. Stratton then observed the political situation in both cities. In Rochester the Republican and Democratic parties were fairly stable and it wouldn't have been easy for Stratton, or any new-comer, to advance too quickly. In Schenectady there was a scandal in the Republican Party, although the Republicans definitely controlled the city. The Democratic Party was weak but it would have been easy for Stratton to make his debut in politics. He realized that, although the Democratic Party was then the minority party in Schenectady, he could make it the majority party. And so he made his choice. He chose Schenectady and became its mayor and congressman.

One of the most conservative New York Democrats in Congress, Stratton was considered to be a possible candidate for the Democratic nomination for governor in 1974, and although he would have liked to run, he didn't. O'Connell didn't want him to run for governor because he didn't want to lose Stratton's seat in Congress. Of course, if Stratton had insisted on running for governor, O'Connell would have supported him. But Stratton didn't have enough money to carry on a statewide campaign, and he isn't known by many people in downstate New York.

A secret White House document released before Nixon resigned disclosed that Charles Colson, one of then-President Nixon's aides, had once recommended Stratton to head the "plumbers" unit established to spy on Nixon's political enemies. Colson described Stratton in a mid-1971 memo to H. R. Haldeman as "an articulate and ambitious" individual who "although a Democrat, is totally on our side on these issues." Stratton denied that he was ever contacted by any of Nixon's aides pertaining to this memo. At times Stratton supported Nixon policies more often than some Republicans.

The state legislature has the power to cut up election districts. They must, however, keep in mind certain requirements. But it is possible, and it happens frequently, that a Republican legislature will cut up a heavily Democratic district (for example, a 32-to-1 ratio of Democrats to Republicans) and reduce the ratio (say to 3-to-1) so that the Republicans will have a better chance on election day.

This process, done by both parties, of reapportioning an election district to the advantage of a political party is called gerrymandering. Politicians have been doing this sort of thing ever since Governor Elbridge Gerry of Massachusetts came up with boundary lines in 1812 that bunched his opponent party's strongholds into a tiny number of weirdly shaped districts, including one that resembled a salamander. Someone called it a Gerrymander, and the name stuck. Gerrymandering is used to strengthen or weaken the number of minority groups in a district. The Republicans have tried to gerrymander Congressman Sam Stratton out of his seat in Congress but he has survived such tactics.

In 1972, State Senator Walter Langley, a Republican, was reelected by about 18,000 votes over Leonard Weiss, an Albany attorney. Former Police Court Justice Michael V. Tepedino, a Democrat, was elected Family Court Judge by about 5,000 votes. Democrat John Clyne was elected County Judge by around 8,000 votes. The Democrats also elected a coroner in 1972.

The charter under which the New York State Bar Association was organized in 1877 tells us that it was formed, among other reasons, "to cultivate the science of jurisprudence, to promote reform in the law, to facilitate the administration of justice, to elevate the standard of integrity, honor and courtesy in the legal profession." The *Knickerbocker News* (Albany) wrote in an editorial that "in the case of the Albany County Bar Association, however, these are just empty words."[35] The newspaper took that harsh position after Albany Police Court Justice Michael V. Tepedino (now a Family Court Judge) was "summoned to City Hall by Mayor Corning to discuss the case of George Bunch before Mr. Bunch was to appear in Judge Tepedino's court on a charge of slapping a twelve-year-old [white] girl," when she called him a derogatory name. Bunch, who was a Negro leader in Albany, was held in jail without bail for the misdemeanor charge by Judge Tepedino until a State Supreme Court judge ordered his release.

At the time, just as in other American cities during the mid-sixties, there was restlessness in Albany's ghetto. The Albany Democratic machine was at odds with many Negroes then. Bunch's imprisonment without bail was one way the machine dealt with its enemies. The newspaper added, "If this type of City Hall meeting between a mayor and a judge had occurred almost anywhere else in the United States, it would have resulted in cries of outrage and demands for investigations, with the local bar association leading the parade." However, the bar association in Albany was different from those in other counties.

Dan Button in his successful campaign for Congress in 1966 used this as one of his campaign issues. Another issue was that of the five-dollar vote, and allegations that the Albany machine bought votes. Button said the continuation of the "machine" rule in Albany is based on a "great myth" that assumes that "one man is infallible, his judgments and his decisions are not to be questioned, and that 'you can't fight city hall.'" He cited six factors that, he said, demonstrated the Albany "machine's contemptuous disregard for people and their needs and their rights." As examples he used the physical condition of the city, the condition of the schools, the lack of playgrounds, the rejection of the antipoverty program, the system of so-called justice and law enforcement in the city, and the "handout system which makes hundreds of men who ought to be proud citizens, beg instead for pittances doled out by the boss to a public payroll that is kept at inhumanly low wages."[36]

Button's major campaign theme of political bossism in Albany helped him win the election. However, his charges were overcritical. Remember that at the time taxes in Albany were among the lowest in the state, while the services provided were not at a critical level. Also the O'Connell organization preferred to give out thousands of low-paying patronage jobs rather than provide fewer, higher-paying jobs.

The 1973 election was a disappointment for the Democrats in Albany. While a struggle was expected, it was a surprise, after the votes were tallied, that the Democrats did so poorly. Mayor Corning was reelected to his $12,000-a-year job as mayor by only about 3,500 votes over the Republican candidate, Carl Touhey. Touhey might have won had he been a better campaigner. He didn't use the results of the recent SIC investigations and other findings against the Democrats. Touhey, however, did spend a lot of money for his campaign. He is the owner of Orange Motors, a Ford dealer in Albany. Mayor Corning generally wins two to one, but real estate taxes have more than doubled since he won his eighth term in 1969. Compared with a 22,663-vote margin in 1969, Mayor Corning didn't do well at all. In fact if the trend continues he might not be reelected in 1977.

The Democrats who ran for county court judge and surrogate court judge both lost. Democratic county legislator Joe Harris ran for the County Court bench against Arnold Proskin, the Republican district attorney. Proskin ran for the judgeship that was created in 1973 by Governor Rockefeller to deal with New York State's tough drug law. A total of a hundred judgeships were created by the governor. This gave Albany County one more judge. So now Albany has one Democrat county judge and one Republican county judge. Dan O'Connell wanted Proskin to win as county judge so the district attorney's office would be open. O'Connell's strategy turned out to be right: a Democratic DA was elected the next year.

Larry Kahn, a former Democrat turned Republican, was elected surrogate court judge over the Democratic incumbent Judge John McCall, an O'Connell crony. Kahn wasn't expected to win. Prior to the election, however, there was an article in the *Knickerbocker News*, Albany's evening newspaper, mentioning that favoritism was shown by McCall in appointing local attorneys to cases brought before his court. Also McCall didn't campaign to any extent, while Kahn had several billboards and ads in the local newspapers. During McCall's term as surrogate, guardianships were awarded almost entirely to Democratic attorneys. This is an important part of the patronage system. A guardian is appointed in settling an estate when a minor or a legally incompetent person is recipient of money from an estate. The attorney serves as the guardian to be sure the rights of the minor or incompetent are not violated. The attorneys rarely overwork themselves in handling these matters, and are paid rather nicely by the estate.

The Democrats won the county clerk's and sheriff's offices as well as president of the Common Council in 1973. The Democratic candidate for sheriff was John McNulty, Jr. McNulty, who was the mayor of the village of Green Island (part of Albany County), wasn't the party's original choice for sheriff. He was placed on the ballot because he won in the primary on June 4, 1973. After that, the Democratic organization backed him. His father was sheriff, but fell to feuding a generation ago with O'Connell, who refused to allow the son to run for the post. Dan backed Chief Deputy Sheriff William T. Mahoney, but in the primary Mahoney lost to McNulty by about sixty votes. McNulty's home village, where he was mayor, provided the margin by giving him a 1,043-to-2 victory there. This was the first major primary defeat of the O'Connell machine since they first got power more than fifty years ago. But the defeat wasn't all that bad because McNulty was a Democrat and he won on election day.

Not only did an insurgent win the sheriff's office, but two insurgents won Democratic primaries for alderman's seats on the Albany City Common Council, where no O'Connell foe has sat since 1929. In fact, when a disillusioned young alderman voted against two measures last fall, one of them the city budget, it made headlines because nobody could recall a vote that wasn't unanimous. The insurgents won in the 1973 Democratic primary because of embarrassingly sloppy petition work, which resulted in the regular Democratic aldermanic candidates being knocked off the ballot in all sixteen city wards. In the two wards where insurgents won, they were listed on the paper ballots and the organization had to mount a write-in campaign. The organization focused on these two wards because they were the only ones where insurgents had filed.

When Albany County Treasurer Eugene P. Devine, a Democrat, became ill in 1974, there was a move to remove control of the county airport and its patronage from the treasurer's office. The move was intended to insure that the numerous patronage jobs linked to the airport would be in the hands of the Democratic-controlled legislature in the event Devine left office and a Republican successor was appointed by Governor Wilson, a Republican. The airport has a payroll of $400,-000 and a budget of almost $1 million.

Dan O'Connell said that Joe Frangella, chairman of the Albany County Republican Committee, had been employing "wetbacks" for years. When then-Governor Wilson spoke at the Albany County Republican dinner on February 12, 1974, he lauded the efforts of the county chairman, Joe Frangella, and said his dedication to the party was so great that he was even neglecting his business interests. The next morning Frangella's mushroom farm was raided by federal agents. They found forty Mexicans who had entered the country illegally, working there for meager pay. An additional fourteen illegal immigrants who also worked at the Fran Mushroom Company voluntarily surrendered to authorities. The fifty-four "wetbacks," none of whom spoke English, represented about half of Frangella's employees. The officer in charge of the Albany office of the U.S. Immigration and Naturalization Services said the men were found largely because "there were so many of them. It's hard to keep that many of them a secret." The workers lived in company-owned trailers located in the plant in Coeymans. Frangella claimed he had no knowledge that any of the Mexicans had entered the country illegally. He said they came to his farm seeking employment. There is no federal law to prohibit hiring or employing an illegal immigrant. Criminal charges could have been brought against Frangella only if he had been found to be harboring aliens secretly or if he had helped them enter the United States.

About four months after the illegal aliens were arrested on Frangella's farm, Governor Wilson vetoed a bill that would have made employers who knowingly hire illegal aliens liable to high fines. Wilson's veto of the bill undoubtedly was cheered by Frangella. Although it would have been possible to charge his employees criminally, they faced only a deportation hearing. The O'Connells made their business politics and the Frangellas made their money in mushrooms; at least they tried to. The wetbacks were sent back to Mexico. But while the regular workers on Frangella's farm were in the custody of federal agents, temporary workers were picking his mushrooms. Those people for whom Frangella had gotten jobs in the state legislature were called from the capital to pick mushrooms.

Dan knew Joe Frangella's father, Nick Frangella, who was a Democratic Committeeman in Coeymans. When Frangella said that the Albany county jail should be closed and the inmates transferred elsewhere while an investigation on conditions in the jail was undertaken, Democratic County Sheriff John J. McNulty, Jr. responded: "I feel certain that he [Frangella] would like the jail closed so there would be no place for the United States immigration officers to board the people they arrest for entering the U.S. illegally to work at Mr. Frangella's mushroom plant, as happened on February 13, 1974."[37]

Nixon tried to bug the Democratic National Committee headquarters in an effort to get information about the Democrats. But Dan O'Connell didn't have to resort to such methods because of someone who worked for Frangella for many years. He visited O'Connell every week and told him what the Republicans were doing.

THE WELFARE DEPARTMENT—
WHY NOT HELP OURSELVES?

The welfare department in Albany is an excellent example of a local bureaucracy that is controlled by politics, although in the past few years, the department has drifted away from the machine's control because of civil service and an uncooperative commissioner. New York State ranks near the top among states paying the highest welfare benefits, and it has long had a reputation as a haven for welfare clients and employees. "Helping People to Help Themselves" is the motto of the New York State Department of Social Services, or, as it is more popularly known, the welfare department. This is ironic because it doesn't help people in the right way. It encourages and enables the welfare recipient to stay unemployed, become lazy, and have more children. Many people are able to help themselves to money through the welfare system. Not only do the recipients benefit, but so do landlords, doctors, dentists, pharmacists, food markets, and "others." The "others" have included some politicians and employees of the department who receive kickbacks, or "gifts," as those who receive them would prefer to say.

The department is located in downtown Albany and is open from nine to four. The employees have an hour off for lunch, and the building is vacated before four by most employees. Since no overtime is permitted, anyone who needs assistance after three-thirty is usually told to come back the next day. The pay is low, and a number of the supervisors therefore have other jobs. For many years, there was no formal training program in the department, although there was a "director of training." Employees learn by trial and error, often at the expense of the recipient. Many of the employees don't stay at the department very long. Many came to the department after they graduated from college. There used to be a lot of summer help also.

There isn't much chance for advancement without political connections, and the pay is only about $7,000 a year for a caseworker. The ambitious worker doesn't have any incentives.

It has been estimated that welfare fraud is around 25 percent. Fraudulent cases are usually just exposed, and changes in the assistance are made if there is an overpayment. A conviction of the recipient on charges of perjury is usually not sought after. Fines or imprisonment don't do much good because the recipient can't afford fines, and sending him or her to prison costs even more money. It is possible for people to use different names and say they have more children than they really have to get more money. Many people who come to the department don't get cash grants but Medicaid and food stamps. The stamps are food coupons that give greater buying power to recipients. Medicaid recipients get all doctor, dentist, hospital, drug, and health-related bills paid for by the government. These two programs are terrific.

A few big landlords, called "slumlords," who rent mainly to low income people receive much business from the welfare department. Their apartments are often poorly kept, unhealthy, and unsanitary. Many have been in violation of many building and health laws. Slumlords charge from $100 to $150 per month for a one- to four-room apartment; frequently the "apartment" is a single room. Needed repairs are often not made. The landlord realizes that he won't hold the building many more years, because the structure is usually in a dilapidated neighborhood in which the buildings will be torn down to make way for new ones. The landlord claims that the tenants don't take care of their apartments and that they also damage the building. Some of this is true, but quite often the landlord exaggerates the condition. The wiring is often unsafe and prone to cause fires; water pipes often leak; ceilings and walls are cracked and need repairing and painting; garbage should be picked up often and on a regular basis. Garbage brings rats and causes unsanitary conditions. Lighting in halls and stairways is often bad. Yet laws affecting slumlords are rarely enforced because of political connections and "gifts" by the slumlords. Such enforcement is infrequent, selective, and doesn't do much good because the fines are so small that it's less expensive for the slumlords to pay the fine than to make any necessary repairs. Most of the tenants of the slumlords are either on welfare or don't make much money anyway and can't afford to move elsewhere. Whether this is the fault of the slumlords or the tenants, some corrective action by the government is needed. These conditions are not unique to any one city, and unfortunately they are widespread.

The welfare department occasionally pays the moving costs of recipients and also gets them needed appliances, such as stoves and refrigerators, at marked-up prices, from "approved" outlets. There were once about five "selected" markets that received the bulk of the orders for food. When a recipient needed food right away, the department would give the individual a food order to present to a local market (usually about fifteen dollars). Democratic headquarters usually had to approve which business firms would supply food or other goods and services to the city and county. Until the food stamp program was started in the sixties the department had a warehouse where food was distributed to welfare recipients *et al.* Then there were more chickens in every pot. If someone (a politician, for example) wanted food, all he had to do was send someone to collect. The food wholesalers received a lot of business through patronage.

One cause of graft and corruption in government is the low salaries paid to public officials and employees. For example, we expect a mayor administering a several million-dollar budget to turn in a $100,000-a-year job for $20,000. We expect an employee with a college degree to be happy with a salary of $150 a week or less. The result is that the city tends to get the mediocre, the incompetent, or those who use the position for temporary training and employment. Public employees should be given adequate salaries with incentives, such as advancement, for doing a good job and working overtime. Many corporations let their employees in on a profit-sharing plan in addition to a good salary.

Some people look at welfare as being only temporary and do not want to depend on it. Some want money only to pay an electric bill or a month or two back rent. This is often arranged because it's cheaper to give someone two hundred dollars or so than to keep him on the welfare roll over many years costing the taxpayers several thousand dollars. The welfare department provides a very valuable service to the needy, and anyone who can use assistance and can qualify should not be embarrassed to apply for assistance. Where else could someone go to get help at a moment's notice? With all its flaws the welfare system has helped many people. It's only too bad that some people try to take unfair advantage of the system.

In Albany County alone, about $40 million is given out in assistance annually, about 85 percent of which is reimbursed by the federal government. Welfare has increased in Albany County. The more money given out, the more votes, contributions, gifts, and popularity the party can expect to receive. Until the past few years, politics played a substantial part in who was hired at the Albany County welfare department, just as at any other city or county department in Albany. Almost no one was hired without being recommended by Democratic headquarters. But civil service and an uncooperative welfare commissioner have changed things. However, things at the department are as bad, or perhaps worse, than they were before. When the caseworkers were mostly Democrats they treated those on welfare better because the employees realized that if the recipients were happy they would vote the straight Democratic ticket. But now there are a large number of antimachine employees at the welfare department who are often cold-hearted, lazy, and unambitious.

In 1974 Dan O'Connell wanted to get rid of the welfare commissioner because some of the reform procedures he had instituted alienated welfare recipients. Also, many employees at the department were Republicans and many did not reside in Albany County. The commissioner, although a Democrat, was hurting the O'Connell machine more than helping it. However, nothing materialized in getting rid of him.

THE STATE CONVENTION AND THE ELECTION OF 1974

About ten days before the 1974 New York State Democratic Convention, gubernatorial candidate Congressman Ogden Reid said that the convention would be a "closed affair" because about ten or twelve party leaders selected the candidates in advance behind closed doors and tried to dictate a state ticket. At the time Howard Samuels and Hugh Carey were running neck and neck for the nomination. Dan O'Connell supported Carey, a congressman from Brooklyn, primarily because he was an Irish Catholic. O'Connell felt that Samuels had his chance in 1966 when he ran for lieutenant governor with Frank O'Connor. As we know, they lost that year. But they lost not because of Samuels but because Rocky was, the people thought, a better candidate than O'Connor. That wasn't a good opportunity to see if Samuels was a good vote-getter.

In response to Reid's statement, Queens' Democratic leader Matthew Troy, Jr., said Reid, who had switched from the Republican Party just two years before, was "acting like a rich spoiled kid who says, 'Either I control the game or I take my marbles.' As far as I'm concerned, you can take your marbles and go home." Troy noted to Reid: "I know you're new to the party but I also know that for the past six months you have done everything but mow my lawn, do my dishes and iron my shirts for my support." Reid said he refused to make deals with Troy and Brooklyn leader Meade Esposito. He said both leaders wanted to be consulted on patronage.[38] O'Connell said he wouldn't back Reid because he was a Republican who had just turned Democrat not too long ago. Even though Reid may not have deserved the nomination, what he said was true. Candidates have long been selected behind closed doors by a small number of party leaders. And reforms are largely "window dressing."

Albany has a large number of votes at the State Democratic conventions, and they are sought by all the candidates. Even more important than the actual votes is their influence upon other county chairmen, especially those near Albany. Although Dan O'Connell is not himself a committeeman and entitled to vote, Albany has seven committeemen who vote according to the way O'Connell tells them.

Their position as committeemen is in name only. The selection of committeemen in Albany, as well as other candidates, has been very secretive, although there are supposed to be provisions for a primary. A large number of delegates to state and national conventions merely vote as their county chairman tells them to. It has been this way in Albany for years.

At the 1970 New York State Democratic Convention, held at Grossinger's Hotel in the Catskill Mountains, Congresswoman Shirley Chisholm had a few harsh words for the delegates. The first black woman ever elected to the United States Congress and a candidate for the Democratic Presidential nomination in 1972, even though she was kind and rather small, she always made her feelings known. Congresswoman Chisholm angrily told the delegates in her always eloquent manner when the nomination process was in progress that "you delegates, you come to conventions consistently and persistently, and you're nothing but robots and automatons who can't answer to the dictates of your own conscience." It was because Mrs. Chisholm was so vocal that former State Senator Basil Patterson, a black man, was nominated to be the Democratic candidate for lieutenant governor that year. Patterson is now vice-chairman of the Democratic National Committee. When Shirley Chisholm was campaigning for the Presidential nomination in 1972 she said, "I'm going to tell them [the delegates]. Money or no money, the delegates will have to reckon with me. There will be a hot time at the convention." Few people, male or female, are as sincere and outspoken as Shirley Chisholm. She has never been afraid to say what she feels. This quality has caused many to respect her and others to despise her.

The 1974 New York State Democratic Convention in Niagara Falls officially began on Thursday, June 13, at two o'clock in the afternoon. But on Wednesday afternoon the candidates started "wining and dining" the delegates. The Ramada Inn in Niagara Falls, where Samuels and Carey stayed, was the place where most of the action took place outside the convention center, a few blocks away. Carey had rented buses to take the delegates from their motels to the Ramada Inn and the convention center, although they were not more than a half a mile away from each other.

The name of former assemblyman Tony Olivieri, a candidate for the lieutenant governor nomination, wasn't well known to the delegates prior to the convention. But on Wednesday night, his birthday, he gave a huge buffet dinner with wine, and about five hundred people attended. Hugh Carey had a singalong with Irish coffee served. Howard Samuels, a self-made millionaire who manufactured plastic baggies, fed the delegates the best. Samuels had an open bar all Wednesday afternoon and evening as well as on Thursday. On Thursday, he had a continental breakfast, a buffet lunch, and a roast beef dinner. At the convention hall the candidates gave out pizza, hot dogs, and drinks. Those who attended the convention (delegates, party leaders, their families, newsmen, and guests) didn't have to buy a single meal or drink.

The candidates started "wining and dining" the delegates at the 1974 Women's Democratic State Convention, held in Albany. Many candidates for statewide office attended and held nice receptions. The female Democrats have an annual convention where they listen to various speakers and have panel discussions. One year U.S. Senator Birch Bayh of Indiana spoke.

On Thursday night before the nominations for governor started, Senator Hubert H. Humphrey gave a keynote address. Humphrey was at the 1966 state convention in Buffalo along with Senator Robert F. Kennedy and former Governor Averell Harriman. In Niagara Falls, the former Vice-President called for unity, and said, "Those who cannot remember the past are condemned to repeat it." Humphrey was warmly welcomed by the convention and received two standing ovations from many of the same people who didn't support him in the 1972 Presidential primary. Sitting in the Niagara Falls convention hall, one couldn't help but think that Humphrey should have been elected President instead of Nixon in 1968 and should have received the nomination instead of McGovern in 1972. An excellent speaker, Humphrey said that although losing helps build character it's nicer to be a winner.

Just minutes after the former Vice-President finished speaking about unity, the Democrats were at it again as candidates who didn't get the party's nomination for governor, lieutenant governor, attorney general, and U.S. Senate threatened to fight for the nomination in the September primary. The only office where a primary wasn't anticipated was the controller's office because Arthur Levitt was unanimously renominated to run for the sixth consecutive time.

Hugh Carey, who lost to Howard Samuels in the nomination for governor, said, "The only circumstances under which I would not run in the primary are if they carry me out of here [the convention] feet first." Samuels, who has wanted to be governor since 1962, got 68.2 percent of the delegates' votes in 1974 while Carey received 31.1 percent. Democratic committeemen from the Capital District provided Carey with 11 percent of the necessary 25 percent to get an automatic spot in the primary. To appear in the statewide primary, a candidate has to get at least 25 percent of the convention vote, or else circulate a petition across the state and obtain 20,000 signatures, a time-consuming and laborious effort.

In 1962 Samuels and Frank O'Connor lost out to U.S. Attorney Robert Morgenthau of New York, who received the nomination. Four years later, Samuels hoped for the gubernatorial nomination, but his efforts were fruitless because O'Connor was practically assured the nomination by the bosses even before the convention began. That year Samuels got the lieutenant governor's nomination. In 1970 Samuels lost to former Supreme Court Justice and U.S. Ambassador to the United Nations Arthur Goldberg, who got the nomination for governor. That year, Samuels ran in the primary but lost to Goldberg by some 50,000 votes.

Samuels was then appointed by New York's Mayor John Lindsay to be the first head of New York City's Off-Track Betting Corporation, the first of its kind in the nation. Shortly before the 1974 convention Samuels left that position so he could have more time for campaigning. At the time he left OTB, the legal bookies earned profits for the taxpayers of over $1 million per week. In 1974 the Albany Democrats didn't like "Howie the Horse," as Samuels was nicknamed, because he was a proponent of off-track betting. Also, the fact that Samuels was Jewish made him a less attractive candidate to the Albany machine. The Albany Democrats are against off-track betting because having it in Albany would hurt the business of the bookies. Bookmakers in Albany have been more or less free to operate. There have been few and infrequent arrests of bookies, and when arrests have been made they are by the state police and federal agents rather than by the local police. Bookies who have been caught have been let off with a light fine with no prison sentence. After paying their fine, they are bookmaking again the same day.

The New York state police does not have jurisdiction in New York City. This is because New York City doesn't want them and the city legislators are powerful enough to keep them away. The degree of corruption can be measured by the number of times the state police makes raids instead of the local police. Gambling (bookmaking) and narcotics are two areas where the local police hesitate to enforce the laws because of payoffs; sometimes the state police or federal law enforcement agencies will make arrests instead.

In 1974, the Republicans of New York State held their convention in Long Island two days before the Democrats held theirs in Niagara Falls. While the Democrats were divided on six of the seven designations for statewide office, the Republicans were unanimous on their seven choices. If the Democrats had lost in November of 1974 their disunity, as usual, would have been a major reason for their defeat. The Republican leaders with Governor Wilson selected their candidates behind the scenes before their convention started. All was nicely packaged; there were no floor fights or challenges, and the Republican committeemen simply went through the motions of nominating the ticket. It is clear that the Republican nominating convention was "concerned not so much with Wilson's credentials, which are taken for granted, as with presenting the kind of united front that is traditional for the GOP and the secret of its success over the numerically superior but divided Democrats."[39]

With former Governor Nelson A. Rockefeller on the sidelines, Democrats had the best chance in sixteen years to win the governor's office in 1974. Some watching the Republican state convention proceedings compared Rockefeller's behavior to that of a happy father attending the graduation exercises of a son. Some believed that Rockefeller resigned as governor in December, 1973, so that Wilson would be assured the nomination, and have an advantage over his Democratic opponent as an incumbent. It was then thought that Rockefeller resigned also to prepare himself for the 1976 Presidential campaign. Since then, however, Rockefeller has been appointed Vice-President.

At the Democratic convention, leaders in huddles on the convention floor or behind closed doors in smoke-filled rooms compromised in an effort to select a balanced and acceptable ticket. Included in these meetings were Meade H. Esposito, the Brooklyn leader; Matthew Troy, Jr., the Queens County Chairman; Pat Cunningham of the Bronx; Assembly Minority Leader Stanley Steingut; and Mayor Corning. Many of the leaders and candidates had little, if any sleep, during the convention, because they were trying to make deals. For example, several people shouted "deal" after every delegate who favored Assemblyman John LaFalce of Buffalo for lieutenant governor voted. The chairman of the State Democratic Committee, when he heard people yelling "deal," told them to keep quiet because every delegate is entitled to vote as he pleases. LaFalce was labeled the bosses' candidate (he withdrew his name).

In 1974 the bosses were careful not to shove any candidate or slate of candidates down the throat of the convention. To prevent animosity, the leaders were as discreet as ever in the selection of candidates. New York's Mayor Beame addressed the convention but left before the nominations started. A seemingly potential influential person, Beame decided to remain neutral. Former Mayor Lindsay, a Republican turned Democrat, didn't attend the convention because he was in Europe. Lindsay, who remained in the background in Miami Beach at the 1972 Democratic National Convention, has yet to enter the ranks of the Democratic leadership. Comptroller Arthur Levitt, also seemingly potentially influential, chose to remain neutral. State Senator Mary Anne Krupsak expected to get the lieutenant governor's nomination before the roll was taken. But what happened showed that a candidate who previously stood a good chance of getting the nomination lost that chance within a matter of minutes. The delegates didn't feel that a woman could be accepted by the voters yet and thus would hurt the ticket. But while she received 27 percent on the first ballot, she received only 13 percent on the second ballot, and even less, 4 percent on the third and final ballot. Even a number of women delegates who had supported her on the first ballot, primarily because they felt obligated because she was a woman also, withdrew their support on the second and third ballots.

After the first ballot for the U.S. Senate designation, millionaire businessman and former Democratic State Treasurer Abraham Hirschfeld told Queens County Chairman Matthew Troy that he intended to swing his delegates to former Congressman Allard Lowenstein. But Troy responded, "Abe, they're my delegates," and Troy was right. Hirschfeld blamed Assembly Democratic Leader Stanley Steingut of Brooklyn for his bad defeat. He walked over to Steingut, and said, "You bastard," and spit in the assemblyman's face. Bystanders had to stop the two from fighting. The incident occurred in a dining room while Steingut was having breakfast the morning after the convention ended. Hirschfeld received less than one percent of the convention vote.

Albany's Mayor Corning successfully led the fight to have Robert Meehan, the Rockland County district attorney and an Irish Catholic, nominated for attorney general. Meehan lost in the primary.

Special efforts were taken by the Democrats in 1974 to have an ethnically and geographically balanced ticket. One reason why the Democrats lost in 1970, when the ticket was headed by former U.S. Supreme Court Justice Arthur Goldberg, was that the ticket wasn't balanced. There were four Jewish candidates and one black candidate.

Under New York State Democratic convention rules, each county has as many votes as the number of persons in that county who voted Democratic during the previous gubernatorial election. Because of the results in the two past gubernatorial elections, the Albany Democrats had fewer votes at the 1974 convention than before. In 1970 voters in Albany cast 10,000 fewer votes for the Democratic candidate than in 1966, a drop of almost 19 percent. At the same time between 1966 and 1970 the average county increased its representation by 7 percent. Albany has seven delegates out of 355, or 2.26 percent of the vote. Not much when Kings County (Brooklyn) has 13.53 percent, Queens County has 10.86 percent, New York County has 10.04 percent, and Erie County (Buffalo) has 9.17 percent. Albany ranks eleventh out of 62 counties in the state in terms of votes. Three delegates from Albany (one was Mary Marcy) didn't attend the 1974 convention, so Mayor Corning cast their votes.

The results of the costly 1974 Democratic primary in New York State were very surprising. The surprise came when Brooklyn Congressman Hugh Carey won the primary in a landslide over Howard Samuels, the convention's choice, and picked up as his running mate State Senator Mary Anne Krupsak. Carey beat Samuels 61 percent to 39 percent. Krupsak managed to win the nomination partially because the Italian and male chauvinist vote was divided between former

Manhattan Assemblyman Anthony Olivieri and Queens lawyer Mario M. Cuomo. The only Democrat who received the backing of the State Democratic Committee and won in the primary also was State Comptroller Arthur Levitt. The results of the primary cause one to wonder if a State Democratic Committee designation is the kiss of death. Samuels was expected to win the primary easily, but shortly after the polls closed Carey was predicted to be the winner. During the 1974 campaign then Governor Wilson said that the primary victory of Carey appeared to him a "charade" arranged by some of the Democratic "bosses," who "put Howard Samuels up front, then proceeded to cut him up." Wilson's observation had, at least, some truth to it.

Carey won the primary largely because of an expensive television campaign, which was made possible by oil industry contributions. Within a relatively short time Hugh Carey went from an unknown Congressman (except in his own district) to a governor-elect because of a well-run media campaign. But Albany Democrats were happy that Carey had won the primary and gone on to win the election over Wilson. The Albany Democrats didn't merely jump on the bandwagon after Carey won the primary, as many New Yorkers did. They backed Carey more than three months before the convention and continued to support him. If Carey owed anyone any favors, it was the O'Connell machine. While the New York City Democrats supported Samuels, the O'Connell clan supported Carey. Carey was not likely to forget that entirely.

The Republicans in Albany, even though they didn't control the city and county patronage, were taken care of with jobs during the Rockefeller and Wilson administrations, for sixteen years. While the Republicans controlled the state patronage, the Democrats in Albany watched, with open mouths, thousands of Republicans filling their pockets with state jobs. The salaries of state employees are much higher than those of city and county employees. There are close to fifty thousand city, state, and federal employees in Albany, which is about one-third of the county's total work force. Most of these workers are employed by the state and the number is rising continuously. Government is the major industry in Albany. While Democrats try to help the Republicans, and vice versa, when they have the power, there is little patronage unless you have power. Power in Albany, just as in Washington, or any capital, goes to the governor (or President) because it is he who has so many jobs at his disposal for patronage. The smell of all those jobs was enough to excite the Albany Democratic organization when Hugh Carey won the 1974 primary. But with a Carey victory in the election, happy days were expected again for the Democrats. The fact that Carey won big in Albany wasn't surprising, considering that about half of Albany's 130,000 population is Catholic, and he was backed by the O'Connell machine.

After Carey took office, Democrats were waiting for Republicans to be fired from their state jobs that weren't protected by civil service. One Albany Democrat said, "If Carey doesn't fire those Republicans and hire Democrats, than he'll be a one-term governor like Harriman." The Democrats didn't like Harriman, who was also a Democrat, because he didn't hire many Democrats. Many Democrats recalled that when Nelson Rockefeller was first elected governor he fired most of the Democrats who held state jobs shortly after his inauguration. After more than a month in office, Carey appointed only a handful of commissioners out of about fifty. It wasn't until months after his inauguration that Carey made most of his appointments. Even the Democratic secretary of state, whom Carey appointed, didn't fire any Republicans in his department in the beginning. Dan O'Connell, like many other Democrats, was annoyed with Carey because he was slow in hiring Democrats. Also, many of the people he appointed to high-salaried positions came from downstate and some were former Lindsay aides who were appointed before Lindsay converted to the Democratic party.

While many Democrats in Albany wanted high-salaried jobs, the Albany Democratic machine never wanted Albanians to get important state positions paying high salaries because the machine was afraid those who received such plums might become independent. However, many high-salaried jobs were available to the machine. It was impossible for an Albanian who wanted a state job, to bypass the machine and go directly to the governor for a job. Any such attempt would be fruitless and a waste of time because their résumés would just be ignored. The Albany machine preferred low-salaried jobs so that they could have a tighter grip on the people in Albany. Dan O'Connell never even liked going outside of Albany County for favors. He always wanted to be independent, and he succeeded, because there was plenty of patronage in Albany. And although people in Albany naturally preferred state jobs because of higher salaries and benefits, they took whatever the machine gave them. As the saying goes, "Beggars can't be choosers."

While the convention selected what appeared to be a balanced ticket, the Democrats who voted in the primary changed the ticket almost completely. In the past, when primaries were held, they were normally a rubber-stamp to the convention. However, as evidenced in the 1974 primary, things have changed. Because four out of five candidates for major statewide office who received the backing of the State Democratic Committee lost in the primary, it appears that the convention process is a waste of time. The New York City bosses who appeared to be governor-makers at the convention couldn't bring out the vote on primary day. Only about one-third of the registered Democrats voted in the 1974 primary. A significantly larger percentage voted in Albany, but there again the turnout in Albany is usually better than the statewide average because of the strong Democratic organization.

When the electorate can come up with a slate of candidates different from the one the bosses and committeemen had, it indicates that the bosses and committeemen aren't truly representative of the people.

Until 1974 Dan O'Connell always said that the convention's choices should be supported. In fact, until 1974 O'Connell didn't even like the idea of having a primary. He also disliked any candidate who tried to win the nomination in the primary after he had lost at the convention. But in 1974 the Albany Democratic organization didn't do as they had preached for so many years, because they supported Carey instead of the convention's choice, Samuels.

Democratic committeemen in Albany worked hard to get Carey elected. Some committeemen who worked at the polls pressured voters and told them who to vote for. Curtains on some voting machines were not on properly, thus permitting the committeeman to see how the voters voted. Election irregularities such as these can be reported either to the county board of elections or the state board of elections, but not many know about the latter and the former is composed of two Democrats and two Republicans. What is supposed to be a bipartisan board is in reality controlled by the Democrats.

Wilson turned out to be a very poor candidate, and to no one's surprise Carey beat him 57 percent to 43 percent. There was a Democratic landslide all over the country because of Watergate. It is somewhat unfortunate that voters simply voted against the Republicans just because of what happened in the Nixon administration. Certainly not all Republicans would participate in so-called "Watergate" activities.

The 1974 campaign was the most expensive campaign ever in New York State. It is unfortunate, to say the least, that money plays so big a part in getting elected. The 1974 election showed what large amounts of money could do. Hugh Carey spent about $4 million to become governor. Carey spent $2.5 million in the primary alone. He borrowed $1.6 million from his brother Edward, who owns New England Petroleum Corp., and others in the oil industry. Carey spent $1.55 million on advertising and $1.3 million on salaries and consultant fees. Wilson spent much less than Carey because he didn't have a primary battle. About $2.2 million was spent in the Wilson campaign, $1.5 million for advertising. Carey's opponent in the primary, Howard Samuels, spent $1.7 million. Carey spent $513,000 in the last ten days of the primary campaign, compared with about $100,000 by Samuels. The large difference came from a massive television campaign for Carey. Wilson's prime source of funds was the traditional wealthy Republican givers. A Republican fund-raising dinner, at $150 a ticket, provided the Wilson campaign with $488,000. Nelson Rockefeller gave $34,000 to the Wilson campaign, and other members of the Rockefeller family gave an additional $47,000.

Carey spent $450,000 more winning the Democratic primary than a new state campaign finance law set. But Carey's aides contend that because the law did not go into effect until June 1, 1974, the campaign's expenditures before that date do not count. He had spent about $850,000 before June 1. The limit under the new law is $2.1 million.

From the time Carey was elected governor until he took office, he acknowledged having some trouble getting people to accept positions in his administration. A number of people who could have got state positions paying $30,000 to $40,000 a year said they could not afford the drop in salary. Many successful lawyers and businessmen are capable of earning more than twice their potential state salary. In addition, some New York City residents were reluctant to take on a state job because it would have meant moving to Albany. The expense of getting a new home and selling their old home discouraged many. A third reason why some people turned down a position with the state is that all high-level appointees had to disclose their finances and recent tax returns. Most people cherish this right of privacy; however, it has been the trend in recent years for officeholders and candidates for public office to tell the public how much they are worth financially. The purpose of full financial disclosure by such persons is to determine if a conflict of interest exists.

When Congress was considering the nomination of Nelson Rockefeller to become Vice-President, he had to disclose his financial worth. While Rockefeller was New York's governor he gave financial help to some of the people he appointed to state positions. He said his gifts and loans were often necessary so that well-qualified individuals could accept a state position. Rockefeller helped compensate for the moving expenses and drop in salary by some of his appointees.

While Rockefeller served as governor of New York, he made many improvements to the governor's mansion in Albany at his own expense. He didn't even have to live in the official home provided for the Vice-President because he has a nicer home in the nation's capital. Rockefeller also didn't have to use the airplane that the Vice-President usually uses because he has a more expensive, and faster, modern jet. It is ridiculous that Nelson Rockefeller was not confirmed as Vice-President until more than four months after he was nominated by President Ford. The delay was largely because the Democrats in Congress didn't want Rockefeller to be approved before election day and help Republicans campaign. As things turned out, however, even President Ford campaigning for GOP candidates didn't help them much.

It is unfortunate that judges have to run for election; it is even more outrageous that judicial candidates have to raise large amounts of money to carry out a successful campaign. Judicial candidates should run on their qualifications and experience. In the race for two seats on New York State's Court of Appeals, the state's highest court, the two candidates who spent the most won. Manhattan lawyer Jacob Fuchs-

berg spent almost $100,000 on the campaign, followed by Supreme
Court Justice Lawrence Cooke, $25,000; Court of Appeals Justice
Harold Stevens, $4,000, and Supreme Court Justice Louis Greenblott,
$1,500. Both Fuchsberg and Cooke were elected.

Not all the Democratic candidates in Albany County in 1974 did
as well as Democratic Congressman Samuel S. Stratton, who beat his
Republican opponent by about 90,000 votes. The Albany Democrats
lost the county treasurer's office by about 500 votes. But the Democratic
machine managed to get back control of the district attorney's office
by a slim 400-vote margin. For both the treasurer's and DA's races, a
recount was called for and it wasn't until three weeks after the election
that the results were made official. There was a question over a number
of absentee ballots that had been changed. Rumor has it that unless a
Republican candidate in Albany can win by more than a thousand
votes, absentee ballots can be changed to permit the Democrat candidate to win.

One result of a Republican county treasurer being elected in 1974
was the immediate firing of deputy treasurer and long-time Albany
County Democratic Committee vice-chairman Mary Marcy, age eighty-
nine. Mrs. Marcy had held the $4,800-a-year post in the treasurer's office
since 1945. Her job was a no-show. The Democratic loss of the treasurer's office meant the loss of much patronage. Perhaps more harmful
to the Democratic machine is the closeness of a Republican to the
financial situation in the county.

Shortly after Theresa Cooke, the Republican county treasurer, took
office, the deputy county treasurer, who was a Democrat, resigned. To
find a replacement for him the new Republican county treasurer placed
an ad in the help wanted section of the Albany newspapers. This
method of attracting city and county employees was different from
what was done while the Democrats controlled the county treasurer's
office. Before, the usual practice to find employees had been to go
through party headquarters. Republicans were also surprised that
Cooke placed the ad instead of contacting the Republican party headquarters.

Republican DA Ralph Smith lost to Democrat Sol Greenberg in
1974. Dan says Greenberg was nominated because he was expected to
lose. Had Dan thought Greenberg would have been elected, he would
have chosen a more qualified lawyer. O'Connell said he didn't care if
Smith was elected DA because Smith treated the Democratic machine
fairly well considering he was a Republican. In the year that Smith
served as district attorney, he didn't prosecute any bookmakers, or
politicians.

Greenberg foolishly acknowledged to the newspapers during the
campaign that Jimmy Ryan asked him to run for district attorney and
as a result the executive editor of Albany's evening newspaper wrote

an article that wasn't complimentary to the Democratic machine. The article pointed out that Ryan is James W. Ryan, a top O'Connell "henchman" and former county purchasing agent who was then under indictment on a misconduct charge. He was accused of illegally adding names of Democratic aldermanic candidates to nominating petitions after the petitions had been distributed and signed by voters. He is the brother of Charles Ryan, "another large wheel in the O'Connell machine," who with Charles's son was under indictment on felony charges involving alleged extortion from gamblers. O'Connell says Jimmy Ryan was "the nicest person I ever knew." Charlie Ryan, O'Connell says, did favors for many people as long as he got something in return: "He always looked after himself."

James W. Ryan II, another of Charles's sons, "a 200-pound-plus broth of a boy," was under indictment on two felony charges and a misdemeanor charge. He was accused of forcibly ousting a poll watcher —a nun—and two women special investigators from the state attorney general's office from a polling place where he was chairman of inspectors on primary day, 1973.

The newspaper editor pointed out that former Democratic district attorney John Garry "fiddled around" with evidence discovered by the State Investigation Commission against Jimmy Ryan, but no action was taken against him. The editor mentioned that Garry "was the DA who, when faced with offers of prospective witnesses to testify about Democratic vote-buying in Albany, threatened to prosecute both the givers and takers of bribes, thereby killing any investigation before it began."

The indictments of the Ryans were before County Judge John J. Clyne, a Democrat, "who somehow hasn't been able to get them on his calendar and set a trial date although the indictments are close to two years old," the editor wrote. The editor concluded: "Albany County can't afford to have another DA who is Jimmy Ryan's favorite. One was enough."[40] As the election turned out, Greenberg was elected by less than four hundred votes.

After Bronx Democratic leader Pat Cunningham became the New York State Democratic chairman in 1975, he called Mayor Corning to get Albany's newly elected Democratic state senator, Howard Nolan, to vote for Senator Jermiah Bloom of Brooklyn as Senate minority leader. Cunningham assumed that Corning would take care of it. As things turned out, Bloom lost to Senator Manfred Ohrenstein of New York, who was a reform Democrat. Nolan voted for Ohrenstein after Dan O'Connell inadvertently told him to vote any way he wanted to. Had Cunningham called O'Connell instead of Corning, Nolan might have voted for Bloom. Cunningham had overestimated the mayor's power. There was a public feud between Nolan and Corning because of this incident.

On November 13, 1974, Dan O'Connell celebrated his eighty-ninth birthday. Considering his age, he looked well. He said he felt well also.

Although his voice isn't very clear, those who know him don't have much trouble understanding him. He's still a big person. He has white hair and dresses conservatively. On his birthday, just as on any other day, he sat in his lounge chair in his living room watching television and talking to visitors. He answers the telephone himself. One caller on his birthday was Governor-Elect Hugh Carey, who thanked him for his support and wished him a happy birthday. More people than usual call O'Connell on the phone and visit him on his birthday. It's sort of like Grand Central Station. However, he liked hearing from his friends.

On his eighty-ninth birthday he received flowers from half a dozen friends, including Mary Marcy, who is vice-chairman of the Albany County Democratic Committee and five months younger than O'Connell. Many judges, politicians, friends and fellow Albanians sent more than seventy cards, letters, and telegrams to O'Connell on his birthday. Although they were mostly from Democrats, there were many from Republicans. The senders thanked O'Connell for what he had done for them and wished him the traditional birthday greetings. But even though O'Connell received more cards, letters, and flowers than most of us, he used to receive many more than he now does.

Alongside O'Connell can usually be found his dog, Mac, a mutt that is part beagle. Two Irish wolfhounds, which belong to his niece, are often in O'Connell's house also. He enjoys having the dogs around. He has had hound dogs all his life. When he was younger, he had bulldogs, hounds, and fighter dogs. He feeds them well (steak sometimes). Dan also has a pair of bronze tiger bookends that were given to him many years ago by a Tammany leader. The tiger was the infamous symbol of Tammany Hall. The symbol was chosen because a tiger was on the fire engine that William Marcy Tweed rode as a volunteer fireman.

While Dan O'Connell has been one of the most successful political bosses this country has ever seen, his Irish temperament, his being stubborn and his being bigoted have emerged, at times, just as with anyone else. Even the best of our country's leaders have had faults. Their position of leadership may give them more power than the average person but it doesn't make them perfect.

Some feel that today Dan O'Connell's bark is louder than his bite. While this may be somewhat of an exaggeration, it is not without some truth, but many are still afraid of him. Up until the past seven years or so, Dan O'Connell's bite was powerful and there was no question that he was in control in Albany. In the past few years, however, although his health hasn't been unusual for a person his age, he is not as visible as he once was, because of a broken hip. In the past few years, he hasn't been attending the meetings of the County committee. However, this does not necessarily mean that he is not still the boss. In the first place, even when he attended the meetings he never was an active participant. He usually just stood in the back of the room talking to friends while the proceedings lasted. In the second place, what takes place at the meetings (such as nominations) is previously arranged behind closed doors long before the meetings.

Many feel that Mayor Corning is the real boss today and that O'Connell is only the titular boss. Because Corning is mayor he is in the media and public view constantly. With his position Corning is able to be a spokesman for the O'Connell organization. Besides O'Connell never liked to have interviews. Also the mayors, even before Corning, always represented O'Connell at the conventions. So while it may appear that Corning is, now, the real leader, it just may be an illusion for the time being. When the times comes, however, either at the request of O'Connell, or more likely when O'Connell dies, Corning will most likely be his successor. It will be a natural succession, but the question remains if Corning will be the leader for long. While no one ever challenged Dan O'Connell for the leadership, it is likely that someone would challenge Corning. The end of the O'Connell leadership will mark the end of bossism in Albany. Of course there will be attempts by some politicians to get control, and it is possible that they may get control for a few years, but it is unlikely that the bosses of tomorrow will be as powerful as O'Connell or any of the other bosses discussed in this book were in their prime. The time when political leaders were bosses is over.

In the summer of 1974 after Mario Cuomo received the Democratic nomination for lieutenant governor, both Cuomo and his campaign manager weren't certain who was the real boss in Albany. Cuomo said that he wrote both O'Connell and Corning letters but received letters from neither. Cuomo was afraid that O'Connell and Corning would back Tony Olivieri in the primary instead of Cuomo. Cuomo's campaign manager said that they were confused about protocol. They didn't know whether to see O'Connell or Corning first. In any case, they knew that the support of the Albany Democratic organization could be helpful.

HOW MUCH LONGER?

How much longer will the Democrats control Albany? All good things usually come to an end. Likewise, based on recent election results, the power of the Democrats in Albany is coming to an end also. The Democrats still control the city and it looks as if they will do so for at least another ten years. But the real immediate problem for the Democrats is the county, because as the population in the towns continues to grow the Republicans gain strength. Losing in the towns isn't anything new for the Democrats. But in the past it didn't matter too much because the Democrats' pluralities in the city always offset losses in the towns, so the county offices were always filled by Democrats. Dan never cared about the towns either. He says, "I didn't bother with them." If he wanted to he probably could have controlled the towns also, but, as he says, "The towns have always been Republican and you're not going to change anybody's politics—not very much." The farmers have always been Republicans. What is new is that the Republicans are catching up. Until 1966 Democratic candidates in the county didn't have to worry about losing but now they must actively campaign.

Even if the Democrats didn't win a seat in Congress or the state legislature it wouldn't matter too much just as long as they controlled the city. The city is the base of all political machines. When Dan ran for assessor he promised to lower real estate taxes. After he was elected he kept his promise. Until only a few years ago, taxes in Albany were relatively low compared to other cities across the country. Now landowners in Albany have an added school tax to pay. The taxes were raised because the voters didn't show their appreciation of having low taxes by voting Democratic. Dan showed those ingrates. Between 1971 and 1973, taxes of homeowners in the city of Albany increased from $33 per thousand dollars assessed valuation to more than $64 per thousand.

Albany has at times been in a world of its own. When Republicans gained throughout the state in 1937 Albany's Democratic candidates won nevertheless. Examples, as in 1937, have helped give the Albany Democrats stature in the state party. Albany is also the only political machine left in the state. At the present time the New York City Democratic organization isn't referred to as "Tammany Hall," but Dan says, "It will be if the Democratic party ever gets going again to represent the poor people." Tammany Hall represented power and stamina just like the tiger—its symbol. In recent years the New York Democrats have been unorganized and divided.

Another example of Albany's uniqueness is the 1972 Democratic Presidential primary. Except in Albany County, McGovern delegates were elected throughout the state. The O'Connell delegates ran as being uncommitted because Hubert Humphrey did not run in the New York primary. Dan supported Humphrey in 1968 and again in 1972. Only after McGovern had enough votes to win the nomination in Miami Beach did the O'Connell delegates change their votes from Senator Henry Jackson to McGovern to get on the bandwagon. After Humphrey dropped out of the race while the convention was in progress, the O'Connell delegates switched their votes to Jackson. Other delegations also changed their votes to get on the bandwagon.

Since before 1919 the Democrats have lost the towns with the exception of 1964 under President Johnson's coattails. The coattails effect was noticeable in 1946 when Dewey ran for governor on the Republican ticket. Nevertheless the Democratic candidates were elected in Albany County, but with smaller pluralities than usual. Another example of the coattails effect was in 1952 and 1956, when Eisenhower was elected President. However, the Republicans failed to elect candidates in Albany during both years. Eisenhower was the only Republican candidate ever to carry the county while the O'Connells have been in power. But while Eisenhower carried the county, in 1952 and 1956, he lost in the city of Albany. While Dan was boss the city of Albany always gave pluralities to Democratic candidates for President, governors, and other state and national offices.

Why could the Albany Democrats never control the towns? Until the sixties it didn't matter whether or not the Democrats had control of the towns. This is because there were more voters in the city than in the surrounding towns. But when this began to change in the early sixties Democratic candidates for county offices began to receive smaller pluralities. While it appears that Democratic candidates for county offices are facing more difficult campaigns than in the past, when they practically didn't have to campaign at all, the Democrats for city offices are still "guaranteed" election. But the time is soon to come when even the Democrats in the city will face some difficult campaigns.

Still, even though it may seem a last hurrah for the longest-lived of city machines, don't bet too much money on it. For one thing, Albany County is about three to two Democratic in enrollment. In the city of Albany, the enrolled Democrats outnumber Republicans by more than ten to one. The most recent enrollment figures show 43,755 Democrats, 4,106 Republicans, 292 Conservatives, and 398 Liberals. The Democrats don't all vote Democratic. Property owners concerned about their assessments have registered Democratic in order to have lower assessments. But even so, in the past, most Albany residents voted Democratic. However, because of the closeness in recent elections the Democrats will have to face some difficult campaigns and elections in the future.

"The old man" was their idol, and although in the last few years he had suffered some losses on election day, there were many in Albany who never wavered in their allegiance to him, and to them Dan O'Connell was a devoted friend. He would go a long way to serve a friend. His influence on the Democratic Party in Albany will be felt after he dies. Great leaders never die; they just fade away.

ELECTION RESULTS IN ALBANY COUNTY,
NEW YORK—1914-1974

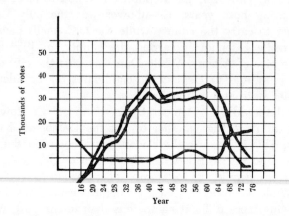

Top line indicates the approximate margins in which Democratic candidates carried the city of Albany.

Middle line indicates the approximate Democratic pluralities in Albany County.

Bottom line indicates the approximate margins in which Democrats lost the towns in Albany County.

APPROXIMATE DEMOCRATIC
PLURALITIES IN ALBANY COUNTY
1946-1964—THE COATTAILS EFFECT

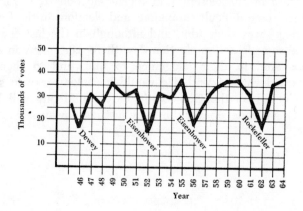

Tammany Hall

Though he may be endowed with the most brilliant of minds, scrupulously honest, morally decent and law-abiding and plentifully supplied with cash, a man without sympathy for the masses never gets far in politics.

MARTIN LOMASNEY

Tammany Hall is the oldest continuous political organization on earth. The organization was founded on May 12, 1789, as the Society of Saint Tammany (or the Columbian Order, as it was also known) by William Mooney. Tammany (Tammanend) was a Delaware Indian chief who was wise and benevolent. Chief Tammanend once told his tribe to "stand together, support each other, and you will be a mountain that nobody can move; fritter down your strength in divisions, let wigwam be divided against wigwam, you will be an anthill which a baby can kick over."[41] And so the organization plan was formed—united we stand, divided we fall—by the famous Indian chief.

"Saint" was added because other societies used the word "saint." The officers held Indian titles, and many of their customs came from the Indians. The head was called the Grand Sachem, chosen from the thirteen sachems. The sachems were chosen annually from the most influential members of Tammany Hall. The Tammany Hall meeting place was called the Wigwam. Although Tammany was originally composed of men from both parties, shortly after its founding they drifted in the path of Thomas Jefferson. The men gathered nightly at the lodge to drink, smoke, and swap stories.

Aaron Burr was the first real leader of the Tammany Society although he was never a sachem. Burr was a United States Senator, an assemblyman, and Vice-President. After Burr killed Alexander Hamilton the Tammany Society disowned Burr because he was impatient in seeking the Presidency. Jefferson became President instead of Burr because of Hamilton. After Jefferson was elected President he rewarded some of his supporters in Tammany Hall with jobs.

The Constitution does not mention political parties. They are governed by no written code other than what is established by the national party conventions held every four years. Political parties arise from the need of the people to deal with political, social and economic problems. A political party is a coalition of many opinions and numerous people. The most successful political party is the party which is able to attract the most support in elections. The right to govern is conferred to the party in control by the voters. In order that there may be an orderly process of change, elections are held regularly. This permits the people to choose their leaders.

The history of the Democratic Party goes back to 1791, when Thomas Jefferson vied with Alexander Hamilton, who was the head of the Federalist Party. The Federalists, the nation's first political party, had arisen from the campaign for adoption of the Constitution. Jefferson believed in a democracy, state rights, and agricultural interests. Hamilton favored an aristocracy, a strong central government, and helping industrial interests. This was the beginning of the two-party system. Jefferson's followers, the Anti-Federalists, were called Democratic-Republicans. By the late 1790s the title was shortened to Republicans. This label lasted until the Jacksonian reorganization conferred the name Democrats. Jefferson was the father of the Democratic Party. The first cause of the Jeffersonians was the Bill of Rights, which consisted of the first ten amendments to the Constitution and guaranteed individual liberties.

The Constitution provided for popular election only of representatives. Senators were chosen by state legislatures, and the President was elected in any manner that the state legislatures directed. For the first Presidential election in 1789, only three of eleven states held a popular vote, and in most states the legislatures themselves appointed the Presidential electors. It wasn't until 1864 that all states had popular balloting for the Presidency.

Jefferson ran unsuccessfully against John Adams for the Presidency in 1796. But in 1800 Jefferson ran again, this time against Burr, and there was a tie in the Electoral College. So the election went to the House of Representatives and Hamilton, who had much influence in the House, even though Jefferson was his rival, supported Jefferson because he didn't trust Burr. As a result the House awarded the Presidency to Jefferson, and there was the famous Hamilton/Burr duel in which Hamilton was killed in 1804. This caused the end of the Federalist Party in 1816. The Republican party didn't have much effective opposition after Hamilton was killed.

Until the Twelfth Amendment to the Constitution was ratified in 1804 the President and Vice-President were not elected as a team. The person who received the most votes was President, and the person who was second was Vice-President. This arrangement had made Jefferson Vice-President to John Adams in 1796 and was the only time that the President and Vice-President were of different political parties.

In 1805 the Tammany Society applied for a charter from the state legislature incorporating it as a benevolent and charitable body "for the purpose of affording relief to the indigent and distressed members of said organization, their widows and orphans and others who may be proper objects of their charity."

Dan O'Connell *(left)* and Albany's Mayor Erastus Corning on November 8, 1945.

Dan O'Connell at his home in 1974, at the age of eighty-nine.

Gubernatorial candidate Hugh Carey woo-ing Mrs. Mary Marcy, then eighty-eight, at the Women's State Democratic Convention in Albany in March, 1974.

Franklin D. Roosevelt, Jr. *(left)* and Judge Bender Solomon in 1964.

Jersey City's Mayor Frank Hague *(left)* and Chicago's Mayor Edward Kelly in 1944.

James A. Farley *(left)* and New York City's Mayor Robert F. Wagner in 1961.

Four former governors of New York State at Nelson A. Rockefeller's inauguration as governor in January, 1959. From left to right: Thomas E. Dewey, Rockefeller, W. Averell Harriman, and Charles Poletti.

William Marcy Tweed.

"Honest John" Kelly.

Richard "The Squire" Croker on a cruise to Ireland.

"Silent Charlie" Murphy.

Thomas Nast, a cartoonist for *Harper's Weekly,* drew many cartoons attacking Tammany's Boss Tweed. This one bore the caption, "No Prison Is Big Enough To Hold The Boss."

New York City's Mayor James J. Walker *(right)* is questioned by Samuel Seabury in 1932. Seabury had been a judge on the state's highest court before he was appointed by Governor Franklin D. Roosevelt to investigate corruption in New York City.

Tammany leader Carmine De Sapio.

President Lyndon B. Johnson is joined by New York senatorial candidate Robert F. Kennedy and his wife, Ethel, in New York on October 14, 1964. The President came to campaign for himself and the former attorney general.

Chicago's Mayor Richard J. Daley (left) and Illinois Governor Otto Kerner at the 1964 Democratic National Convention in Atlantic City.

"The Louisiana Kingfish"—Huey P. Long.

U.S. Senator Russell Long.

Mayor Richard J. Daley in 1974.

Chicago Boss Patrick Nash.

Senator Harry S. Truman *(left)* of Missouri and Thomas J. Pendergast of Kansas City at the 1936 Democratic National Convention in Philadelphia.

Mayor Frank Hague, then seventy-three, casts his ballot in the 1949 election.

"Nucky" Johnson, of Atlantic City.

Boston Mayor John F. ("Honeyfitz") Fitzgerald.

The current mayor of Boston, Kevin H.
White. Mayor White is also the leader of
the Boston Democratic organization, which
is not as strong as it was when Curley was
mayor. Prior to being elected mayor in
1967, White served as Massachusetts secretary of state.

Massachusetts governor James M. Curley *(left)*, President Franklin D. Roosevelt, and his
son James Roosevelt *(right)* on their arrival in Boston by train on February 22, 1936.

Tammany Hall was always charitable, but the leaders seemed to feel that charity begins at home. Benjamin Romaine, a Tammany Grand Sachem, was removed from the office of city controller for malfeasance even though the Common Council was controlled by his own party. As a trustee of corporation property he had fraudulently obtained valuable land without paying for it. The Tammany Society's founder, Mooney, was appointed in 1808 as superintendent of the almshouse. Mooney took from the city supplies, about $1,000 worth of articles, and had expended about $4,000 for, as he said, "trifles for Mrs. Mooney."

By 1815 Tammany Hall had obtained control of the state and in 1816 it completely regained control of the city. Step by step the organization obtained control of the state legislature, the City Council, and the mayor's office. The mayor's office was very important because the mayor made numerous appointments and it was through patronage that the machine power grew. Control of the state legislature helped in getting certain bills passed or defeated. Tammany Hall sought suffrage reform, and as a result there were more people who could vote for its candidates. The last remnant of the property qualification was abolished in New York State in 1826. Mordecai Noah was a sheriff and later elected Tammany's first Jewish Grand Sachem in 1822.

In 1822 the abolition of the Council of Appointment carried with it a clause vesting the appointment of the mayor in the Common Council. The Council of Appointment was composed of four state senators who appointed the mayor and all state nonelective officers.[42] It was not until 1834 that the mayor was elected by the people. The closed nominating system reached a crisis in 1824, when the Republicans, by then the nation's only major political party, cast up four candidates for the presidency. Andrew Jackson won the popular vote and received ninety-nine electoral votes to eighty-four for John Quincy Adams, forty-one for William H. Crawford of Georgia, and thirty-seven for Henry Clay of Kentucky. There was no electoral majority, and for the second time the House of Representatives had to decide. It chose Adams to be the sixth President. As you can see, it is possible for a person to win the popular vote but not become President. This is one example of why the Electoral College should be abolished.

There was the reduction of the five-year naturalization period for aliens between 1825 and 1828. Therefore more immigrants could vote and support the organization. When immigrants came to America in the closing years of the nineteenth century and the opening decades of the twentieth, they came by ship, and New York was the principal port of entry in the United States. It is because of this that the largest political machine was located in New York City. Conversely, it is because of this that California is rarely mentioned as a locality where political machines were vibrant then. As the immigrant population grew in

New York City and the city became congested, many immigrants left New York City and went to other cities in the United States, primarily in the East.

The first thing the immigrants saw when they traveled by ship into New York harbor was the Statue of Liberty. The proud lady holding a lamp was a welcome sight. It is the world's largest statue. The immigrants had to go through United States immigration before they were permitted to enter the mainland. They did this at Ellis Island, which is a small island near the Statue of Liberty. The island was a United States immigration station for more than sixty years (1891-1954). During that time, officials examined more than twenty million aliens at the island. Immigrants who were sick when they arrived at the island, depending on the illness and their condition, were either kept on the island until they got better or were deported. Ellis Island was a hectic place at the peak of immigration. Tammany Hall had numerous workers on the island who met the ships and helped the immigrants get situated. Tammany Hall thus provided an invaluable service, which was appreciated after the immigrants were naturalized as citizens and were able to vote. But some people who weren't eligible voted, and some voted more than once at different polling places. Votes were bought.

Thus the success of the Tweed Ring, and other political bosses, depended largely upon their control of the immigrant vote, which consisted about half of the entire vote in New York City. This made naturalization an important factor in the control of elections. The *New York Tribune* reported that in 1868 citizens were made "at the rate of a thousand per day with no more solemnity than, and quite as much celerity as is displayed in converting swine into pork in a Cincinnati packing house." Judge George G. Barnard was a Tammany Supreme Court Judge during the Tweed era. He was later impeached. From October 8 to 23, 1868, he naturalized 10,093 men. This was before women got the right to vote.

Tammany Hall established offices in the city where immigrants could obtain naturalization papers and witnesses would swear that they had been in the country long enough to become citizens. According to testimony before a House of Representatives committee investigating election frauds in New York City in 1868: "There are men in New York whom you can buy to make a false oath for a glass of beer. These men hang around such places, and are always ready to go into court to represent parties, one assuming such a name, the other assuming such a name."[43] Tammany Hall paid the fees required by the court for the naturalization papers.

The congressional committee reported "On the 30th and 31st of October, when only two days intervened until the day of election, gangs or bodies of men hired for the purpose, assembled at these headquarters where they were furnished with names and numbers, and under a leader or captain, they went out in ones and twos and threes and tens and dozens, in nearly every part of the city, registering many times each, and when the day of election came these repeaters, supplied abundantly with intoxicating drinks, and changing coats, hats, or caps, as occasion required to avoid recognition or detection, commenced the work of 'voting early and often,' and this was carried on by these vagabonds until wearied and drunken, night closed on the stupendous fraud which their depravity had perpetrated."[44]

Some men, who were cheated out of some money for voting several times, testified that they were given liquor so they would get drunk and not remember voting so many times. One person testified having voted fifteen or eighteen times on the same day. He said, "The evening previous to the election I was met by two men, who asked me if I wanted to make a few dollars. They said there was no risk in it. They furnished drink and liquor, and cigars. . . . We had drinks between each voting. I put in two votes at the next place, changing my hat and coat after the rest had voted. Then we came to East Broadway and I put one vote in there. They promised to give me $10 for each vote; but they got me so drunk that I did not know what I was about. I found them next morning in the bar-room of the New England Hotel, and asked why they did not pay me. They said, 'You have put in 28 votes, and we have paid you $28.' . . . When I asked for more money they licked me."[45] Many of the election inspectors were threatened with violence when they attempted to interfere with the voting irregularities.

The boss, like the Mafia chieftain, exerted so much power and influence that few dared to testify against him in court for fear of what would happen. The congressional committee found a lack of cooperation, either on the record or off the record, because people were afraid to become involved. The House said: "With all the concealment which cunning could invent, or perjury secure, or bribery purchase, or the fear of punishment inspire, or the dread of violence from bands of conspirators and democratic desperadoes could command, or the blandishment of more accomplished knaves could entice, or the hopes of office could buy, or fear of the loss of place could bring, all of which naturally conspire to throw obstacles in the way of or defeat the investigation of the committee, it is by no means possible that the extent of these frauds has been revealed even in any one ward."[46]

After a three-year campaign, perhaps the longest in American history, Jackson was elected the seventh President in 1828. He was the first President to be elected under the "Democratic" name as the party is known today. This ended the system of party or congressional caucus as a means of nominating Presidential candidates. A part of the old Republicans split away to become the National Republican Party. By the mid-1830s, under the leadership of Henry Clay, they had become the Whigs.

In 1829, under the direction of its banker, merchant, and lawyer leaders, Tammany Hall had been made a medium for either coercing or bribing the legislature or Common Council into passing dozens of bank charters and franchises with scarcely any provision for compensation to either state or city. But when going to the polls the voter sometimes has to ask himself which is the better of two evils. Even if Tammany Hall was bad their opponents were no better and were perhaps worse. In any case, there wasn't always harmony in the Tammany Wigwam (clubhouse). Occasionally members were divided according to their interests, financial or otherwise.

President Jackson's fight against the United States Bank established the Democratic Party's historical hostility to banking interests. Jacksonian democracy included broad political participation, the secret ballot, abolition of property qualification for voters, free education, and the right of labor to organize. In 1832 Jackson became the first President ever nominated by a national political convention. To be nominated a candidate had to have at least a two-thirds majority. There was a unit rule that required a delegate to vote as the majority of his delegation directed. Jackson, so that his friend and Vice-President Martin Van Buren would be nominated, called for the convention to be held in 1835, which was eighteen months before the election, before other candidates entered the field. President Van Buren helped labor by establishing a maximum ten-hour day for workers on federal projects. Historically the Democrats have supported labor.

The Democratic convention in 1848 created the Democratic National Committee. The committee is the permanent agency of the Democratic Party. Its function is to organize the party on a nationwide basis. The convention delegates, 3,016 in 1972, elect at the end of each national convention, held every four years, 110 members (a man and a woman from each state and territory) to serve on the national committee. They meet at least twice each year. The committee is the oldest continuing national party committee in the United States. It was originally composed of one man from each state, but when women got the right to vote in 1920 women were added to the committee.

There are three standing committees of the Democratic National Committee. The Credentials Committee decides which delegates will be seated at the convention; the Rules Committee recommends the rules of the convention; and the Platform Committee drafts the party's major policy statement. The platform is usually broad so that the Presidential candidate may revise it according to his views.

In 1850 Tammany Hall adopted the convention system of nominating candidates. Even though delegates were elected to the conventions they could easily be controlled. The new method made it appear that candidates were selected in the "open" rather than in a prearranged nomination by the leaders behind closed doors.

The Republican Party was founded in 1854 by Free Soilers, antislave Whigs, and Democrats opposed to the Kansas-Nebraska Act. The Kansas-Nebraska Act of 1854 authorized the two territories to determine for themselves whether they would be slave states or free states. Senator Stephen A. Douglas, a Democrat from Illinois, advocated the states' rights bill, and in 1860 he ran for the Presidency against the Republican candidate Abraham Lincoln but lost.

The Democratic Party as well as the country was sectionally split because of the slavery issue. Lincoln was the first Republican elected President under the party we know today by that name. The Southerners who were for slavery did not like the Republicans (Northerners) who were against slavery. It is because of this that the South has been traditionally Democratic.

In the heyday of Tammany Hall, the police did not interfere in election irregularities because they were hired by the aldermen with consent of the mayor for one-year terms. If the policeman wanted to keep his job he looked the other way and stayed away from polling places on election day. Even if any arrests were made the lawbreaker wouldn't be punished, because aldermen sat as justices in the mayor's court, where the jurisdiction would be placed. Even though at one time twenty-nine aldermen were under judgment for contempt of court and under indictment for bribery, they continued acting as judges in the criminal courts. Aldermen also granted licenses to saloons. A bill was passed in 1855 that ordered the saloons to be closed on Sundays, but because there was no provision for enforcement they kept open. After 1854 aldermen could no longer sit as criminal court judges or appoint policemen. Also in 1854 Fernando Wood became the first Tammany mayor of New York City. In 1859 a registry act was passed by the legislature. It often redistricts the city to its advantage.

By 1863 Tammany's organization was well established. According to its newspaper, *The Leader*, in each of the city's 220 electoral districts "there are representatives delegated by Tammany Hall, captains, lieutenants, and corporals, to organize, discipline and to look after the interests of the district votes."[47] But there *were* reform movements in Tammany Hall. It is interesting to note that Tweed was elected to the City Council on Tammany's reform ticket. One faction would promise "better government," but when it was in power things would be no better and even perhaps more corrupt.

WILLIAM MARCY TWEED

William Marcy Tweed became the boss of Tammany Hall in 1861. The best known of the Tammany leaders, he was also the most corrupt of all the bosses. Since Tweed the bosses have refined their methods. There are no longer crude Tweed stealings. They are more careful than the Tweed ring was. They learned their lesson so they wouldn't be sent to jail like Tweed. But through subtler means, largely "honest graft," the Tammany bosses still became wealthy through politics despite their humble beginnings. Hard work pays off for the politician also. Because even with little work and "no-show" jobs those with political plums manage to earn a better than average living. It is kind of a survival of the fittest. There is an upward struggle, with severe competition, but by playing the game better than others one succeeds in politics.

Tweed was the first Tammany boss to obtain notoriety. The circumstances in the city of New York (mass immigration, voter apathy, and ignorance) made it possible for Tweed to obtain power in 1861. He held power for only about ten years, but during that time Tammany Hall started its reputation, which was to last sixty years. Although Tammany Hall actually existed longer than sixty years, its real power and notoriety covered that span. During those sixty years of power, Tammany Hall had four bosses, an average of fifteen years each, who didn't have continuous power as Dan O'Connell did in Albany. The Tammany bosses lost an occasional election but were able to regain power. Dan O'Connell held power for more than fifty-five years.

William Marcy Tweed was born on April 3, 1823. He didn't go to school but he always read the newspapers. Tweed learned the chair-making trade from his father. He and his brother Richard owned a chair factory and a store that sold the chairs they made. Tweed was a hard worker. When he was twenty-five he worked as a volunteer fireman. The tiger became the symbol of Tammany Hall because it was the emblem on Boss Tweed's fire engine. Thomas Nast used the tiger in his cartoons to signify the ferocity of Tammany Hall.

Around Tweed's generation there were volunteer fire departments in most major cities. The members of Tweed's fire company were all friends and worked for Tammany Hall. Although most big cities today have their own professional fire departments, in the nineteenth and early twentieth centuries professional fire departments were a new concept. In order to protect their neighborhood the residents formed volunteer fire departments. Even today there are more volunteer fire departments than full-time professional departments, but the volunteer departments are usually located in towns and villages that cannot afford a full-time department. Tweed, Kelly, and Croker were all volunteer firemen. Although there was a volunteer fire department in Albany, Dan O'Connell never joined the department as his colleagues did in New York.

Tweed, like many other young New Yorkers, believed that the highest aim in life was to be the leading member of a good volunteer fire company. His ambition was gratified, for he became the foreman of his company. Tweed's chair business declined because he devoted more time to his fire department than to his factory. In 1861 he was adjudged a bankrupt but meanwhile he was a successful politician. Within ten years he made millions of dollars.

In 1850, he ran for assistant alderman but lost. He was elected in 1851 and served on the "Forty Thieves" Board, as the City Council was nicknamed because it was corrupt. At the age of thirty-nine he was elected to the bipartisan Board of Supervisors. Tweed was a supervisor until 1870, when the board was abolished by the new charter. The board passed resolutions dealing with expenditures and the giving out of contracts, in addition to appointing election inspectors. Although there were six Democrats and six Republicans on the board, Tweed was able to bribe one Republican supervisor to stay home. This enabled the Democrats to have control.

Tweed ran for sheriff in 1861 but lost. Also in that year he was elected chairman of the Tammany General Committee. In 1863 he was appointed deputy street commissioner and could employ thousands of workers. He held that job until 1870. Ward supporters got jobs through their alderman from Tweed. In 1867 he was elected to the State Senate. Tweed was elected Grand Sachem of the Tammany Society in 1868. The title of "boss" he earned by his despotic action in the Tammany General Committee. When a question was to be voted upon that he wished to have determined in his favor, he would neglect to call for the negative votes and would decide in the affirmative.

In 1868 the Democratic National Convention was held at the new Tammany Hall building on Fourteenth Street. Former governor Horatio Seymour was nominated for President but lost, partly because he was labeled the candidate of the big city bosses. In 1868 and 1872 Union (Northern) General Ulysses S. Grant was the successful Republican candidate for President. Grant was supported by rich businessmen both times and would have tried for a third term except for his ignorance of business schemes and much patronage. The Republicans aided their supporters (the rich businessmen) by sponsoring a series of high tariffs (taxes) on imported goods that protected American manufacturers from international competition. Historically high tariffs occurred during Republican administrations. It was disclosed that a Republican congressman distributed Credit Mobilier railroad construction stock to other members of Congress to influence the 1872 election in favor of Grant.

Tweed owned the Manufacturing Stationers Company, which he formed for the purpose of supplying stationery to public offices. People who did business with the city and county gave a percentage to Tweed. Contractors who built new streets, widened them, and did other improvements gave him a cut of their enormous profits. A great amount of money was spent on streets around this time.

The swindles of the Tweed Ring were covered up by issuing various stocks and bonds, and the creation of a floating debt that was never shown in the comptroller's statements. In 1870, to improve the ring's image, Comptroller Connolly, a member of the Ring, had a respectable committee examine his books. This report was in his favor. The committee even commended him for his honesty. It wasn't that the committee was fixed, it was just that Connolly covered up what the Tweed Ring stole.

A charitable person, Tweed gave $50,000 for Christmas, 1870, for the poor relief in the Seventh Ward.[48] He was on the board of directors of the Erie Railroad and made plenty from the railroad's income. It was estimated that from 1865 to 1871 the Tweed Ring stole about $200 million from the city, and only $876,000 was recovered.[49]

Tweed profited personally by all the printing that was done for the city. He was part owner of the New York Printing Company and the *Transcript,* an obscure newspaper that received the city's legal announcements. Tweed later acknowledged that the bills of his printing company were 25 percent higher than they should have been. The Tweed Ring also organized its own bank, the Tenth National Bank, which became a depository for city funds.

Members of the Tweed Ring secured city business. One member, Andrew J. Garvey, did all the plastering for New York City. Not only did Tweed's associates get city business but they charged exceedingly high prices. For just two days' repair work, on December 20 and December 21, 1869, Garvey was paid $133,187.20. Garvey did plastering work free of charge for various members of the Tweed Ring in their own homes and charged the work to the city. To show Tweed his appreciation, Garvey gave the ring a cut of his profits.[50]

Tweed contractors profited greatly when they built the New York County Court House at a cost of $13,000,000. It's hard to believe that when the original law authorizing the courthouse construction was passed in 1858 it provided for an expenditure of $250,000. Perhaps the original estimate was a little low, but no one would have guessed, except for Tweed, that the total cost when the courthouse was completed in 1871 would be as high as it was. A similar situation occurred with the Albany South Mall project built by Governor Rockefeller.

Tweed had to pay off many state legislators, and he said "It was impossible to do anything without paying for it."[51] Kickbacks were a prime source of income. Tweed said he paid at least $600,000 in bribes, entertainment, and other expenses to state legislators to pass a new city charter which said that the mayor would appoint the comptroller and other department heads. Also the Board of Supervisors would be replaced by a Board of Audit to audit all city and county bills. The new board would consist of the mayor (Oakey Hall, another member of the Tweed Ring), the comptroller (Dick Connolly, also in the ring), and the commissioner of the public works—Tweed.

At the Tweed Ring investigation, Tweed testified that you can't buy all the people of the state but you can buy their representatives in the legislature. Himself a state senator, Tweed said that "there was an organization formed of men of both parties, Republicans and Democrats, called the Black Horse Cavalry, composed of twenty-eight or thirty persons, who would all be controlled by one man, and vote as he directed them. Sometimes they would be paid for not voting against a bill, and sometimes they would not be desired, if their votes were not necessary. When the vote was called, they would step into the anteroom of the lobby, and if their vote was required, someone would step out, and have them vote; if they wasn't, they wouldn't come in at all."[52]

The Tweed Ring might have lasted a few more years, at least, had it not been for the death of James Watson, who was the city auditor. After Watson was killed while driving one of his fast trotters behind a sleigh during the winter of 1870-71, a person named Copeland was appointed to work on the books on his office. Around this time, Jimmy O'Brien, the sheriff of New York, was refused by the Board of Audit on a bill of "extras" that he submitted; it amounted to a quarter of a million dollars. The greedy O'Brien was angry with Tweed because of this. Unfortunately for Tweed, Copeland discovered some suspicious accounts and he told his friend O'Brien. The latter, still angry at Tweed, went to the *New York Times* with his information, which the newspaper thereafter printed. This caused the fall of the Tweed Ring.

In 1871 the ring was exposed through Thomas Nast's cartoons and the *New York Times* during July and August. The owner of the *Times* turned down a $5 million bribe not to print the exposés. Nast also turned down a $500,000 bribe. Newspapers that attacked Tammany and other political machines lost public notices from the city, a large amount of paid advertisements.

Tweed was arrested, on the affidavit of Samuel J. Tilden, on October 27, 1871, and bail was posted in the sum of $1 million. Tilden was an opportunist Democrat who was later elected governor of New York. He ran for President in 1876 and won the popular vote but lost to the Republican candidate, Rutherford B. Hayes, by only one electoral vote.

On November 19, 1873, Tweed was found guilty on 104 counts and sentenced to twelve years in prison. After one year behind bars, he was released by a decision of the Court of Appeals because of a legal technicality. As soon as Tweed was released from the penitentiary he was rearrested on a civil suit and held in $3 million bail. On December 4, 1875, while visiting his home in the custody of two guards, he escaped. He left the country and on November 23, 1876, he was rearrested in Cuba. Tweed was married and had eight children. A big spender all his life, he died a poor man at the age of fifty-five in prison on April 12, 1878. He died from pericarditis, complicated by pneumonia and kidney disease. His last words were "I have tried to do some good even if I have not had good luck."

The *New York Times* obituary on Tweed noted that "the story of his rise is the very romance of professional robbery thinly disguised under the pretense of political activity. . . . But for such a career, and all that it represents, society itself is mainly responsible. Such a product could not have been reared except on favorable soil. The indolence, the apathy, and the self-seeking of his fellow citizens gave him the opportunity he coveted."[53]

Still, Tammany aided the people in their fight against poverty, helped them in their difficulties, was their friend in need, their provider of amusement, their adviser in daily life, and their rescuer when they were in difficulties with the police or the courts. Natural human sympathy and bold political scheming go into the building of a powerful political machine.

HONEST JOHN KELLY BECOMES BOSS

John Kelly took over as boss in 1871, while Tweed was in prison. Honest John arranged with Tweed that if the former boss would testify before a committee of the Board of Aldermen he would be released from prison and receive immunity from prosecution. Tweed testified, as we have seen, but the attorney general, Charles S. Fairchild, and the governor, Lucius Robinson, refused to carry out the bargain. Kelly was furious because he didn't like having fooled a broken old man, even though Kelly was not part of the Tweed Ring.

Kelly never forgot what Robinson did, and at the next Democratic state convention in 1879, when Robinson was renominated, boss Kelly withdrew the Tammany delegation and had himself nominated for governor by Tammany. Kelly never expected or wanted to be governor; he just didn't want Robinson to be elected again, even if there wouldn't be a Democratic governor. As expected, the Republican candidate, Alonzo B. Cornell, was elected.

In 1871 Tammany Hall did poorly at the polls because of the Tweed Ring exposé. There was a call for reform. But although there were some new faces, true reform was only a dream. Nevertheless Tammany Hall was a mess and in need of a new leader who could help it improve its public image and regain its power. John Kelly, who had been a prominent Democrat in local politics, took over the job. He was boss until his death in 1881.

According to Dan O'Connell, Kelly was Tammany Hall's best organizer. O'Connell says that Kelly was able to take a "rabble and make an army of it." One of his first moves to rebuild Tammany was to appoint prominent persons as sachems of the Tammany Society. He originated the system of having candidates pay the party for being nominated.

He thought it would be better for Tammany to campaign for the whole ticket than have a person campaign only for himself. Kelly also compelled city employees to contribute a percentage of their salary to the party.

Businessmen, owners of houses of prostitution, builders, *et al.*, contributed annually to the party's campaign fund. The contribution was "insurance" against having their store windows smashed by the district leader's gang or being unnecessarily bothered by the police. Also a contribution could help a businessman increase his business with city contracts. Then too, while Kelly and Murphy were the bosses, the Monday before election day was known as "Dough Day" because the organization distributed the money that was to be spent on the next day. (Other bosses did the same thing.) Each ward leader got as much money as was needed to do his job properly.

Kelly was born to a poor Irish family on April 20, 1822 in New York City. As a youngster he contributed to his family small sums that he earned selling newspapers. He got a job as a "fly-boy" on a printing press of the *Herald*. But he didn't like that job so he became a soapstone-and-grate setter. In his youth and early manhood, New Yorkers did not have the many resources for amusement that they now have. Some enjoyed the theater in their free time, but more favored politics. The young men were divided into factions, each with a leader who was the strongest. Although Kelly didn't talk much and was reserved, he obtained control of his gang. He sought no quarrels but he retreated from none. Like Tweed, he was also a volunteer fireman.

In 1851 he ran for assessor but was defeated. Having been beaten in his first race for office, Kelly thought he was not fitted for politics. At first he did not want to run in the next year for assistant alderman, but he did and lost. In 1853 he ran for alderman again and this time he was elected.

Kelly ran for Congress in 1854 and won by a small margin. When the polls closed, Kelly thought he had lost, so he went to bed early. But about midnight a friend woke him and told him he had won by a small margin but that the ballots were being changed so that Kelly would lose. Kelly immediately went down to the police station where the ballots were kept and he noticed that they were written in pencil. To prevent alteration, he demanded that they be written in ink. Kelly won. If his friend had not waked him up that night he might not have served in the House of Representatives that term.

He was the only Roman Catholic in the House. On the House floor Kelly denied that Roman Catholics were loyal only to the Pope. He did not like the title of "the Irish Know-Nothing," which his opponents called him. Dan O'Connell says the Republican Party today is a "knownothing party." O'Connell adds that "it didn't change a Goddam bit"

from the way the Know-Nothing Party was around 1900. As congressman, Kelly obtained much patronage for his constituents.

In December of 1858 he gave up his seat in Congress so that he
could become sheriff. Kelly wanted to be sheriff because he didn't
have much money. The office of sheriff attracted Kelly just as it did
many others because of the lucrative fees. He was sheriff until 1861.
One is usually poor when elected sheriff, but few men have left the
office that way. The New York sheriff was an unsalaried post but its
fees were profitable. During Kelly's six years as sheriff he was said to
have made about $800,000 "honestly and fairly."[54]

Kelly was nominated for mayor in 1868 by the anti-Tweed reformers
to oppose Tweed's mayoral candidate, Oakey Hall. But Kelly withdrew
from the race just nine days after he was nominated because his son
died that year and his first wife died two years before in 1866. He went
to Europe to recuperate at the advice of his doctors. Mayor Hall
quipped, "I am the medical advisor who drove Kelly to Europe." But
considering Kelly's family life and his ambition, Hall's comment wasn't
justified.

In 1870 Kelly's daughter died. Within four years he had lost his
entire family. It is understandable that, at the time, Kelly even thought
of spending the rest of his life in a monastery. He once wanted to
become a priest.

Kelly, like O'Connell and other old-time bosses, did not like reformers, so he tried to discredit the independents who were elected
in 1871. When Mayor William F. Havemayer, a reform mayor, publicly
called boss Kelly corrupt, Honest John sued him for libel. The day the
trial was to begin the mayor, who was then almost eighty years old,
dropped dead of apoplexy in his office. Kelly then successfully ran a
Tammany candidate for the mayor's office, and things were again the
same.

John Kelly was the first Irish Catholic Tammany boss, and it was
during his tenure as boss that the first Irish Catholic mayor of New York
was elected. He was William Grace, an immigrant waiter who later
owned the Grace Shipping Line. However, Kelly broke with Grace when
the boss could not have his own way.

While Kelly was the boss the election results were not always
favorable for Tammany. He would say on those occasions, "We have
been beaten this time, but we will win the next." There was always
hope, and this hope, along with being a considerate and honest person,
helped Kelly keep his leadership. A charitable person, he helped bring
Tammany Hall together into a strong machine after it was tarnished by
Tweed. While Kelly was boss, Tammany Hall was free from scandal.
Kelly's stealing was kept to a minimum during his long tenure as boss.
Because of this he was called "Honest John."

He was married for the second time in November, 1876. His bride was a niece of Cardinal McCloskey. From December, 1876, to December, 1880, Kelly was city comptroller. He was sick about a year before his death. When he died, in June, 1886, his son John was nine and his daughter Josephine was seven. His last words were "I have tried to live a good Catholic life and I want to be buried in the Catholic Church with no pomp or ceremony." His overworking himself and being upset about the deaths in his family caused his death.

In an obituary editorial, the *New York Times* wrote that members of the Democratic Party "will lament his death as a kingdom mourns its sovereign or a republic its founder." The *Times* added that John Kelly "was an honest and incorruptible man. But he was so little careful about the company he kept that he was constantly in the most intimate and confidential relations with men of notoriously dishonest and corrupt lives." The *Times* further said that "when the bribe-taking Alderman is sent to Sing Sing the 'boss' who sent him to the Board of Aldermen must not altogether escape censure."[55]

It was estimated that Kelly, at the time of his death, was worth from $300,000 to $500,000. Public offices were ordered closed by the Board of Aldermen on the day of Boss Kelly's funeral. Also the flags on public buildings were placed at half-mast out of respect to the boss's memory. Thousands of New Yorkers attended his burial. His funeral was simple, as he requested, but impressive. He was put to rest in a tomb in the old St. Patrick's Cathedral on Mott Street.

CROKER BECOMES BOSS

As leader of the Eighteenth District, Richard Croker made it one of the strongest Tammany districts in the city. His success placed him in the position of being the natural successor to Kelly. During the last year or two of Kelly's life, Croker assumed many of Boss Kelly's duties. After Kelly died the twenty-four leaders of the assembly districts, constituting the executive committee of Tammany Hall, announced that there would be no further "boss" and that the party would be run by the executive committee. However, Richard Croker, Kelly's protégé, was able to secure power and was the boss for about fourteen years.

Richard ("The Squire") Croker was born in Ireland on November 24, 1843. Croker's father found living difficult in Ireland, so he, his wife, and his seven children immigrated to New York in 1846 when Richard was three years old. Richard went to school for only a few years, and even then his attendance wasn't good. His neighborhood was tough, and Richard became the leader of the Fourth Avenue Tunnel Gang. It wasn't unusual for teenagers to form gangs in their neighborhoods. He learned to fight well. In one fight in a bar, Croker's opponent lost an ear.

When Croker was twenty-one, he voted for the first time. He then said that the Democratic Party was the party for young men. At the next election, when he was twenty-two, he said he voted seventeen times in the same election. Like Tweed and Kelly, Croker was also a volunteer fireman. In 1868 and 1869 he was elected an alderman, and in 1873 coroner. He was a coroner when Tweed died.

Croker was indicted for murder in 1874. He was accused of shooting and killing a supporter of Jimmy O'Brien, the ex-sheriff who helped expose Tweed and was then running for Congress. At the trial eye-witnesses gave conflicting testimony. The jury, six Democrats and six Republicans, remained out for seventeen hours and was divided: six for conviction and six for acquittal. Because the jury could not reach a verdict, Croker was released and never tried again. In later years it was believed that he was protecting someone else and had not killed the man.

In 1883 he was appointed fire commissioner. From April, 1889, to February, 1890, Croker was city chamberlain at a salary of $25,000 a year. The chamberlain was in charge of selecting banks for the deposit of city funds. The state legislature authorized the chamberlain to pocket some of the interest.

One of Croker's first important actions as leader of Tammany Hall was to surround himself with advisers who possessed qualities he himself lacked. He picked Bourke Cochran, Hugh J. Grant, and Thomas E. Gilroy. They, with Croker, constituted the "Big Four." In 1884 he got Hugh J. Grant elected sheriff. While sheriff, Grant gave $25,000 to Croker's two-year-old daughter, saying the gift was made because the little girl was his godchild.

Boss Croker instituted the system of having his lieutenants give reports. He always kept his word and expected others to do the same. There were 90,000 men on the roll of the Tammany organization and thirty-five district leaders. Once a number of the leaders planned to overthrow the boss. On the hour set for the overthrow, Croker walked into their room and asked, "Is anyone here dissatisfied?" There was no answer, and he ordered them all back to their districts.

Croker himself had been a "reformer." In 1868 he was elected a member of the Board of Aldermen on the anti-Tweed ticket when Tweed was the boss of Tammany Hall. Croker later made peace with Tweed, though, and received many favors from Boss Tweed. Croker was in the real estate business and believed in honest graft. He had seven homes, traveled to Europe every year, and journeyed in a private Pullman car to the national conventions and to his winter estate ("The Wigwam") in Palm Beach, valued with its long shorefront property at $800,000.[56]

Under Croker, Tammany Hall made the most of its opportunities of "honest" graft. Every year millions of dollars of graft was collected by Tammany Hall. One source of Croker's personal fortune was the United States Fidelity & Casualty Company. The company bonded city employees whose positions required it.[57] The Park Row Building, owned by Croker, had city offices in it. There the city paid rents higher than it could have obtained elsewhere. Croker's son, Frank, when he was only twenty-one years old, was a partner in the Roebling Company, which fireproofed city buildings. Croker was accused of getting $140,-000 worth of stock from the Auto Truck Company, a trucking firm that did business with the city. He was charged with taking money from the New York Telephone Company for a city contract.

The Tammany Police Commissioner in 1894, James J. Martin, admitted that from 85 to 90 percent of the appointments, transfers, and promotions were recommended by district leaders of Tammany Hall.[58] The police officers had to pay to get their jobs and to be promoted. During Croker's reign, anyone who wanted a job as an ordinary policeman had to pay $300. For $1,600 you could be promoted to sergeant and for $14,000 you could be made a police captain.[59] The policemen didn't mind paying so much to get their jobs because there was so much graft to be had. Prostitution flourished, saloons stayed open after-hours, and gambling was widespread.

In May, 1894, Croker announced his retirement from politics because of his health. He then went for a few years to England and Ireland, where he had estates and owned several race horses. But even though an ocean separated him from his base of power in New York, he was still the boss. Whenever any problems arose, nothing was done until word was received from Croker.

Tammany Hall lost the election in 1894 because of the police corruption that was exposed in the Lexow Investigation. While Croker was in Europe there was no real leader of Tammany, and because the Republicans were in power the Democrats had to lay low. When Croker returned to the United States in 1897 and resumed his role as Tammany leader, the Democrats were again victorious at the polls.

After being leader of Tammany Hall for fourteen years Croker decided to retire for good. The son of a poor immigrant, he had made millions through politics and wanted to spend the rest of his life enjoying the better things. When Croker's favorite horse, Orby, won the Epsom Derby, Croker confessed that the proudest moment of his life, above his election victories, was leading Orby past the royal grandstand as King Edward VII and others stood at attention.

On January 13, 1902 it was announced that Croker had selected Lewis Nixon as his successor. Nixon was a graduate of the United States Naval Academy and a shipbuilder. Croker bowed out as boss after he saw the public beginning to show their discontent with Tammany Hall's police graft. After his first wife died in 1914 (he was separated from her), he, then seventy-one, married a twenty-three-year-old Indian girl a few weeks after the funeral. Croker's children thought their father's second wife married him for money, so they went to court and argued that their father was mentally unfit to handle his own affairs and that his second wife had obtained control of his property through undue influence over her aged husband. The court decided in favor of the former Tammany chieftain, who was then blind. When Croker died in Ireland, on April 29, 1922, his estate, left to his second wife, was estimated to be worth more than $5 million. In his later years, Croker lived bigger than any of the other Tammany bosses. Also, he was the richest. When he died, the flags of Tammany Hall and every district clubhouse flew at half mast. He was buried in Ireland.

Croker's death was due to a prolonged illness after he caught a cold. When he returned to Ireland from the United States, in October, 1921, there was trouble in Ireland. Martial law was in force, and this resulted in a ban on passengers landing at Queenstown. So Mr. and Mrs. Croker had to go to Liverpool, where a wait on a drafty pier, while their luggage was being examined, with exposure to a snowstorm, caused his illness.

The *New York Times,* in its obituary editorial, said, "In the dynasty of Tammany bosses Richard Croker stood midway, both in time and in methods, between Tweed and Murphy." The *Times* noted that "No man could have won and held an evil leadership as Richard Croker did without great native ability. He literally fought his way to the top of Tammany. And once there he maintained himself by an iron rule and a system of personal terrorism." Croker even admitted that in his public activities he was "working for his own pockets all the time."

From 1900 to 1901 Nixon was chairman of Croker's Anti-Vice Committee. The committee was established during the campaign to offset growing public indignation that Tammany Hall had profited from the system of police protection. Nixon didn't last long as chairman of Tammany's finance committee. On May 14, 1902, he resigned because he said all of his important acts had to be checked with Croker before they became effective. Every boss of Tammany Hall was chairman of the finance committee.[60]

For a short time in 1902 there were three leaders of Tammany Hall: Charles F. Murphy, Daniel F. McMahon ("Two-Spot"), and Louis F. Haffen. Murphy was soon the Tammany boss. McMahon was chairman of Tammany's executive committee and the head of the contracting firm of Naughton and Company. Much money was made through that company. Haffen was later borough president of the Bronx and removed from office by Republican governor Charles Evans Hughes.

MURPHY BECOMES BOSS

On September 19, 1902 at the age of forty-four, Charles Francis

Murphy became the boss of Tammany Hall as well as the treasurer of Tammany. "Silent Charlie" was boss for twenty-two years until he died on April 25, 1924, at the age of sixty-five.

Murphy was born in New York City on June 20, 1858. Like Croker, he was a good fighter and a member of his neighborhood gang. Murphy saved $500 by working in various jobs and opened his own saloon in 1879. He sold a mug of beer and a bowl of soup for five cents. Those were the days! The saloon business was prosperous and by 1890 Murphy had four saloons. One of them served as the headquarters for a Tammany Hall district association. He never allowed women in his saloons.

"Silent Charlie" was a charitable person and in 1892, at the age of thirty-four, he was made a district leader. One of his brothers was on the police force, and two of his other brothers were aldermen. Robert Van Wyck was elected mayor in 1897, and Murphy was appointed a dock commissioner. When he took this post, he was worth about $350,000 or $400,000, the profits of his saloon business. Murphy was proud of the title "Commissioner," as he was often called. It was the only important office he ever held. In 1903 the Dock Department in New York City had "exclusive and private and secret control of the expenditure of $10,000,000 a year."[61] No wonder Murphy chose to control it! When he left office he was said to be worth a million dollars. In any case, he was rich because, in addition to a home in the city, he had an estate in Good Ground, Long Island, where he built a nine-hole golf course.

Murphy made millions through politics. He got large contracts awarded to Tammany-affiliated businesses. Murphy stole through legitimate firms. In 1901 he started the New York Contracting & Trucking Company. The company leased two docks from the city at $4,800 a year. The firm then leased the docks and made a profit of about $200 a day or 5,000 percent on the company's investment. It also excavated the site for the Pennsylvania Station and did improvements on the New York, New Haven & Hartford Railroad.

There were times when the mayor was not a Tammany man, as well as times when the governor did not go along with Tammany Hall. But even when the Tammany boss did not control the mayor or the governor he still survived, because there were always the borough presidents, city councils, and the state legislature they could control. Such was the case with Boss Murphy and Governor William Sulzer. Murphy wanted Sulzer to appoint a friend of his state highway commissioner but Sulzer said no. Governor Sulzer paid the consequences for not going along. Murphy had a great deal of influence in the legislature, and Sulzer was impeached in 1913.

Sulzer was a Tammany congressman and it was Murphy who nominated him for governor. Murphy later said it was the biggest mistake of his life. Sulzer made an honest mistake in his gubernatorial campaign statement. He omitted certain checks for sums he had received and used for personal expenses. This charge is frequently heard today and just another reason why we are in need of campaign reforms.

D-Cady Herrick, boss of the Albany Democrats before O'Connell, said during the impeachment proceedings that "the bringing of these impeachment proceedings is lamentable because of the object lesson of what may occur to any man in public life who dares stand and oppose the wishes of those who may know something about the private life and history not known to the general public."[62] On October 17, 1913, Sulzer was impeached by a vote of forty-three to twelve. It was the only time in the history of the state of New York that a governor was removed from office. Not surprisingly, Republican Boss William Barnes of Albany went along with Murphy for Sulzer's impeachment.

Sulzer was replaced by Martin H. Glynn of Albany, who was then the lieutenant governor. Dan O'Connell knew Glynn. O'Connell says that McCabe wanted Sulzer impeached so that Glynn, a fellow Albanian, could be governor. He says "Glynn was no Goddamn good, he wasn't loyal to McCabe. Then Glynn, the Goddamn fool, appointed McCabe a commissioner that lasted about three or four years when he could have appointed him a commissioner that would have lasted ten years."

"Big Tim" Sullivan, Tammany's leader in the Bowery and a cousin of Christopher D. Sullivan, who was later boss, gave a Christmas dinner every year to about five thousand men at his political headquarters. In the summer, the Tammany Hall district associations had clambakes and steak roasts. During the winter, they had dinners and dances. Each association would boast that its members could eat more steak, drink more beer, and consume more bread than any other organization. At the dinners they would sing their favorite songs. Everyone bought tickets to these events even if they couldn't attend, just to reassure Tammany Hall that they weren't antagonistic toward them.

Murphy was the only Tammany boss able to gain control of New York State. Dan O'Connell says, "I always thought Murphy was the best politician of them all." Measured by results, Murphy was the most successful leader of Tammany Hall, and his term of office was the longest (twenty-two years). He elected three governors in a normally Republican state and three mayors. One of the governors, Alfred E. Smith, was Presidential timber. Boss Murphy dominated the state Democrats more than his predecessors did. He united the Democrats statewide.

Theodore Roosevelt described the relationship of Murphy and William Barnes, Jr., the Republican boss of Albany and also the leader of the GOP in New York State, in the following manner because Barnes did not support Roosevelt: "Now, no doubt, Mr. Barnes and Mr. Murphy would like to have everything all the time, but they are perfectly willing each to take half instead of the whole, but we don't care anything about dividing the state equally between them, instead of giving it all to one. What we intend to do is take it from both and we intend to take the nation from both."[63] The working relationship between Murphy and Barnes made it possible for each to share the spoils.

Boss Murphy generally refused to notice attacks upon him, and although he brought a number of libel suits against newspapers, these were largely for political effect. Murphy summed up his attitude toward critics when he said: "It is the fate of political leaders to be reviled. If one is too thin-skinned to stand it he should never take the job. History shows the better and more successful the organization and leader the more bitter the attacks. Success is always a target."

Mr. Murphy was a Roman Catholic who regularly attended services. He was never talkative in public and always shy of the limelight. He believed in "practical" politics. He was a "good, sensible man," Dan O'Connell says, having known Murphy personally. Instead of fighting the civil service, Murphy instructed his workers to organize classes so that their constituents could pass the tests.

At one of the Tammany Hall Fourth of July celebrations, a newspaperman noticed that Murphy was not joining in the singing of the "Star-Spangled Banner." The reporter asked a leader in the organization, "What's the matter with the boss, can't he sing?" Murphy's friend responded, "Sure he can. Perhaps, he didn't want to commit himself." That remark was probably made in jest, but bosses don't usually want to commit themselves until as late as possible. It is a good strategy because it permits them to keep their options open and gives them flexibility. The more options a person has, the better position he is in. That way he doesn't get boxed into a corner and is able to think about his position longer. To many people it may seem as if the boss is stalling because he is afraid to commit himself. This may be true. However, it is usually good strategy to follow. A political strategist should also try to preserve a winning image.

George Washington Plunkitt was one of the thirty-five Tammany district leaders. His uniqueness stems from his willingness to talk about politics. His remarks were published first in the newspapers and then in a book in 1905. Most politicians dislike publicity, but Plunkitt was used to it because he had been a state legislator. Like Dan O'Connell and other political bosses, politics was a way of life for Plunkitt. He was not a philosopher by trade, but his philosophy is now famous because of what he had to say and his honesty in saying it.

He was leader of the Fifteenth Assembly District. During his political career he was a sachem of the Tammany Society, chairman of the elections committee of Tammany Hall, a state senator, assemblyman, police magistrate, county supervisor, and alderman. He once filled four public offices in one year and drew salaries from three of them at the same time. He made a lot of money through politics. A contractor, he built some of the Hudson River docks. He was a close friend of the former Tammany leader Charles F. Murphy. Plunkitt died in 1924 at the age of eighty-two.

"I seen my opportunities and I took them," Plunkitt used to say. He distinguished between "honest graft" and "dishonest graft." According to Plunkitt, dishonest graft is blackmail, robbing the city treasury, or working with gamblers or lawbreakers. An example of honest graft is Plunkitt taking advantage of what the city has to offer. If the city is repaving a street and has many old granite blocks to sell, according to Plunkitt, he would buy them and later sell them at a greater price. Plunkitt said that a newspaper once sent two outside men to bid against him at an auction. He went to each man and asked him how many of the 250,000 stones he wanted. One said 20,000 and the other 15,000. Plunkitt promised he would give them what they wanted if they would let him bid for the entire lot. They agreed and when the auctioneer asked for a bid, Plunkitt said, "Two dollars and fifty cents." He got what he wanted.[64]

Plunkitt said civil service reform "is the curse of the nation." He added, "How are you going to interest our young men in their country if you have no offices to give them when they work for their party? Tammany is for the spoils system, and when we go in we fire every anti-Tammany man from office that can be fired under the law."[65]

He said, "The politician who steals is worse than a thief. He is a fool. With the grand opportunities all around for the man with a political pull, there's no excuse for stealin' a cent." If only people would be satisfied with making an ordinary profit and not be so greedy and try to get rich quickly!

THE DECLINE OF TAMMANY HALL

The election of 1913 was disastrous for Tammany Hall because all of the anti-Tammany candidates for city offices were elected. The patronage was cut off and the machine practically broke down. What were some of the reasons for Tammany's defeat? The city was becoming more populated. People were moving both in and out of the city. There was a progressive (reform) movement. Many people felt sorry for Sulzer. Many people were tired of being swindled for so long. They wanted more responsive government. But here we are sixty years later, and are things much better?

Keeping control of the city is important to any machine because once it loses control it becomes powerless. That is why Dan O'Connell never really cared about any place except the city and county of Albany. Losing a Presidential or state election doesn't mean the end of a machine, but to lose the mayoralty of a city is quite the opposite. The loss of patronage terminates the once powerful machine.

In 1915 Tammany Hall elected Judge Edward Swann as district attorney of the county of New York and Alfred E. Smith as sheriff. There were signs that Tammany was recovering, but would it ever be as strong as before?

Murphy had indigestion pains for several years before he died. Because he complained of indigestion, his maid sent for the doctor a few hours before he died on April 25, 1924. The physician found Murphy, in great pain, sitting on a chair in the bathroom. He was put to bed and he died. Murphy was married but had no children. About sixty thousand people, according to newspaper estimates, lined the streets while Murphy's body was carried to St. Patrick's Cathedral for a high requiem mass. The church was packed for the solemn occasion. Governor Smith, Mayor Hylan, Bernard Baruch, United States Senator Copeland, several judges, and some Tammany district leaders were among the honorary pallbearers. Murphy's estate was estimated at more than two million dollars.

After Murphy died a committee of seven ran Tammany Hall for a while. Surrogate James A. Foley was selected as Murphy's successor, but he declined to take over the leadership of Tammany, so Judge George W. Olvany was selected. Olvany, formerly a leader of the Tenth Assembly District, and at that time a judge of the Court of General Sessions, was thought to be the only other candidate who would be regarded with favor by the public. The selection of a judge would give Tammany a better public image and perhaps higher ethical standards than it had had in the past. Mayor Walker once said that he would make no political appointments without consulting the Tammany leader.

In 1924, Olvany succeeded Murphy as the Tammany leader. With the exception of Lewis Nixon, he was the first Tammany leader with a college degree since Aaron Burr. Olvany's law firm had deposited more than $5 million over seven years, with most of the fees coming from clients who had dealings with the city. Judge Olvany resigned as Tammany's leader on March 15, 1929, for health reasons.[66]

John F. Curry, age forty-eight, replaced Olvany as boss on April 23, 1929. Curry was born in Ireland and came to New York with his parents as a small boy. He milked his father's cows as a boy on a farm near West Sixtieth Street. He was a telegrapher and bookkeeper for the Union Stockyard and Market Company. Curry was popular in his neighborhood and good in sports. His first political job was as a clerk in the tax department at three dollars a day. Later he became financial clerk in the paymaster's office. In 1902 he was elected to the state assembly. Curry became a district leader in 1905. He had an insurance business, and was commissioner of records of the Surrogate Court from 1911 to 1929.

Tammany's Big Four in 1929 were Al Smith, governor and Presidential candidate; Jimmy Walker, mayor of New York; Surrogate James Foley, Murphy's son-in-law; and United States Senator Robert F. Wagner, who had been elected in 1926. Walker resigned as mayor in 1932 when he was about to be removed from the office. The Democrats lost the mayoralty in 1933 when the Republican candidate, Fiorello La Guardia, won. Governor Lehman and President Franklin Roosevelt opposed Tammany Hall because Curry didn't support them.

On April 20, 1934 Curry was ousted as Tammany Hall's leader. It was the first time that a Tammany leader had been removed from office by the executive committee. The committee voted 14⅓ to 10⅚ to remove Curry after he refused to resign. He was ousted because of a number of "mistakes" he had made. He opposed the nomination of Franklin Roosevelt for President, and Herbert H. Lehman for governor.

Curry supported John Boyd Thacher, mayor of Albany, for the gubernatorial nomination. But actually Curry was hoping that there would be a deadlock at the convention between Thacher and Lehman so that Samuel Levy, borough president of Manhattan, could get the nomination. However, Curry's strategy didn't work and Lehman was nominated. Also Curry pledged to renominate James J. Walker for mayor after Mayor Walker resigned while facing charges resulting from the Seabury investigation. Instead of being removed from office by then-Governor Franklin Roosevelt, Mayor Walker resigned. In addition, Tammany did poorly on election day in 1933. The Seabury investigation on Tammany corruption hurt the machine during Curry's tenure.

A story is told that around the time of the Seabury investigation, there was a Tammany boss who asked a henchman to name the priest who went easiest on you, as far as confessions were concerned. He told him of Father O'Brien, who also happened to be a little hard of hearing, and they went to him. At the church, the henchman went into the confessional box first. When he emerged he was pale and shaken. "What happened?" the Tammany leader asked. "Father O'Brien isn't hearing confessions tonight," he said. "Seabury is substituting for him."

Dan O'Connell's friends, Edward J. Ahearn, Billy Solomon, and Clarence H. Neal, Jr. (all district leaders), voted to remove Curry. Clarence H. Neal, Jr. was Ahearn's lieutenant. They were all close friends. Ahearn's father, John, a Murphy puppet, was borough president of Manhattan but was removed from office by Governor Charles Evans Hughes. O'Connell says, "He didn't do nothing that I know of." Dan became friendly with several Tammany leaders when they came to Albany while the legislature was in session. Ahearn, Neal, and Solomon got hold of Tammany Hall at one time. At the time of Curry's ouster

Ahearn of the Fourth District was mentioned to succeed him because it was Ahearn who had led the group to remove him. Ahearn had been defeated by Curry in a race for Tammany leader five years before. Neal had made an appeal for Curry's resignation. He said, "John, this is not a reprisal. We are not trying to get even. We are doing this for the good of the party and to restore harmony."[67] O'Connell says "You couldn't take Curry's word for anything. He was unreliable. You couldn't depend on him. . . . That's what got him out of Tammany."

A committee, similar to the committee in 1902, which had been composed of Murphy, McMahon, and Haffen, ran Tammany Hall until James Dooling, forty-one, an attorney, was elected leader. Born in 1893, Dooling had succeeded his father as district leader when the elder Dooling died in October, 1931. The younger Dooling was a deputy public administrator from 1923 to 1932 at $5,000 a year. It was the only political job he ever held. When he became leader of Tammany Hall there was political chaos and factionalism in the organization because of Curry's ouster. Dooling was like former leader George Olvany because he wasn't an old-time boss. The youngest man ever to head Tammany, he was hailed as a leader of a new type, frank and open, where his predecessors had been devious and secretive.

Dooling was elected leader, just as Curry was ousted, largely through the efforts of Postmaster General James A. Farley. In spite of this, Dooling resented Farley and Ed Flynn because the former wanted to make the Tammany organization a minor factor in the city's Democratic setup, giving Flynn of the Bronx most of the power. Flynn was a good friend of Farley and Roosevelt and thus received most of the federal patronage that went to New York City. Dooling made it clear that he had no intention of being guided by Flynn. Dooling never really came to power in a full sense as leader of Tammany because of a Republican mayor in New York City at the time and because most federal patronage went to the Bronx.

Ed Flynn was a lawyer, assemblyman, and sheriff. While sheriff in 1922 he was selected by Boss Murphy to run the Bronx organization. Flynn was the Bronx leader until he died in 1953 at sixty-one. He made much money from his law practice. Flynn was close to Franklin Roosevelt and Jim Farley. He had a summer estate at Mahopac in Putnam County. Once a yard there was paved with city paving blocks and installed by laborers from the Bronx borough president's office on city time. This scandal cost him a post as ambassador to Austria. President Roosevelt withdrew his nomination because of this.

Flynn was picked by President Roosevelt to succeed James Farley, also a Roman Catholic, as chairman of the Democratic National Committee. A long-time personal friend of Roosevelt, Flynn was appointed regional administrator of the NRA program for New York, New Jersey, and Pennsylvania. Mayor Walker had appointed Flynn city chamberlain. In 1929, when Roosevelt was governor of New York, he had appointed Flynn secretary of state, Dan O'Connell once said that Ed Flynn helped kill Tammany Hall.

Flynn broke with Tammany when John F. Curry supported Al Smith at the 1932 Democratic National Convention in Chicago while Flynn supported Roosevelt for President. Tammany blamed Flynn for splitting the Democratic Party in New York City and causing the election of Mayor Fiorello H. La Guardia, a Republican. Flynn had supported a Recovery Party candidate in 1933, Joseph V. McKee. Flynn said the Republicans in 1914 kept "themselves alive during the long droughts by accepting handouts from Tammany's back door." When Flynn died, Congressman Charles A. Buckley took over the Bronx leadership.

New York City is divided into five boroughs (counties). The Democratic Party has always been the dominant political party in New York, but there is no New York City Democratic Party as such. Instead it has five groups, sometimes united and often divided. For example, Flynn, former boss of the Bronx, supported Roosevelt for President in 1932, while Tammany boss Curry and Brooklyn boss John H. McCooey opposed Roosevelt.

Up until 1898 New York County contained all of New York City. But in that year the area was divided into five boroughs. Tammany Boss Murphy was able to name the Bronx leaders and told them what to do. After Murphy died, however, there was frequently a struggle of power among the mayors, Tammany bosses, and leaders of the boroughs. The boroughs posed additional problems for Tammany Hall. Undoubtedly, the leaders of Tammany Hall would have combined the five boroughs into one unit if they had had the chance. The mayor of New York, even if he was a Tammany man, had to give out patronage to the other boroughs as well as Manhattan, which was the Tammany borough.

Until Mayor Jimmy Walker established a citywide department of sanitation, two of the five boroughs had their own departments to give out patronage. Also until Mayor La Guardia established a citywide department of parks, every borough had its own department, which caused some duplication of equipment. The consolidation might have saved the city some money, but the bosses would have preferred to handle their own departments for patronage reasons even at the additional expense. Until 1937 each county elected its own sheriff, county clerk, and register. Also until 1937 every borough president built all the public works in his borough. Even until 1961 every borough president controlled all of his borough streets and sewers. Until Mayor Wagner set up a site-selection board the borough presidents decided where public buildings would be built.

Today there are surrogates and district attorneys in each of the counties, so the patronage is kept close to home. At its height the

New York City Democratic organization had 32,000 committeemen spread over five counties. Madison Square Garden was the only place large enough to hold a meeting. By a comparison, in 1964 there were 510 committeemen in Albany.

Vincent Impellitteri ran for mayor in 1950 as an independent. Carmine De Sapio, who was then the Tammany leader, and Ed Flynn of the Bronx didn't support him. Mayor Impellitteri in 1953, when he sought nomination for reelection in the Democratic primary, lost to Robert F. Wagner, Jr., then Manhattan borough president. Mayor Wagner appointed Impellitteri to a low court judgeship. Although De Sapio made Wagner mayor, Wagner went along to get rid of Carmine De Sapio, as the Tammany leader, so that Wagner would look like a reformer.

Both Wagner and Franklin Roosevelt were against Tammany. As Dan O'Connell says, "The Wagners were never much good for Tammany Hall." Wagner expanded the civil service with collective bargaining for pay raises and benefits, and promotions by taking exams. Wagner served as mayor of New York City for three terms, running once on an "anti-bossism" ticket. He won despite opposition of the city's top Democratic leaders. Tammany Hall, Dan O'Connell, and other Democratic politicians didn't like Robert Wagner because when he ran for reelection as mayor of New York City in 1961 he broke with the Tammany leader, Carmine De Sapio, not wanting to be associated with the boss label. A few years later, Wagner charged the State Democratic chairman, Bill McKeon, with offering bribes to legislators. Many Democratic politicians were further annoyed with Wagner because of this, and the State Investigation Commission cleared McKeon of any illegal actions. The collapse of political machines was partially a result of the social reforms of Roosevelt's New Deal, which provided for welfare, unemployment insurance, social security, and union pensions.

Roosevelt and Farley tried to break the boss rule of Tammany Hall by cutting its federal patronage. As postmaster general, Farley distributed a lot of patronage, and until recently, the post office was the biggest department for party patronage. Earlier, Farley had been chairman of the New York Boxing Commission. He had also been a town committeeman in Rockland County. In 1920 he was appointed port warden in New York City, where he was supposed to inspect all ships sailing into New York's harbor. Dan O'Connell says, "I think Farley's the most disloyal man that ever lived. He quit Smith, went from Smith to Roosevelt and from Roosevelt to himself." Farley made money in the Coca-Cola business. "I know the first time Farley spoke to me about Smith I was very much surprised. I told him. I said, 'I can't understand how you'd ever get away from Smith. I wouldn't know you if it wasn't for Smith.'" Dan says, "I think Farley was the most ungrateful man that ever was in politics." But then Dan O'Connell always believed in loyalty to one's friends and party. According to him, "Farley would still be selling sporting goods if it hadn't been for Roosevelt."

Since Murphy's death Tammany Hall had gone downhill. Immigration had reached its peak in 1907 with 1,285,000. By 1933 it was down to 23,000. This was the result of restrictive immigration laws passed by Congress after World War I. These laws were passed because many Americans, especially organized labor, complained that immigrants competed with and took jobs away from native Americans. In addition, immigration had created ghettos in large cities, which bred disease, crime, and other problems. The Emergency Quota Act of 1921 limited the annual number of immigrants from each nation to 3 percent of the foreign-born persons from that nation residing in the United States according to the 1910 census. The Immigration Act of 1924 reduced immigration quotas to 2 percent and shifted the base date to 1890. No more than 150,000 immigrants from outside the Western Hemisphere were permitted to enter the United States as a result of the National Origins Plan of 1929. Each was given a quota, and many of the quotas remained unfilled because of this act, coupled with the Depression of 1929. Welfare and Social Security displaced the ward leader's food baskets and other help. There was a shrinkage of Tammany's power base. In 1900 more than half of the city's population was in Manhattan; by 1930 only 25 percent lived there.

Then, James Dooling died of a stroke at age forty-one, on July 26, 1937, Tammany needed a new leader. Christopher D. Sullivan, sixty-seven, got the nod. Sullivan was a member of the House of Representatives from 1910 until 1940. On February 6, 1942 he was removed as the Tammany leader by a vote of the executive committee (145 to 136) because the Democrats hadn't won a city election since 1932. At the time Sullivan was ousted as Tammany's leader there was interest in the removal of the headquarters of the Manhattan Democratic organization from Tammany Hall and the abandoning of the 150-year-old name of Tammany.

The next "leader" was Congressman Michael J. Kennedy. He had been a city marshal for fifteen years. He resigned as Tammany's leader in January, 1944, after gangster Frank Costello said he helped Kennedy get his position as the Tammany leader.

Edward V. Loughlin of Yorkville was elected as Tammany's next leader. But in 1945, after three terms as mayor, La Guardia chose not to run again. Bill O'Dwyer, an immigrant from Brooklyn, was elected mayor as a Democrat. Loughlin didn't get along well with O'Dwyer, so Loughlin was forced to resign.

Frank J. Sampson replaced Loughlin as the Tammany leader in 1947 but he lasted less than a year.

Borough President Hugo E. Rogers was elected the new leader

of Tammany Hall. Rogers was the first Jewish leader of Tammany Hall. (Mordecai Noah was Grand Sachem but not the political leader.) Rogers was replaced by Carmine De Sapio on July 20, 1949.

Born on December 10, 1908, Carmine De Sapio was both the last of New York's old-time bosses and the first leader of the modern machine. His machine was the least corrupt ever in New York. He lasted until September 7, 1961. During his political career, De Sapio was a precinct captain, deputy sheriff, and member of the Board of Elections. In December, 1953, he became Tammany's first boss to be a member of the Democratic National Committee. When Averell Harriman was elected governor in 1954 he appointed De Sapio secretary of state as appreciation for his support. His tenure as Tammany boss was a victory for the Italians because the Irish were usually in control. De Sapio was put in as leader of Tammany Hall with the help of gangster Frank Costello.

De Sapio's decline began in 1958 when, against the wishes of Harriman and Wagner, he got the Democratic senatorial nomination for Frank Hogan, New York's district attorney. (Hogan was defeated but continued as DA until he resigned in 1974, dying soon after.) New York's reform Democratic movement began to rise as De Sapio declined. His fall was due to his overconfidence and his desire to present himself as a reformer. He would have lasted longer had it not been for his own reforms, which happened to be the first major reform of Tammany Hall since its founding. He pushed through rules requiring the direct election of Tammany district leaders by the enrolled voters instead of by the election district captains. While leader of Tammany Hall, De Sapio remained a district leader. In 1961 he lost the leadership of his own district and of Tammany Hall. As Norman Thomas and Paul Blanshard in 1932 wrote, "to lose your district in a primary is political suicide." So Tammany got a new leader.

Many stories have been told about De Sapio, for example, in 1957 a cab driver found a paper bag containing $11,200 in cash in his back seat shortly after having had De Sapio as a passenger. De Sapio claimed the money wasn't his. However, New Yorkers smiled and made wisecracks about the incident. In another incident, an important roll call was about to be taken in Congress. One congressman called Carmine De Sapio and said, "We need two more votes. Where are your two congressmen?" De Sapio replied, "They'll leave for Washington on the next plane." Sure enough De Sapio delivered the two representatives, who rarely stayed in Washington because they were either in their New York business or on the golf course.

De Sapio was not a licensed insurance agent, but after he left as leader of Tammany Hall he worked for an insurance company "to promote the good will . . . through acquaintances that I have acquired over a period of years." Later he was convicted by a federal jury of "having conspired to bribe a public official and share in the proceeds of selling influence." He was sentenced to two years in prison.[68] The commissioner of the Department of Water Supply, Gas and Electricity, James Marcus, was involved with the former Tammany leader in the incident, described below, that caused both of them to be sent to jail.

The story of how James Marcus ruined a promising career is sad. Shortly after John Lindsay was elected mayor in 1965, Marcus joined his administration. In March, 1966, he became commissioner of the Department of Water Supply, Gas and Electricity. Within two years he was sentenced to eleven months in the Lewisburg Federal prison.[69] Had it not been for his obsession with playing the stock market and his greed he might not have been sent to jail. He lost much money of his own and borrowed money in the market. When he could not pay back the money he borrowed and the high interest, which was at usurious rates charged by the Mafia, he got in trouble. Instead of his situation improving it got worse as he sank deeper into debt. His love of money and dream of striking it rich did him in. Marcus found a way to make some extra money. He accepted a bribe whenever he could. But even if he had been able to pay off the loans, he would probably have accepted another bribe. Those he did favors for would come back again and again. Thus Carmine De Sapio tried to obtain a building permit for Consolidated Edison (the electric and gas supplier in the New York City area) from Marcus. In return Con Ed would pay off Marcus and De Sapio. This time, however, the deal didn't go through. In 1968 De Sapio was sentenced to two years in prison for his part in the scheme.

Edward Costikyan, thirty-seven, took over as the Tammany leader. He had been a partner in Adlai Stevenson's law firm. When he resigned in 1964, Mrs. Charlotte Spiegel took over as Tammany's first female leader. She held office only for about a month until the executive committee could elect a new leader. On December 6, 1964, J. Raymond Jones was chosen as boss. Jones was the first Negro to head Tammany Hall, and in 1968 he was the only Negro county leader in America. Born in St. Thomas, Virgin Islands, in 1899, he came to New York when he was eighteen. He became a Harlem district leader in 1944 and later was appointed a deputy United States marshal. Mayor O'Dwyer appointed him deputy buildings commissioner. In 1958 Jones was Congressman Adam Clayton Powell's campaign manager. A member of the City Council, he resigned for reasons of health (ulcers) and was followed by New York Assemblyman Frank Rossetti, now in his late sixties. Rossetti was once chauffeur for Carmine De Sapio.

Officially, Tammany Hall is the executive committee of the New York County Democratic Committee. After the fall of Carmine De Sapio, this group of party leaders from thirty-three districts in Manhattan preferred to be known as "Chatham Hall" after their meeting place in the Chatham Hotel.

For many years the Manhattan Democratic organization, known also as Tammany Hall or the New York County Democratic Committee, has had the most powerful leader in New York City. However, since Boss Murphy died in 1924 the Manhattan Democratic organization hasn't had effective leadership all that time. Because of this the Manhattan leaders have from time to time, due to circumstances beyond their control, been put in the background by one of the leaders of the other counties in New York City. We have seen Bronx boss Ed Flynn grow more powerful than Tammany boss John F. Curry, and there has been a struggle for power among the leaders of the five counties. We now see Meade Esposito, the Brooklyn boss, overshadowing the Tammany leader Frank Rossetti. While Esposito was one of the top leaders, if not the top, at the 1974 New York State Democratic convention, Rossetti attended the convention physically but he wasn't influential in selecting the ticket. The newspapers didn't even mention Rossetti's presence at the convention. Because of this, Manhattan Borough President Percy E. Sutton, a black man, took over. Sutton, a leading spokesman for New York's black community, backed Harold Stevens, the only black person ever to serve on the state's highest court, as Democratic candidate for the Court of Appeals in 1974. Stevens lost in the Democratic primary, and when he ran in the general election as a Republican he was defeated.

Meade H. Esposito, now in his mid-sixties, became the leader of the Brooklyn Democratic organization in 1969. He succeeded former State Assembly Speaker Anthony Travia, who resigned to take a federal judgeship. Meade is the son of a saloon keeper who came to the United States from Italy in 1900. Like Dan O'Connell, he lived over his father's saloon. Most of the Italians were registered Republicans, and Esposito's father was treasurer of his Republican club. Like Dan, Meade viewed the Republican Party as the party of the rich and powerful, although his father was not rich, while the Democrats were more for the common people. Meade became a Democrat and so did his father, although the two did not talk for six months when Meade became a Democrat.

At the age of eighteen, Meade started his own political club with a couple of dozen of his friends. Married at eighteen, a father at nineteen, he worked as a wholesale beer salesman during the Depression years, and later went into the bail-bonding business. Today Meade is in insurance and serves as a consultant to two banks. He lives modestly. Meade's father wanted him to become a doctor, and his mother wanted him to become a lawyer. He dropped out of high school, and got a job as an office boy in an insurance business run by Jim Powers, a former U.S. marshal and a local Democratic sachem. Esposito is a partner with his predecessor as leader, Assembly Speaker Stanley Steingut, in a large insurance company in Brooklyn. With his political position, however, he doesn't have to spend much time selling insurance.

The mere size of Kings County, which is made up of Brooklyn (population 2,700,000) and has twenty-one assemblymen, gives Esposito his power. He controls 13.53 percent of the State Democratic convention votes, more than any other person. The size of his constituency, geographical location (neighboring Manhattan), and, of cource the great amount of patronage (although not as much as it once was) nicely complement one another. Although Esposito was not chosen as a delegate to the 1972 Democratic National Convention (many other political leaders were also not chosen), he supported McGovern in the general election. While Hubert Humphrey carried Brooklyn by 208,867 votes over Nixon and Wallace, McGovern carried Brooklyn by only 1,141 over Nixon. New York City's Mayor Beame is himself a product of the Brooklyn machine, and, as expected, Esposito has much patronage to dispose of. Just as long as the mayor of New York is Democratic, to supply jobs and other patronage, Esposito's power should continue.

Meade's base of power is the Thomas Jefferson Democratic Club in the Canarsie section of Brooklyn. The club has more than two thousand members who each pay five dollars a year in dues. The club annually publishes a journal, filled with ads, of some three hundred pages. Residents still go to the clubhouse for recreation and to seek help in solving problems.

While successful Democratic political organizations have been popularly referred to as "machines," the successful Republican counterparts have been called "societies." By and large, however, there is little difference between the two.

The suburban Republican machine in Nassau County, New York, is run by Assemblyman Joseph M. Margiotta, now in his late forties. The Margiotta organization is located on Long Island, which by nature of its relatively homogeneous and affluent population makes the suburb more manageable politically than New York City, where the population is diverse racially, ethnically, and economically.

Margiotta is currently New York State's most powerful Republican county leader, largely because Nassau County is the most populous Republican county in the state. If Ralph Caso, the Nassau county executive, had been elected lieutenant governor with his running mate, Malcolm Wilson, in 1974, Margiotta's power would have been enhanced because of the large patronage at stake. However, the fact is that Caso and Wilson lost didn't do much to help Margiotta, and might have hurt him somewhat, because the Republicans were expected to do better in Nassau County than they did.

Margiotta expects an annual contribution by more than 17,000

county and town employees, in Nassau County, equivalent to one percent of their yearly salary.[70] On December 6, 1974, the *New York Times*
reported that Caso and Margiotta had been named in a lawsuit filed
the previous day and alleging kickbacks to the Republican Party by
civil service employees as a condition of employment or promotion.
The United States Attorney for the Eastern District of New York was
reportedly investigating the allegations of kickbacks. The lawsuit contended that "as much as $6 million may have been extorted" through
kickbacks to the Republican organization for jobs or promotions.

Receiving kickbacks, along with high-priced dinners, gives the
Republicans at least a million dollars to spend annually. Whereas
tickets for Democratic fund-raising dinners are rarely more than $100
a ticket, the Nassau GOP sold 4,700 tickets at $125 a person for their
annual dinner in June, 1974, held in the Nassau Coliseum. They also
had a $500-a-plate-dinner in September, 1974.

The Nassau County GOP operates out of a brand-new high-rise
office building in Hempstead, with a full-time staff of twenty-three
workers. They also have a printing plant nearby. In comparison, the
Brooklyn Democratic organization, controlled by Meade Esposito, operates out of a small suite of rooms in downtown Brooklyn and has a
staff of three. It has been said that if Margiotta wants to know what
his constituents think, he takes a poll. Mr. Esposito talks to three of
his district leaders to know what his constituents think. Both Margiotta
and Esposito control most of the legislators from their district. The
thirteen-member Nassau County Republican delegation in the state
legislature is the largest single Republican bloc in the legislature; its
members are unaffectionately called "Margiotta's puppets." Esposito,
however, exerts even more control in the legislature than Margiotta.

Democrats have been doing favors for the Republicans for years,
and vice versa. For example, in 1971, when Boss Esposito "delivered"
Democratic votes in the legislature for Rockefeller's tax package, the
governor rewarded him with several patronage posts for his followers,
some in the $30,000 to $40,000 a year range.

Political bosses, today, can't deliver the vote as well as they used to.
Today's voters are more educated, affluent, and independent than the
voters of the past. They don't like to be told whom to vote for. The
bosses realize this and would rather have the voters vote for the local
candidates first. Even though a county chairman may support a gubernatorial or other candidate for statewide office, unless the district
leaders and ward workers also support him, the large organization
doesn't help the candidate much. Party workers will usually work
harder for a local candidate because they know him. They realize that
once someone is elected governor, they'll never see him again.

In 1972, the New York Democratic organization seemed more like
a pussycat than the Tammany tiger when delegates supporting George

McGovern were elected over regular organization delegate candidates who were neutral or supported other Presidential hopefuls. The anti-machine candidates won all over the state except in Albany, where the O'Connell delegates won. What happened in 1972 showed which bosses actually control their cities. The record often speaks for itself, and leaders like Esposito and others in New York City would like to forget what happened in 1972. Also, Esposito's support of Howard Samuels for governor in 1974 might have hurt him somewhat after Samuels lost and Hugh Carey won. Even though Carey is also from Brooklyn, Esposito backed Samuels originally until Samuels lost. At that point Esposito got on the Carey bandwagon.

Many political leaders feel that service is even more important than handing out jobs in keeping control. One reason is that the number of political jobs is limited. However, making sure that the voters get what they pay for in taxes affects everyone. The bosses are able to do favors for the voters, cut government red tape, get assessments lowered, see to it that there is adequate police protection in high-crime areas, and help the voters in any way they can. Their ombudsman-type function is necessary. Their service is voluntary. All they ask in return is the support of the party candidates on election day.

Political leaders in New York City, like Frank Rossetti, Patrick J. Cunningham, and more recently Matthew J. Troy, devote more time fending off dissident Democrats than to fighting Republicans. In September, 1974, Queens Borough President Donald R. Manes, who had sought the Democratic nomination for governor a few months earlier, deposed Councilman Troy as leader of the Queens Democratic organization. The vote on the surprise defeat of Troy was forty for Manes and twenty-one for Troy. Troy was in the unsuccessful camp of Howard Samuels for governor, while Manes supported Carey after he dropped out of the race.

Disagreements among the five Democratic county leaders in New York City have caused a decline in their power. One example was in 1969 when three of the five county leaders supported former Mayor Robert F. Wagner in the Democratic mayoral primary in New York City and all five backed Mario F. Procaccino in the general election after he won the primary. Nevertheless, Wagner lost the primary election and Procaccino lost the general election. The New York leaders have each tried to get the most power. And while Meade Esposito of Brooklyn has the most power today, his power merely shadows the power of Boss Tweed, who controlled not only a party organization but an entire city. The public feuding does not enhance the power of any one leader. If the leaders don't discipline and unite themselves, how can they expect their followers to do differently? It simply shows which leader has the biggest mouth. The desire for party reform by the voters hasn't added to the power of the leaders either.

But while the leaders today have little power compared with the Tammany leaders of fifty and more years ago, whenever they support a candidate, there are cries of "bossism" from reformers and editorial writers. The open support of a candidate by the leaders can be a kiss of death for a candidate because the voters still retain the Tammany image, even if the bosses' power is mostly an illusion of what happened a long time ago. The ideal situation for a candidate is to have the leaders as a friend but not out front.

For the past twenty years there have been attempts by reform members to get control of the New York County Democratic Committee. The present chairman, Frank Rossetti, said in 1971 after being elected chairman to a third two-year term, "I'm tired of trying to bring peace to the party and always getting knifed in the back."[71] In an editorial following that election the *New York Times* said: "Mr. Rossetti is an old-line, machine-type political totally out of tune with modern times and demonstrably unsympathetic to the desperate need for party, political and electoral reforms. His re-election in Manhattan is a defeat for enlightened local government."[72] Mr. Rossetti inherited the problems of the New York County Democratic Committee when he first became its chairman in 1968. The organization, Tammany Hall, suffered its decline long before Rossetti took over, and he cannot be blamed for its problems. Leaders like Tweed, Kelly, Croker, and Murphy wouldn't believe that the chairman of the New York County Democratic Committee has so little power today compared with what they had. It is unlikely that anyone could be as powerful as the Tammany leaders once were. The New York organization has diminshed greatly. Its leader is no longer called a "boss," and the organization is no longer a "machine" in the true sense of the word.

The issue of "bossism" during campaigns has often been overplayed, especially in recent years. It is often a principal issue, but quite often it is not a valid issue. In many cities the power of the local political organization is overestimated. It is ironic that in one year a candidate will yell "bossism" because he did not get the support of the political leader, and four years later the same candidate will "walk arm and arm" with the same political leader because he supported him this time. Such an inconsistency occurred with Howard Samuels. In 1970, when former U.S. Supreme Court Justice Arthur Goldberg got the Democratic nomination for governor instead of Samuels, the latter said that leaders like Joseph Crangle (then State Democratic Committee chairman), Meade Esposito, Patrick Cunningham, Assemblyman Stanley Steingut (former Brooklyn Democratic leader), and William F. Luddy (Westchester Democratic leader) are "part of a political system that is not responsive to the people. Their politics is the politics of another decade, and it has to go."[73] Samuels said those are the men who initiated Goldberg's candidacy for the Democratic nomination. Samuels sought their support then and four years later when he got the nomination. In 1970 he said he "would only accept their support if they accepted my commitment to reform the party."

Joseph F. Crangle, now in his early forties, was State Democratic Committee chairman until Hugh Carey was elected governor in 1974. Shortly after the election Crangle, also the Erie County (Buffalo) Democratic leader, announced his resignation. The reason was that Crangle had supported Howard Samuels. The Carey forces urged Crangle's resignation. Albany Mayor Erastus Corning II would have liked to become the state chairman then, but Bronx leader Patrick Cunningham, who is in his mid-forties and an attorney, got the position instead. An Albany reporter went to New York City at that time and asked New Yorkers if they knew who Erastus Corning II was. His findings didn't please the mayor, who said New Yorkers don't know much anyway. One New Yorker said "Erastus" sounds like a colored fellow from down South. Crangle was almost chosen as chairman of the Democratic National Committee during the Nixon administration.

Although the five counties of New York City make up more than 42 percent of the vote at the state Democratic convention, no one person, today, controls all of that as the leader of Tammany Hall once did when the machine was at its height. Today Kings County (Brooklyn) has 13.53%, Queens, 10.86%, New York 10.04%, Bronx 7.47%, and Richmond (Staten Island) .78%. The Tammany leader used to control virtually all of the votes of the five counties, but today no one person can control all the votes in any one county. The time when leaders were bosses in New York City is gone.

★ 3 ★

Mayor Richard Daley
of Chicago

I don't even go to the bathroom without checking first [with Daley].
— A Chicago Congressman

"There were reports and intelligence on my desk that certain people planned to assassinate the three contenders for the presidency; that certain people planned to assassinate many of the leaders, including myself. So I took the necessary precautions." So stated Chicago's Mayor Richard Daley in his attempt to explain the massive show of police force during the 1968 Democratic National Convention.[74] These reports have never been substantiated; however, it was entirely possible that such assassinations would take place.

Until the 1968 Democratic National Convention, Richard Daley was just another mayor of a big American city. But the events that took place in Chicago while the Democrats nominated Hubert Humphrey as their Presidential candidate brought national attention to Mayor Daley. Many people were injured by the police, who were swinging their clubs. In addition to the demonstrators, newsmen and innocent bystanders were injured. Senator Abraham Ribicoff, at the Convention Hall, referred to the Chicago police as "the Gestapo." It was an unfortunate occurrence. Then, on Thursday night, at the last convention session, Daley packed the gallery with his loyal workers who screamed, "We love Daley, we love Daley" all night long.

Vice-President Hubert H. Humphrey easily won the nomination in 1968. Senator Eugene J. McCarthy, also of Minnesota, sought the nomination too. Humphrey got 1,760¼ first ballot votes, McCarthy got 601 votes, and Senator George McGovern of South Dakota got 146½ votes. McCarthy was supported by many young people and liberals who were against the Vietnam War.

After the convention, Daley tried to make Humphrey and President Johnson scapegoats for the convention disorders. He said that "it wasn't the people of Chicago who brought those people [the protestors] here. It was the candidacy of Humphrey and the policies of the administration on Vietnam."[75] This was inconsistent, because Daley had supported both Humphrey and Johnson.

The Walker Report, in examining the convention's violence, found that much of the violence was the result of a "police riot." It should be noted that no one was killed or shot in Chicago.

It is clear that Mayor Daley has been quite powerful and admired in Chicago. Because of the convention disorder, he has been the most publicized political boss in recent years. Thus it is hard to believe that just four years after the 1968 convention in Chicago Mayor Daley and his delegation were not seated at the 1972 Democratic National Convention in Miami Beach. The Albany delegates supported the seating of Mayor Daley and his 59-member delegation. Many people had promised to repay Daley for what had happened in Chicago. Just four years later he was repaid. But Daley is still the boss in Chicago, and there appears to be no question about who will succeed him, because he will most likely be in power for many more years.

Many people think that it was the fault of the policemen that many demonstrators got hurt. It is important to realize that the demonstrators went to Chicago for trouble. They threatened the people before the convention opened that if it were held in Chicago, and if the candidate they wanted were not nominated, there would be trouble. Most of the trouble occurred in the park, where the demonstrators wanted to protest. It was not the "peaceful protesting" that the police objected to. It was that, in Chicago, no one is allowed in the park during the hours of darkness. The demonstrators also "disturbed the peace" in front of and in the lobbies of hotels near the Conrad Hilton, which was the headquarters of the Democratic party.

Security was tight because of the recent assassinations of Senator Robert F. Kennedy and Dr. Martin L. King, Jr. There were 6,500 Illinois National Guardsmen, 5,000 regular army troops, and thousands of police and federal agents. Police were helmeted and stationed at every half block in the downtown area. The convention site was surrounded by a chainlink fence topped by barbed wire. Police and Secret Service agents patrolled the roofs of buildings where the candidates were. Helicopters flew over the city continuously. You could be sure that you were safe. I know because I was there. Chicago policemen were helpful and courteous to the conventioneers. They would tell you where a good restaurant was, what was going to happen, and when it would happen.

Why was Chicago chosen as the location for the Democratic convention? Chicago was not an ideal city for a convention because the hotels and Convention Hall are spread apart and it wasn't convenient. The convention was held in Chicago mainly because Daley had such a powerful machine. The 1956 Democratic National Convention was also held in Chicago. Some people felt that what happened in Chicago in August, 1968 (the demonstrations, violence, and lack of tickets for the convention), hurt the Democrats' chance of winning the Presidency in 1968.

A host committee arranged events, shows, and parties for the people who wanted to attend them. There were many volunteers who donated their time to chauffeur people in new cars provided by the manufacturers. Many volunteers for Senator Gene McCarthy, a Presidential candidate, also donated their time to chauffeur people in their own cars.

The news media made it seem that the police were going around clubbing demonstrators without telling why they were doing so. It is true that a couple of policemen probably got "carried away," but for the most part they were just doing their job. Carrying out orders that came from their boss, Mayor Daley.

Richard Joseph Daley was born in Chicago's South Side on May 15, 1902, where all the Irish lived. His father was a sheetmetal worker. In 1919, while Daley was a teenager, there was the biggest race war in Chicago's history. Part of it occurred in Daley's neighborhood. It lasted four days and left 15 whites and 23 blacks dead, 178 whites and 342 blacks injured, and about 1,000 homes were burned.[76]

Daley was a young man during Chicago's "Roaring Twenties." He worked during the day at City Hall and at night he went to De Paul University School of Law. He was also involved with ward politics and the Hamburg Club, a neighborhood social and athletic place. He served as the club's president for about fifteen years. At twenty-one Daley was a precinct captain, and got a job in the city council's office. In 1931, he was given a better job in the treasurer's office. He was a hard worker and was well liked. Daley got his law degree in 1934 but he never practiced law.

In 1936, only fifteen days before the November election, an elderly state legislator from Daley's district died. His name had already been printed on the ballots. It was too late to reprint the ballots so a write-in campaign was organized for Daley. Daley won his first elective office as a Republican. The legislator who died was a Republican running unopposed, so Daley's name had to be written on the Republican side of the ballot.

Two years later Daley was elected, as a Democrat, to the State Senate. Daley was a state legislator for eleven years. During this time he also served as the Cook County comptroller, a nonelective office. As comptroller, he kept the county books and knew who was on the payroll and at what salary, and what expenditures were made by the county.

In 1946 Daley ran for sheriff but lost. He was appointed state director of revenue after Adlai Stevenson won the governorship in 1948. In 1950 the county clerk died with less than a year left of his four-year term, so Daley took over.

In July, 1953, Daley, at the age of fifty-one, thirty years after he entered politics as a precinct captain was elected chairman of the Cook County Democratic Central Committee. This was the beginning of Daley's regime.

Chicago had been Democratic long before Richard Daley became its mayor. Anton J. Cermak, who was once a pushcart peddler and

later secretary of a saloonkeepers' league in Chicago, put together a
powerful Democratic organization. Cermak became president of the
Cook County Board, and in 1931 he ran for mayor. He was Chicago's
only foreign-born mayor, having immigrated to the United States from
Bohemia in 1874. Tony Cermak's political career would have lasted
much longer had he not been killed in March, 1933. He died in Miami,
Florida, in an assassination attempt on President Franklin D. Roosevelt.
Cermak had gone to see Roosevelt about obtaining some federal patronage. He was shot. It was rumored that gangsters from Chicago had
Cermak killed and that it wasn't an accident. However, most believed
that the assassin, who was mentally ill, meant to kill Roosevelt. Cermak's
funeral was the biggest in Chicago's history.

Patrick Nash, who was Cermak's chief lieutenant, succeeded him
as leader of the Chicago Democratic organization. Nash had Edward
J. Kelly, former chief engineer of the Chicago sanitary district, named
to finish Cermak's unexpired term as mayor. In 1935, the Kelly-Nash
machine was so powerful that it was able to select Kelly's Republican
opponent. Kelly won that year by a majority of 543,853 votes. While
Pat Nash ran the party organization, Ed Kelly ran the city government.

Nash had been a sewer contractor, and his business was so profitable that his name was included in a list of the ten Chicagoans
having the highest incomes.[77] From 1918 to 1924, Nash was a county
reviewer, an elected office dealing with tax assessments. It was while
he was an assessor that Nash became friendly with Kelly. After Pat
Nash died in 1943, Kelly ran both the party and city government, but
didn't do a good job in either. He served as mayor until 1947, when
he was urged to retire. This meant the end of the Kelly-Nash machine,
which was powerful in its day. However, its demise did not mean the
end of the Democratic rule in Chicago, because a faction in the Democratic Party took control. Martin Kennelly, who had a successful moving
and storage business, succeeded Kelly. Kennelly's nomination was
planned to improve the image of the Democratic machine. Mayor
Kennelly held that position until Richard Daley became mayor in 1955.

Daley gets along very well with organized labor. On every policy-
making city board or committee there is a labor leader. Even Republican
businessmen contribute money to Daley's machine, because the Republicans can't do anything for them—but Daley can.

Daley never has had any opposition from an independent candidate.
The laws discourage an independent from running, whereas in New
York a regular party candidate needs 5,000 signatures on his nominating
petitions and an independent must have 7,500 signatures, in Chicago
a Democrat or Republican needs a figure based on one-half of one
percent of the previous total votes cast, and then only the signatures of
legally defined independents, those who have not voted in the recent
partisan primaries.[78]

Even with Democrats far outnumbering Republicans in Chicago the machine violates voting laws. Most of the violations occur in the wards where the voters are black, poor white, and lower middle class. While there are election supervisors these judges rarely protest. Absentee ballots are cast by the sick. And just because a person died does not necessarily mean that his vote is not being cast.

Most of the candidates come up through the system—ringing doorbells, collecting signatures, doing favors, selling tickets, and waiting for someone to die to get a particular job. Daley got lucky because of people passing away. The committeemen help get the voters out on election day. During the year they sell tickets to dinners, clambakes, and picnics, and ads for the county committee's annual magazine.

Daley saw to it that his relatives got jobs. He didn't come from a big family but he married into one. In *Boss* Mike Royko says that the parents of Daley's wife "might well have said that they did not lose a daughter, they gained an employment agency."[79] Daley calls his wife "Sis" (Eleanor).

In 1955 Daley first ran for mayor and won. A few elections later in 1967 Daley won bigger than ever before, obtaining 73 percent of the vote and carrying all fifty wards. His opponent did not even carry his home ward. In 1975 Daley was elected to his sixth term as mayor.

Daley lives in a modest neighborhood. He attends daily mass and eats at home most of the time. He has four sons. Daley's eldest son, Richard Michael, is a partner in the law firm of Daley and Simon. He is also a State Senator. Daley's second son, Michael, is practicing law with a former law partner of the mayor. The third son, John P., is an insurance broker with a big Chicago firm. The firm, Heil & Heil, is owned by one of the mayor's old friends. Not surprisingly, the city of Chicago gives a large amount of insurance to Heil & Heil, and big clients use the mayor's two sons as lawyers. A fourth son, William, is still in law school.

In the spring of 1974 Mayor Daley suffered a mild stroke, and some people speculated that it marked the end of the Daley era. While he has since returned to work, Daley would be smart to pick a candidate who could win so that he wouldn't have to run for mayor again. If Daley should run again the pressures of that office could be too much for him. And if he should die, without grooming a successor, the end of the Democratic rule in Chicago would be imminent. While there are many Democrats who would like to take Daley's place, only the future will tell if his successor will be as successful as he. In all probability, the machine would fold. There are a number of ward leaders and aldermen who could take at least his title as chairman of the Cook County Democratic Committee. But as with the recent leaders of the once powerful Tammany Hall, their power is largely titular.

In the fall of 1974 two of Mayor Daley's chief political allies were convicted, one for mail fraud and the other for income-tax evasion. Chicagoans were calling the situation "Daley's Watergate." Observers said that one effect of the criminal cases is a further weakening of Daley's iron control over Chicago's machine. Even so, the Republican candidate for mayor in the 1975 election withdrew from the race because of the "raw power and brute force" of the Daley organization. He said, "It's impossible in the climate of total control by the Democratic organization for any opponent to survive."

Mayor Daley built Chicago (the expressways, public buildings, the civic center, and the airport) and gaves jobs to his supporters and friends. Many people owe Richard Daley more than they can ever repay him. He has done a lot and will be remembered for many years to come.

★ 4 ★

Huey Long
of Louisiana

A Great Dane always has a few poodles yapping at his heels.
JAMES MICHAEL CURLEY

He made the state militia his personal army, the judges were his friends, his attorney general could supersede any district attorney, his school budget committee could pass on the appointment of every teacher, his state tax commission was able to change any local assessment to help or punish businessmen, his bank examiners controlled the banks, and his civil service board could hire and fire police chiefs. This powerful man was Huey Pierce Long, known as the "Kingfish" of Louisiana.

Huey Long had no ward leaders or committeemen as the O'Connells and the bosses of Tammany Hall did. He had an organization built on patronage given to supporters. He used the state's payroll to his advantage. His own men did not rebel against him because they signed undated resignations before they collected their first paycheck. Politics in Louisiana was not Democrat versus Republican but the Longs versus the anti-Longs. You either loved Huey or you hated him. Not many people felt neutral. But it was better to be neutral than be against Huey Long.

During his short life Huey was governor of Louisiana and a United States Senator. While Huey was serving in the Senate he was assassinated when he was only forty-two years old. But the Long name continued to be heard in the political arena. After Huey died his brother Earl became Louisiana's governor.

Earl became known as the crazy governor after he was able to leave the mental institution to which his wife committed him in 1959. He was only at the institution for a short time. And when he left, the hospital superintendent left also because Earl fired him.

His brother George became a Congressman. And Huey's oldest son, Russell, was elected to the United States Senate the first year he was old enough to run.

The Longs held power by providing the voters with better than average public services. Welfare recipients in Louisiana got three times the national average in welfare benefits because of Huey. Schoolchildren, going to public and private schools, got free lunches, pencils, and erasers. The old-age pension in Louisiana is one of the nation's highest because of Huey. He built charity hospitals and many roads.

Huey use to say "Share the wealth." Poor people supported Huey because of his antipoverty programs. The people remembered the Depression and looked forward to better times with Huey's campaign promises, which called for the previously mentioned items. After he was elected Huey kept his promises, but he found that in order to do what he promised the taxes would have to be raised. So the taxes were raised and the citizens got their added services and Huey got his power.

Huey got his start in politics, at the age of twenty-five, when he was elected to the Railroad Commission, a forerunner of the Public Service Commission. Prior to that he practiced law. His parents were not wealthy, so Huey worked his way through college and law school. He got married at the age of twenty. After attending law school for only one year he took the bar examination and was able to practice law at age twenty-one. Huey made his reputation as a railroad commissioner fighting the big interests. He ran for governor in 1924 but lost. In 1928 he ran again for governor, and this time he won.

Still fighting the big interests, after he was elected governor he wanted the state legislature to pass an "occupational tax" on the Standard Oil Company. The oil company threatened to close their refineries in Louisiana if the tax went through. Because of this, in 1929 the Louisiana House impeached Huey and the State Senate was to hear the case and decide whether or not Huey should be removed as governor. However, Huey was not removed because he was able to get fifteen senators to side with him. This prevented a two-thirds majority needed for removal. All the senators who sided with Huey were later rewarded with high-paying state jobs.

Louisiana law prevents the governor from succeeding himself, so Huey could be governor for only one term at a time. This law prevents a governor who has a great amount of power, like Huey had, from holding office for more than four years at a time. But Huey still controlled his successor and could have run for governor again four years later just as his brother Earl did. In 1948 Earl Long was elected governor, and he couldn't run for reelection in 1952. Earl was elected governor again in 1956. I don't think Huey would have run for governor again after serving in the Senate, except as a last resort, because he had presidential aspirations. Had Huey been alive in 1936 he might have run against Franklin D. Roosevelt.

Because his term as governor would expire in 1932, Huey ran for the U.S. Senate in 1930. He was elected to the Senate, but he continued to serve as governor, and did not go to Washington until 1932. While Huey served in the Senate, a friend of his was governor and he did whatever Huey wanted him to do. In the Senate Huey continued to speak against the big interests and in favor of his special programs. He became popular across the country.

Huey Long, like the Kennedys, had charisma, and was able to excite people emotionally by appearing before them. Dan O'Connell says Huey Long was "a great orator." O'Connell heard Long give a speech at the Democratic National Convention in 1932.

In 1932 Huey helped nominate Franklin Roosevelt for President. Shortly after the election, however, Huey broke with Roosevelt because he felt FDR was moving too slowly in solving the economic problems caused by the Great Depression. Also Huey realized that he couldn't control President Roosevelt, as he would have liked to, and that FDR would run again in 1936. Roosevelt didn't distribute patronage to Long's people, and this annoyed Huey, although he didn't need any favors from him because there was plenty of patronage in Louisiana.

Had Huey lived he might have run as a third-party candidate in 1936 because FDR would have been renominated by the Democrats. Historian T. H. Williams wrote in his biography that according to some of Huey's close friends, in 1936 he "intended to run a liberal Democrat as a third-party entry and so divide the liberal vote that the Republican candidate would win. The Republicans would be incapable of dealing with the depression, the economic system would go to pieces, and by 1940 the country would be crying for a strong leader to save it."[80] That strong leader would be Huey Long. The strategy seems logical. However, no one will ever know if Huey could have become President.

Considering his dictator-like tactics perhaps we are lucky. But perhaps what Robert Penn Warren wrote in *All the King's Men* applies to Huey Long, Richard Nixon, and other politicians. Warren's thesis was that the politician who wishes to do good may have to do some evil to achieve his goal. But what happens to many people who desire to reach some high goals, happened to Huey. He did whatever he saw fit to reach his goal. It is questionable, however, whether his means justified the end.

Knowing that voters vote for their own kind, Huey boasted about his ethnic background (English, Scotch, Irish, German, and French). His older brother, Julius, annoyed at this, said that "Huey would claim he had Negro blood if he thought it would get him any colored votes in the North."[81]

Huey did not come from a wealthy family. He had to work his way through college. The voters felt that here was a man who came from modest surroundings like their own and wanted to help them. After being elected, Huey kept his promises, and his power base grew.

In 1928 Louisiana State University had an enrollment of only 1,800 students, ranking eighty-eighth in size among American universities. By 1935 it had an enrollment of 5,200 students and had risen to twentieth in size among American universities and eleventh in size among state universities. LSU's rapid growth was because of Huey's interest in the university. Millions of dollars were spent on new facilities. LSU charged practically no tuition and offered numerous scholarships so that anyone who wanted a college education could obtain one.

When Huey found out that LSU's band had only 28 pieces he ordered it increased to at least 125 pieces. Huey often attended the weekly band practice and would assist the band leader. He occasionally led it in parades and at football games. Once he led it through New Orleans in the Mardi Gras.

Huey was a strong supporter of LSU's football team. Instead of sitting in the governor's box he would sit on the LSU bench. Before the games and during halftime Huey would give the team a pep talk. He would hold towels packed with ice to injured players' bodies. Once, when Huey found out that three injured football stars were in LSU's infirmary he invited them to move into the governor's mansion to recuperate. The players would have steaks twice a day in order to regain their strength. Huey's treatment was semisuccessful. The players regained their strength, but one player put on fifty pounds and collapsed after five plays in a game.[82]

In 1934 Huey chartered six trains of fourteen cars each to carry fans to Nashville, Tennessee, to see LSU play Vanderbilt. About 4,500 LSU fans, including Huey, went to see LSU win 29 to 0.

Huey established his own newspaper, *The Louisiana Progress,* a weekly, in 1930, so that he could present his views. If another newspaper wrote anything bad about him he would set the facts straight in his newspaper. From the time he ran for railroad commissioner, he compiled a mailing list of people who helped him campaign and supported his programs. By 1930 he had about 40,000 names. It was a good business practice for a businessman to buy an ad in Huey's newspaper. In 1932 the *Progress* ceased publication, but in 1933 Huey established *The American Progress,* another newspaper, this time with a national scope. In 1935 it had a circulation of 375,000. Some were paid subscriptions but more than half of the copies were sent to people on Huey's mailing list free.

In his speeches and articles Huey would use words even someone with an elementary education could understand. He made his points clearly, without going in circles. This helped him communicate with all the people. Educated people could understand him, and uneducated people would feel at ease with him. Adlai Stevenson was a good speaker and had a lot to offer, but people with a simple vocabulary couldn't understand him. Stevenson spoke above the people's heads and was thus ruined as a successful vote-getter.

In 1934 Huey spoke on nationwide radio and called for a program of "Share Our Wealth," with "Every Man a King." Share-Our-Wealth clubs were organized across the country, with most clubs naturally in Louisiana. There wasn't a different or new policy in this publicity campaign, but it was successful. It was just a reiteration of Huey's antipoverty and antibig-business programs. Had he run for the Presidency, the club membership would have been a good start for campaign workers. Club members got a copy of Huey's autobiography and newspaper. At the time of his death, there were 27,431 clubs, with a total membership of 4,684,000.[83]

Just like other Southerners, Huey was for segregation and white supremacy. However, he believed the Negroes should benefit from his programs just like anyone else. In this respect Long was better than most Southerners. Actually Negroes benefited more from Huey's programs than most whites because they were poorer than the whites. But whether a politician came from the North or the South, the Negro vote was sought on election day.

During the last two years of the Hoover administration the Internal Revenue Service received many letters, most of them unsigned, from anti-Long people in Louisiana saying that Huey and his associates were stealing large sums of money. While the Treasury Department could not prosecute Long lieutenants for corruption, they could for income-tax evasion. Many criminals have been sent to jail this way. Former Vice-President Agnew was convicted on income-tax evasion. One government professor in college told my class that if any of us go into public office the first thing we should do is get a good tax lawyer. The federal government disposed of the Al Capone gang this way. Agents first went after the little men and worked their way up to the leader.

The federal government didn't prosecute the Long men until 1934, when Roosevelt's Secretary of the Treasury, Henry Morgenthau, Jr., ordered his agents to continue the investigation. Roosevelt had reasons to get rid of Long. The most immediate one the 1936 election. A similar situation occurred in 1972, when it was speculated that President Nixon could have stopped the Department of Justice from prosecuting Agnew had he wanted to. There was even speculation that Nixon and his close associates wanted to get rid of Agnew as Vice-President. We have seen numerous examples of the power of the President, especially during the Nixon administration.

The government did manage to indict a few of Huey's associates for not reporting income and not paying taxes on that income, but they never came close to Huey.

Huey Long was shot in Baton Rouge on September 8, 1935, while he was in the state capitol building. His alleged murderer, Dr. Carl Weiss, was killed by bodyguards seconds after Long was shot. No motives have been given for the killing. It was rumored that one of the bodyguards actually shot Huey because, with the Kingfish dead, the federal government might stop its investigation in Louisiana. However, most feel that it was the doctor who killed Huey. Dr. Weiss, age twenty-nine, an eye, nose, and throat specialist from Baton Rouge was the son-in-law of Judge B. H. Pavy, a leader of an anti-Long faction. Long was planning to gerrymander Judge Pavy's judicial district so that his reelection would have been impossible. Two days after Huey was shot he died. Huey's wife served his unexpired term in the Senate.

An obituary editorial in the *New York Times* on September 11, 1935, "In reality, Senator Long set up a Fascist government in Louisiana. It was disguised, but only thinly. There was no outward appearance of a revolution, no march of Black Shirts upon Baton Rouge, but the effectual result was to lodge all the power of the State in the hands of one man."

The *Times* continued: "If Fascism ever comes in the United States it will come in something like that way. No one will set himself up as an avowed dictator, but if he can succeed in dictating everything, the name does not matter. Laws and Constitutions guaranteeing liberty and individual rights may remain on the statute books, but the life will have gone out of them."

Voters, who are ordinary citizens like you, elected Huey Long as governor. It just shows how gullible and naive people can be. Huey Long is by no means the only person who has been elected by the people and has become as powerful as a dictator in a Fascist state. Richard Nixon as President thought he was above the law and could do whatever he wanted to. The sad thing is that American citizens and the Congress let him do whatever he wanted to. It need not be that way, but when our state representatives and our representatives in Washington are afraid or are being paid off by the person in control or by a special interest group, then our country is really in very bad shape. We may improve our annual gross national product and make other advances but we should not boast of our progress until our representatives really represent the people who voted for them. The time has long since come when we must rid ourselves of the special interest groups and individuals who feel that with money you can buy power.

Huey's estate had a value of about a hundred thousand dollars. So, like Barnes and other bosses, his estimated wealth when he died wasn't nearly anything what it was thought to be. In all reality, the estates were kept low for tax purposes. Also it would be a post-mortem confession to leave a large estate. He was said to have been a millionaire. It was felt that his money was held by his close associates.

Long's last words were pertaining to the students of Louisiana State University. He said, "What will the boys and girls do if I should die?" A few hours before his death he said, "Oh, Lord, don't let me die, for I have a few more things to accomplish."[84]

★ 5 ★

Thomas J. Pendergast
of Kansas City

A politician is a person with whose politics you don't agree. If you agree with him he is a statesman.

DAVID LLOYD GEORGE

Thomas J. Pendergast was born in St. Joseph, Missouri, in 1872. His brother Jimmy was a political leader in Kansas City and he owned several saloons. Although Tom had ambitions of playing professional baseball after he finished college, he didn't do that because his father thought it wasn't very respectable to play baseball. Instead Tom worked in one of his brother's saloons until Jimmy got him a job as a police officer in Kansas City. Tom Pendergast was one of the few bosses who went to college. In 1911 Jimmy died, so Tom took over the political organization. He made the organization stronger and within five years he acquired statewide power.

Boss Pendergast had a practical approach to politics. When a poor man came to him or his ward leaders for help, he said, "We don't make one of those investigations like those city charities. No, we feed 'em and we vote 'em."

Pendergast made judges, representatives, governors, and even a President. At every Democratic National Convention, he controlled Missouri's big bloc of votes, and many sought his support. Although Pendergast died three months before Harry Truman made it to the White House, it was Tom Pendergast who gave Truman his start in politics. In 1922 Truman was elected a county judge, and in 1934, again with Pendergast's support, he was elected to the United States Senate.

Truman's political career began when the brother of Pendergast walked into his haberdashery store, which was then not doing well because of the Depression, and asked whether Truman would be interested in running for county judge in Jackson County, which includes Kansas City. This offer was apparently made because Boss Pendergast's nephew Jim had served in Truman's regiment. Truman accepted the position, which was administrative rather than judicial. The county judges were concerned with roads, hospitals and political patronage, and were similar to county managers.

One instance that is illustrative of the integrity of Harry Truman came when he sold his family farm of 360 acres about ten miles from Kansas City instead of using his influence as a U.S. Senator to obtain a loan. In the early thirties Truman's mother mortgaged her farm for $30,000; at that time the farm was well worth the amount of the mortgage. His mother was then aged and his father was dead. The Depression ruined farm values, and as a result the Truman mortgage could not be paid. While a U.S. Senator, Truman put the farm up at auction and sold it for the price of the mortgage. Almost any bank would have renewed the loan for him if he had asked them to, but he didn't ask any of them because he didn't want to be under any obligation to anybody while in the Senate. How many elected officials today would have done as Truman did?

In 1943 the Republican National Committee sent an investigative team to Kansas City in an attempt to find evidence of corruption in the public career of Truman, which included being road overseer of Jackson County and judge of the Jackson County Court. After about five months of intensive work they came up with absolutely nothing.

As President, Truman granted pardons to members of the Pendergast machine who had lost their right to vote because they had served time in jail. President Truman also fired the United States attorney who attacked the Pendergast machine. Both of these things occurred after Pendergast died.

Harry Truman said Tom Pendergast was a good and loyal friend. Many times Truman said that Pendergast never asked him to do a "dishonest deed." Truman said, "I did my job in the way I thought it ought to be done. And he never interfered, not even when he was in deep trouble himself."[85] When Pendergast died, on January 26, 1945, Truman was discouraged from attending the funeral. But Truman didn't care what anyone said; he went to the funeral. The newspapers criticized him for this, but Truman could not desert an old friend. People mistakenly and foolishly thought that if Truman were friendly with Pendergast he must be corrupt also. This was not the case. People said if Truman wasn't corrupt, why didn't he denounce Pendergast? Truman responded, "I wouldn't kick a friend who was in trouble no matter what it might do to win votes."

Harry Truman was like Dan O'Connell in many ways. They both believed in loyalty, friendship, and the Democratic Party. Perhaps that is why O'Connell admired Truman so much. Like O'Connell, Truman's words were never fancy. While some politicians have a public face and a private face, Truman and O'Connell were never anybody except themselves.

Kansas City boss Tom Pendergast was a Democrat but not a New Deal Democrat. The same was true of Dan O'Connell. Although Dan O'Connell got along all right with FDR and Farley, he did not like the way they treated his colleagues, the bosses of Tammany Hall and Pendergast. O'Connell says, "Roosevelt was a phony." He didn't like FDR's New Deal either. He spoke with Pendergast from time to time, mostly about national politics. Dan O'Connell's advice was sought by

Pendergast and other bosses. He says Pendergast used to go to the horse races in Saratoga every summer, about thirty miles from Albany.

Pendergast used to bet many thousands on the races. He should have stuck to politics to make money, because he wasn't very lucky at the races. Tom owned a few horses. Although Missouri had a law against horse racing, Pendergast saw to it that a racetrack was opened in the state. When citizens complained to Circuit Judge Guy B. Park and read him the state constitution, Judge Park said, in effect, "So what?" For this, Park was made a governor by Pendergast. To thank "Big Tom," as Pendergast was called because he was six feet tall and overweight, one of his first acts as governor was to order a highway built from Kansas City to the racetrack, which was an hour away.

At one time the judges in Kansas City refused to contribute to the Pendergast machine, and in the next session of the legislature their salaries were reduced by three times the amount of the requested contribution.

The Treasury Department caught up with Pendergast, and on April 7, 1939 he was indicted for evading income taxes totaling $265,465 for 1935 and 1936. He was also charged with receiving a $315,000 bribe from a group of fire insurance companies for helping to settle a rate-increase controversy. After pleading guilty, he was sentenced to a year and three months in Leavenworth Penitentiary and given a $10,000 fine. Pendergast was broken in health and in spirit while in prison, and had several heart attacks. After serving a year and a day of his sentence he was released from prison on May 30, 1940. The terms of his probation included a provision that he abstain from politics for five years. While in prison his machine continued to operate with his lieutenants in control. However, in 1940 and again in 1942 they were defeated in local elections. The Pendergast machine was gone.

Frank Hague
of Jersey City and
Nucky Johnson
of Atlantic City

Words were given men so they might conceal their thoughts.
TALLEYRAND

FRANK HAGUE OF JERSEY CITY

Frank Hague was the mayor and Democratic boss of Jersey City, New Jersey, from 1917 to 1947. During those thirty years, Hague's political influence spread throughout New Jersey and was even felt on the national level. Many Democrats got their start in politics through Hague. He made numerous judges, state legislators, congressmen, senators, and governors.

He was born in 1876, the son of poor immigrant parents. Hague didn't have much of an education, and started working young. Like many other young men, he got interested in politics. Even though he was a leader and a good fighter, his shrewdness enabled him to get the other boys to do the dangerous fighting for him. He grew up in a tough neighborhood that was predominantly Irish.

By the time he reached voting age, he was elected to what was then called constable (policeman). In 1906, he was made sergeant-at-arms of the State Assembly, which was then controlled by the Democrats. He was named City Hall custodian, a patronage position, in 1908. As custodian, he became friendly with A. Harry Moore, whom Hague later made governor for three terms. In 1911, Hague became a member of the Street and Water Board.

The Walsh Act of 1911, passed by the state legislature, permitted the municipalities of the state to change to the commission form of government if and when they chose. Hague realized at the time that it would be easier to control a five-man commission than a large city council. In 1913, Hague and Moore were elected to the city's first Board of Commissioners from a list of ninety-three candidates. The new commission made a Republican, Mark Fagan, mayor; Harry Moore, commissioner of parks; and Hague, commissioner of public safety. Because he felt that he who controls the armed forces controls the state, Commissioner Hague got rid of those policemen he didn't trust and hired others who were loyal to him.

Hague was tough and worked hard for the party. It was while

he was a member of Jersey City's Board of Commissioners that he got control of the Democratic organization, which was then not too powerful. It was partly through making deals that Hague was able to get his power; he was a shrewd and lucky politician. In 1917, Democrats were elected to replace Republicans on the commission, and the commission appointed Hague mayor of Jersey City. He served as mayor longer than any man before or after him. The new Hague administration had numerous political debts to pay; the government payroll increased and taxes were raised to pay for the patronage.

One of the many patronage-filled departments in Jersey City was the police department. It was the largest police department for any American city with 300,000 to 400,000 population. As the accompanying table, compiled from the 1940 *Municipal Yearbook*, will show, its salaries and costs were also the highest.

City	Population, 1930 (000 omitted)	Total police department employees, 1938	Minimum salary for patrolmen	Salary of chief of police	Total Wages and salaries paid, 1939	Total costs of department, 1939
Indianapolis	364	567	$1,700	$4,800	$1,162,011	$1,369,543
Jersey City	317	968	3,000	9,000	3,009,624	3,552,624
Louisville	308	432	1,417	4,050	696,922	893,926
Portland, Ore.	302	438	1,950	4,800	964,064	1,119,380
Rochester	328	477	1,785	4,900	1,000,308	1,224,063
Seattle	366	574	1,920	5,000	1,196,508	1,439,836

As mayor, Hague literally controlled what went on in the city. Hague boasted in 1937 in an address that "I am the law in Jersey City." Any opposition to the Hague machine was easily dealt with. One opponent of the machine was James J. Burkitt, who attended a meeting of the Jersey City Commission to have "the limits of his police permit to speak at certain corners defined by the commission. Mayor Frank Hague, who presided, was clearly amused by the sight of Burkitt as the later approached the assembly rostrum to speak. 'What's the matter with your face?' asked the mayor. 'Some of your thugs beat me up,' Burkitt replied. The mayor laughed heartily."[86]

Hague made all appointments and distributed the patronage. Like Dan O'Connell of Albany, he preferred to put fellow Irishmen in the best public jobs. People from other ethnic and religious groups would be given small positions. However, the Irish made up only 10 to 15 percent of the population of Hudson County where Jersey City is located. Like members of other political machines, the men of Hague organization did much to help the poor, and they also did much to fill their own pockets. The more a person made in politics, either through a job or a contract for goods and/or services, the more he was supposed to kick back to the party.

The Hague machine took no chances of losing on election day; violence and threats, vote-buying, and vote fraud were common. Ballots were cast even in the names of dead people. In some instances, the official number of votes cast exceeded the number of registered voters. On April 14, 1926 the *New York Times* reported that in one district where there were 662 names on the poll books, 683 votes had been cast. In most cities today if 65 percent of those registered vote it is deemed satisfactory; however, in cities where machines existed, such as Jersey City and Albany, an 80 percent voter turnout was common.

Among the numerous examples of the abuses of government in Jersey City and Hudson County that were brought to light by a New Jersey State Senate investigation committee in 1929 was that of Albert H. Mansfield, an employee of the Hudson County Board of Health, who served as a health inspector at a salary of $4,000 a year. The Senate committee said: "He has worked in that capacity for twenty-five years. He was unable to give the Committee the name and address of the owner of any place that he had ever inspected, and testified that he had never made a complaint or arrest, and that if a man has a job he is 'supposed to get the vote out.' "[87]

Governor Moore offered Hague a chance to serve an unexpired term in the United States Senate in 1938 but he turned it down. In 1947, Hague retired as mayor after serving eight terms. He never lost an election, but his successor as mayor, Frank Hague Eggers, served as mayor for only two years until he was defeated in the next election. Eggers was Hague's nephew. This defeat was fatal to the Hague machine and Hague was deposed as state boss in 1949, although he remained a member of the Democratic National Committee until 1952. He was elected to serve on the national committee in 1922. Hague had served as vice-chairman of the Democratic National Committee when James Farley was its chairman.

A couple of years before his death, Hague, his nephew, former Mayor Eggers, and former Deputy Mayor John F. Malone were named defendants in a $15-million suit brought by the Jersey City administration, which was then not controlled by Hague. The suit was taken in behalf of city employees who had allegedly kicked back as contributions 3 percent of their salaries from 1917 to 1949. Nothing materialized in the lawsuit because of Hague's death.

Hague once said that he was worth two million dollars, but there were estimates that he was worth much more. As boss, he ran New Jersey from a plush Manhattan penthouse, at 480 Park Avenue. He also had a home in Jersey City and one in Miami Beach, Florida. He was a very flamboyant boss; also he was charitable. He once donated a $50,000 altar to his church. The boss was married and had a son and an adopted daughter.

In 1939 Frank Hague, Jr., was appointed by Governor Moore as a judge of the state's highest court less than three years after being admitted to the bar. Young Hague, who was then thirty-four, failed nine of the twenty courses he took at the University of Virginia Law School, and then transferred to the Washington and Lee Law School but never graduated. However, he was able to pass the New Jersey bar examination. Shortly after he was admitted to the bar, he became a secretary to a Supreme Court justice. Many New Jersey lawyers were against his appointment because of his lack of experience; there was no record of his ever having tried a case before he became a judge.[88] In 1972, Frank Rossetti, Jr., the son of the New York County Democratic chairman, was appointed a judge of the state's Court of Claims at the early age of thirty-seven.

Hague died on January 1, 1956, some two weeks before his eightieth birthday, after a long bout with bronchitis and arthritis. More than 6,000 people viewed his body in a Jersey City funeral home, and 1,400 persons attended a high mass in his memory.

While Frank Hague was the boss of the New Jersey Democrats, Nucky Johnson of Atlantic City was the Republican leader in Southern New Jersey. Hague, however, was the more powerful of the two leaders, because the influence of the Jersey City Democrat was spread over a greater area.

NUCKY JOHNSON OF ATLANTIC CITY

Enock L. (Nucky) Johnson was the Republican boss of Atlantic City, New Jersey. Nucky was born in Atlantic County, New Jersey, in 1883 of Scotch and Irish parents. His father was a sheriff, and, because the local law prohibited consecutive terms for the sheriff, Nucky became sheriff at the early age of twenty-five. He then took over the county leadership of the Republican Party from his father. When Nucky was elected county treasurer, his brother took over as sheriff. While treasurer Nucky was appointed clerk of the State Supreme Court. He held both jobs at the same time.

Nucky was a big spender and had an expensive taste even during the Depression years. He had four Cadillacs. He slept until four o'clock in the afternoon. After a few hours of talking business, he would go out on the town, enjoying what his resort area had to offer. Before he got married he would go from nightclub to nightclub on the boardwalk looking for a girl to sleep with. He didn't have to look hard because the lucky girls were given expensive gifts such as furs and jewelry. Also Johnson was a popular man in Atlantic City. After he got married, he spent most of his evenings in the casinos.

Johnson was clever enough to list from $20,000 to $60,000 on his income-tax statement as "other commissions." These "other commissions," not itemized, were payoffs Nucky received. However, the amount was nowhere near the true amount he received. Should any frightened gambler, madam, or any other person who paid off Johnson admit paying him a large amount of money, he only had to say that he had declared the sum in question in "other commissions." Nucky had to declare "other commissions" because it was obvious that he was spending much more money than his salary. He was safe unless mass confessions were to point out that he received more than he reported. Mass confessions were unlikely because prison was preferable to what Johnson would do. The Treasury Department got Johnson the same way they caught Al Capone and Tom Pendergast. They investigated and prosecuted the little man right up to the top.

In Atlantic City there were twenty-five race rooms employing five to seven hundred people; eight brothels employing between one and three hundred prostitutes; and nine numbers banks employing about a thousand workers.[89]

The race rooms, brothels, and numbers banks did about ten million dollars in business a year. For providing protection to operate, Nucky received about $300,000 a year. He was the only person who had to be paid off. The police did nothing about the illegal rackets and they did not mind that Nucky was the only one to be paid off because he gave them their jobs. Also the police chief was his friend and the sheriff was his brother.

Although Johnson was required to pay additional income taxes in 1928 and 1934 which he omitted, he was not criminally charged. However, in 1941 he was sentenced to ten years in prison for income-tax evasion and accepting payoffs for providing protection from the police.

Nucky died in 1968.

One of Nucky Johnson's friends was Moe Annenberg, the father of Walter Annenberg, who was appointed United States ambassador to England by President Nixon. Walter Annenberg contributed heavily to Nixon's campaign fund in 1968. Moe Annenberg provided bookies all over the United States with racing forms since 1922. He had a nationwide monopoly on racetrack wire services and was the owner of a large publishing empire. As the leader of the Republican Party in Pennsylvania, Moe Annenberg became quite powerful.

On November 17, 1932, a federal grand jury indicted Moe and Walter, *et al.*, for sending obscene literature through the mail. The material was printed in one of Annenberg's magazines. However, the case against the Annenbergs was dropped.

But on August 11, 1939, Moe Annenberg was indicted for evading $3,258,809 in taxes from 1932 to 1936. A multimillionare, Annenberg agreed to pay $8,000,000. This was the largest amount ever paid by an individual tax evader. He also served three years in prison.

★ 7 ★

James Michael Curley
of Boston

It isn't what a politician says, but what he whispers that gives a slight clue to what he is thinking.

JAMES MICHAEL CURLEY

In the history of American city politics, the ward boss has often been replaced by the citywide boss. It is much more difficult to control a city than a ward because a city comprises several wards. Because it is more difficult to control a city the boss has to be a more exceptional and capable individual than the ward boss. The power of the citywide boss is much greater than that of the ward boss because the patronage and opportunities are greater. In Albany, during the O'Connell years, there have been ward "leaders" but not ward "bosses." There is a difference between a "boss" and a "leader." This is because in Albany there is only one boss. He is Dan O'Connell. The ward leaders are his lieutenants. They each coordinate the activities of the committeemen and other ward workers. They do favors for the residents in their neighborhoods and make sure everything runs smooth on election day. In some cities where there is no one powerful boss, the ward "bosses" have more power.

In Boston it has never been easy for one man to control votes. One writer on Massachusetts politics said this is "perhaps because of the mercurial feuding nature of the Boston Irish, reluctant to be led and, when led, easily tempted by an alternative leader."[90] This so-called "feudal" situation also occurred in Ireland, where the Irish were dependent on local chieftains, self-styled "kings" who were easily toppled from power.

James Michael Curley came nearer to attaining the position of "boss" of Boston than any other politician, including John F. ("Honey Fitz") Fitzgerald, who came before him. Honey Fitz, also a mayor of Boston, was the father of Rose Kennedy, mother of President John F. Kennedy and wife of Joseph P. Kennedy. Joe Kennedy's father, Patrick J. Kennedy, was also active in Boston politics. He was a saloon owner who became a state senator. Curley was a rival of both Patrick Kennedy and John F. Fitzgerald; all were ward bosses. John F. was the first American-born son of Irish parents to become mayor of Boston. He sang his favorite tune, "Sweet Adeline," and was the first to introduce modern advertising techniques in political campaigns. One of his slogans was "A bigger, better and busier Boston." Honey Fitz, during his career, was a councilman, alderman, representative in the state legislature, congressman, and chairman of the ward committee. His career paralleled Curley's in almost all respects, except that he reached each office a decade earlier. John F. Fitzgerald was eleven years older than Curley. However, Curley's power remained personal, and rarely could he transfer his support among the voters to a candidate other than himself.

One cannot defend the graft that took place during his terms as mayor, even though both sides might rationalize their motives. The givers, often businessmen, gave to the machine as a means of carrying on legitimate business. And the takers, like Curley and his associates, took as a means of obtaining a fair return on their efforts.

Mayor Curley's chief biographer writes that "Curley had accepted the system as he found it. It was his ambition to master it, not reform it. What other ward leaders had done, he would do in a larger way, even on a magnificent scale. He had vision and inventiveness. Greater skill would come in time."[91]

Curley's record of victories and defeats and his long political career is impressive. From city councilor to alderman, from state representative to congressman, and from mayor to governor of Massachusetts he went. He lost to Henry Cabot Lodge in 1936 in his try for the U.S. Senate. He also suffered defeat twice for governor and six times for the mayoralty (which he won on four occasions). His two terms in prison didn't hurt his being reelected mayor because he once ran for the mayor's office while in jail. His first time in prison was in 1903, for impersonating a constituent at a civil service examination. For this, he was sentenced to sixty days in the city jail. While in jail he was elected to the Board of Aldermen. He served on the Board of Aldermen from 1904 to 1909. The second time he was involved in a mail fraud.

Curley, like Daley of Chicago, was not entirely a backroom politician but an active candidate who used his office, when in power, to patronize the voter in terms of jobs, improved city services, and facilities to attract support in order to build his power base (which included the Irish and other immigrant groups). Curley's power ended because he, like the bosses of Tammany Hall and other American cities, lacked the abilities to survive in a more complex urban age.

James Michael Curley was born on November 20, 1874, in Boston, the son of Michael and Sarah Curley. In 1905 the future political leader worked in a saloon. Curley's parents had come to Boston from Ireland after the potato famine. Boston had a population of 260,000, including 5,000 Irish immigrants, in 1847, the year before the famine. Ten years later, it had a population of 310,000, including 50,000 Irish. The Irish in Boston had grown from one-fiftieth to a sixth of the population and accounted for more than a third of the city's voters.

Immigrants came to America traveling by ship in steerage class. The "cattle Irish," as the immigrants were called, were packed together on the ships like animals. They came to this country when they could afford the eighteen dollars fare, and they didn't usually have much money to spend on necessities when they got here. The Irish came to escape the poverty that the English absentee landlords had bequeathed to them in Ireland. To their misfortune, however, when they arrived they found the same poverty.

Because they could not afford the cost of the food served on ships, families lived on porridge, bacon, and hardtack, which they brought along with them. They frequently arrived penniless, or with only enough money to provide food and shelter for a week or two. When a shipload of immigrants arrived, the ward bosses waited to greet the passengers at the immigration center.

They were lucky to find work at no more than about ten cents an hour and be able to pay eight dollars a month rent in 1891. Coal was also cheap, compared with today's prices, but they couldn't always afford to buy even a twenty-five pound bag, so they would go to the dump for wood, except when the ward workers would give them some coal.

The Irish didn't have as much trouble with the language in the United States as the Italians, Germans, and Jews did. Wolfinger's study in New Haven observed that the Irish took over the Democratic Party and they wouldn't let the Italians join, so the Italians joined the Republican Party. There was a struggle between the old ethnic groups (the Irish) and the new ethnic groups (the Italians). Also, the Irish seemed to have had a natural affinity for politics. When three Germans got together they were likely to open a saloon, but when three Irishmen got together they were likely to form a political club.

Curley's father worked in the city of Boston's paving division. He died when Curley was ten years old. His mother worked as a cleaning woman in downtown buildings. In his autobiography Curley says that, during his first term as mayor, he thought of his mother one night and told one of the scrubwomen cleaning the corridors to get up. He said, "The only time a woman should go down on her knees is when she is praying to Almighty God." The next morning he ordered long-handled mops.[92]

To earn a little spending money and help support the family, young Curley sold newspapers, worked in a drug store, and delivered groceries for a market. He didn't have an easy life. He worked hard and didn't have much of a formal education, going only as far as the sixth grade.

As a young man Curley got interested in politics and, like Dan O'Connell, admitted that he didn't have time for steady girl friends because of his ward activities. He chose politics because working conditions were deplorable, the hours were long, and the wages were poor. In addition, the prospects of getting anywhere seemed remote to Curley.

Curley first ran for election in 1898, when he wanted to be on the Common Council. However, he lost by about five hundred votes. Curley thought he had won but there was no way he could prove the election fraud. But the next year he was elected to serve on the Common Council.

In 1900 he became a ward boss, then being the youngest in the city, at twenty-six. Around that time, Curley went to New York City, where he studied the Tammany organization. When he got back to Boston he duplicated, as best he could, Tammany Hall's great political model. He, like Murphy, used to conduct classes on naturalization, teaching immigrants the things they had to learn to qualify as citizens. He and the other ward leaders used to help the people find jobs, fill out job applications for them, intervene on their behalf in court, give them food baskets and coal, pay for funerals and delinquent rent and thereby prevent families from being evicted by landlords. In 1907 there was only one bathtub for every twenty-five families in Boston, so Curley established public bathhouses. The same thing was done in Albany.

By serving himself the political boss served the public good. As the trickle-down economic theory goes, when a political boss is successful, some of his success passes down to his subordinates and the voters. The wise politico carefully adheres to a bit of advice given by the late George Bernard Shaw: "Treat a friend as a person who may some day become your enemy; an enemy as a person who may some day become your friend." You may never know if a person will help you or oppose you until the time comes. It is the many surprises which happen to us that help make life interesting and eventful.

From 1914 to 1921 Curley served as a trustee, vice-president, and president of the Hibernia Savings Bank. He also had a real estate business. His first wife died in 1930. And seven months after she died his oldest son, James Michael, Jr., a student at Harvard Law School, died also. Of Curley's nine children, seven of them died before he did.

When Franklin Roosevelt was elected President, Curley wanted to be Secretary of the Navy, but President Roosevelt told him that he could not appoint him to that cabinet post because two Catholics, James A. Farley and Senator Walsh of Montana, had already been chosen for his cabinet. Instead Roosevelt offered Curley an ambassadorship to Poland, but Curley did not accept because the salary was only $17,500 a year and he would have preferred to be an ambassador to a more important country, like Italy. Curley felt he was betrayed by Roosevelt because he had supported FDR when he first ran for President. Supporting Roosevelt made Curley an unpopular man among many in Massachusetts because the state not surprisingly wanted New York's Governor Al Smith, an Irish Catholic. Roosevelt promised Curley a cabinet level post if Massachusetts voted for him.

After it was announced that Curley would support FDR instead of Smith, Bostonians viewed Curley as a traitor, a betrayer, and a double-crosser. City Hall employees glared at him. Even his children were disappointed. Standish Willcox, Curley's secretary and closest friend, asked him, "Are you sure you know what you are doing?"[93] His move was viewed as political suicide. Needless to say, Curley's enemies were privately happy that Curley supported FDR but publicly they criticized him.

In the primary for delegates to the Democratic National Convention in 1932, Smith won an easy victory in Massachusetts. At the convention in Chicago, however, things were different. Although Curley did not have credentials as a delegate from Massachusetts to get into the convention hall he managed to get in and was seated as a delegate from Puerto Rico. James Michael Curley was called, at the convention, Alcalde Jamie Miguel Curleo.

The Boston Irish loved a fighter and that's what Curley was at the convention. They realized that Smith had been beaten once and if he was beaten again it would mean four more years of Hoover and that was frightening. New England felt the hardships of the Depression greatly. Also Smith didn't have a chance of getting nominated.

The convention was deadlocked between Jack Garner of Texas and Roosevelt. To try to break the deadlock, Curley spoke to the influential William Randolph Hearst, his friend, and urged him to support Roosevelt in exchange for guaranteeing that Garner would be nominated as the Vice-Presidential candidate. Hearst agreed and the Democrats nominated the Roosevelt-Garner ticket. The mercurial Boston Irish changed their attitude toward Curley and they made up, luckily for him.

He had a right to be angry at President Roosevelt when he didn't make him Secretary of the Navy. Curley had campaigned hard for Roosevelt. At his own expense, he had traveled 10,000 miles, made 140 speeches in 23 states in just 41 days.

In 1945 Curley married for a second time. Also in that year he was ordered to return $42,629 ($500 a week for 86 weeks) to the city of Boston. The judges decided that Curley had received $30,000 (the difference was interest and costs) in 1933 for helping to settle a case between the General Equipment Corporation and the city. Curley claimed he was broke and unable to pay the large amount of money. Around this time detectives went to banks in Montreal and Toronto and elsewhere looking for a million dollars Curley was believed to have in his name or his daughter Mary's name. They didn't find anything. To pay the sum an estimated two thousand people from all over the city went to Curley's house in Jamaicaway to give him money. Also the Boston Teamsters' Union held a testimonial dinner in Curley's honor to raise money for him. Curley helped them in times of need and now Curley needed their help. They waited in lines in front of his house to see him.

For about a year before Pearl Harbor, Curley was the president of Engineers Group, Inc., a company organized in Washington to provide engineering services to business. The actual organizer and manager of the company was James G. Fuller, a confidence man with a long jail record. Franklin Roosevelt was against all big-city bosses and that included Curley, so President Roosevelt instituted court proceedings against him. Roosevelt was angry at Curley, who had criticized him for giving him the runaround on many occasions. Curley went to President Harry Truman, hoping that he would stop the case from being prosecuted, but Truman didn't do this because the proceedings had been instituted by Roosevelt.

Curley was found guitly, in 1946, of using the mails to defraud, from his connection with Engineers Group. He was sentenced from six to eighteen months in the Federal Correctional Institution at Danbury, Connecticut. Curley claimed that he was merely a figurehead of the company and that because he had complete faith in Fuller, he had never asked any questions and never knew about any illegal activities. While at Danbury, Curley was not allowed to communicate with aides at City Hall in Boston, although he was still mayor and still received that salary. A temporary mayor was appointed, however, while Mayor Curley was in jail. Congressman John McCormack from Massachusetts (then the Democratic whip in the House, later Speaker), Postmaster General Robert Hannegan (former chairman of the Democratic National Committee), and other well-known people signed a petition so that Curley would be pardoned. President Truman pardoned Curley after he had served five months in jail.

During campaigns Curley's prison record was made an issue by his opponents. But taking an examination for a friend who needed a job to support his wife and four children wasn't such a crime that justified Curley's opponents castigating him as a felon. A good orator, Curley rationalized his conduct that an unlawful means to achieve an end was right if it could be established that the end itself was just and desirable. Such is the way he explained his taking a civil service exam for a friend.

Curley's first campaign for mayor was based on reform. He was critical of the ward bosses, and made it clear that he would have no part of them and would run the city as he saw fit without making any deals. When elected, he insisted on a full day's work for a full day's pay, especially from all city employees who didn't support his candidacy. It was a change from the no-show and "soft" jobs. While Curley was mayor it was he who gave out the jobs and other patronage and not the ward leaders. The Curley era was known as Curleyism. Perhaps Curley made a mistake by taking so much power from the ward bosses. After all, the ward bosses helped keep the voters in line.

While Curley was the boss of the Boston Democrats from around

1914 until the mid-fifties, there were about twenty years during that period when he did not hold public office because of losing an election, and his power and patronage were then limited. Curley's control was similar to that of Mayor Richard Daley of Chicago. Both men were powerful because of the nature of the mayor's offices they held. However, the longest time Curley was mayor at one time was four years; Daley has been mayor continuously for more than nineteen years.

Boston's city charter prevented Curley from succeeding himself, but it was amended to permit Mayor Maurice J. Tobin, Curley's opponent, to succeed himself. Because the state legislature was against Curley, they passed a law that prohibited him from succeeding himself. This meant that he had to look around for an interim office. But the circumstances did not make it possible for Curley to alternate neatly between the statehouse and city hall, because he lost many elections. Curley's political career has been irregular, with both successful and unsuccessful election attempts. While in office, Curley was powerful, but much of his power was that associated with the offices he held. James Michael Curley might have been more successful had he not taken so much power away from the ward bosses. While many political bosses have made other people senators, governors, congressmen, judges, and presidents, Curley was more interested in making himself. Curley was mayor of Boston for sixteen years, member of Congress for eight years, and governor of Massachusetts for two years. He hoped to be remembered as the "Mayor of the Poor," champion of the oppressed and underprivileged. On November 12, 1958, Curley passed away.

CURLEY'S PUBLIC OFFICES AND CAMPAIGNS

1900-01   Boston Common Council
1902-03   Representative (State Legislature)
1904-09   Alderman
1910-11   City Council
1911-14   Congressman from Massachusetts
1914-18   Mayor of Boston
1917   Defeated for Mayor by Andrew J. Peters
1922-26   Mayor of Boston
1924   Defeated for Governor of Massachusetts by Alvan T. Fuller
1930-34   Mayor of Boston
1935-36   Governor of the Commonwealth of Massachusetts
1936   Defeated for U.S. Senate by Henry Cabot Lodge, Jr.
1937   Defeated for Mayor of Boston by Maurice J. Tobin
1938   Defeated for Governor of Massachusetts by Leverett Saltonstall

1940   Defeated for Mayor of Boston by Maurice J. Tobin
1943-46   Congressman from Massachusetts
1945-49   Mayor of Boston
1949   Defeated for Mayor of Boston by John B. Hynes
1951   Defeated for Mayor of Boston by John B. Hynes
1955   Defeated for Mayor of Boston By John B. Hynes
1950-58   National Committeeman, Democratic State Committee
November 12, 1958   Died

Patronage

The politician who thinks he can get away from the people who made him, usually gets what is coming to him—a swift kick in his political pants.

MARTIN LOMASNEY,
Boston ward boss and
associate of James Michael Curley

Patronage is the offering of a favor to someone by a person in public office. It is partially through patronage that an incumbent is reelected. Patronage occurs at all levels of government. It rewards the giver's supporters and is used to get more support. Patronage has been used in the United States extensively by politicians ever since its founding. The more patronage a politician is able to distribute the more powerful he is. Patronage is a give-and-take situation. Favors are performed by politicians in return for votes and sometimes financial help. Patronage is legal except when laws are violated, but usually even flagrant violations are overlooked by the people who could do something to stop it if they wanted to. Once in a while a columnist such as Jack Anderson or some consumer advocate will make public the uses and abuses of political patronage.

Even though many people have benefited from patronage it can cause a few problems. Patronage made our withdrawal from Vietnam more difficult because the end of the war would mean a cut in defense spending and therefore many people would be out of work. Congressmen took their time in letting the Vietnam War go on because of the contributions they received from the corporations who benefited from defense contracts.

Many people face losing their jobs when another party is in power. In 1969, for example, 10,000 state employees were fired by the new governor of Illinois, Richard B. Ogilvie, a Republican.[94] Even civil service jobs don't really provide the job security that most people think they do. Workers can be transferred to another city and be inconvenienced to the extent that they are forced to resign. Also the governor may abolish a category of jobs under civil service by saying that the state no longer needs that job performed or that there are too many people doing that job.

Former Tammany Hall leader George Washington Plunkitt said that "dishonest graft" included blackmailing and bribery and that "honest graft" was availing oneself of inside information for personal enrichment.[95] Many people, including Plunkitt, have made a fortune in politics by purchasing real estate with the advance knowledge that something would be built on the land and therefore the property value would increase a great deal.

Patronage includes giving out jobs, fixing parking tickets, lowering property taxes by the way of lowering assessments, and other big and small favors. Legislators help companies in their district get government contracts. Architects want to design government buildings (an architectural firm in Albany received over a million dollars in fees for drawing up plans for a new high school), doctors and dentists want to get increases in Medicaid and Medicare fees, lawyers want to become judges, insurance companies want to insure government property, banks want to have government deposits, contractors want to build government-funded buildings, companies want government contracts, and the list goes on.

Mayor Corning's insurance company has received about $200,000 in annual premiums for insuring the property of Albany County. The business was obtained without competitive bidding because the uniform insurance rates are fixed by law by the State Department of Insurance and no insurance company can undersell another. His insurance company also has written insurance on plumbing and heating contracts for the Empire State Plaza in Albany.[96]

Peter D. Kiernan, president of Rose and Kiernan insurance company of Albany and a contributor to the Albany Democratic Party, received annual insurance premiums totaling $200,000 from the South Mall project.[97]

Until the past two years, Albany County kept its money in local banks, receiving little or no interest. The county is now earning about $500,000 per year in interest as compared with only $10,000 in 1972 and $88,000 in 1973. Naturally, the local banks made out quite well not having to pay the county interest for so many years.

People who are given jobs or other favors through patronage are party supporters. Occasionally a Democrat will do a favor for a Republican, or vice versa, with the hope of getting a favor in return.

Why do people go into politics? Many people take a cut in salary by entering public office. It is often a thankless job and is frustrating at times when you think that just a couple of years later you might be out of a job. Yet many people love politics as if it were in their blood. Politics permits an individual to become involved with his government, rubbing shoulders with important people, and sometimes permits one to increase his bankbook. But you might ask yourself, is it worth it? The cost of being elected is increasing all the time and campaigning is tiresome. Because you can't please everyone you tend to make enemies while in public office.

Some people think that the "old politics" is bad and the "new politics" is good, but there really isn't much difference with the tactics used by both. The young people of today will also get old. Former

New York State Senator Joe Zaretsky, a well known and elder politician, told me, when I sat next to him on the airplane going to Miami for the 1972 Democratic National Convention, that he was the same way the young people are today when he was younger and first entered politics. He confided to me that the elder politicians don't mind letting young people into politics, it's just that they don't want the young people to destroy what they have worked hard for. The youth of all generations want change and reform, and in this century they have been more liberal than their parents and grandparents were. Thomas Jefferson said, "The boys of the rising generation are to be the men of the next, and the sole guardian of the principles we deliver over to them."

It is possible to go around civil service rules by using "temporary employees." However even though "temporary employees" may be appointed for a hundred and eighty days, they are reappointed and it is possible to hold a job for several years that was intended to be filled by civil service.[98]

A U.S. Civil Service Commission report, issued after Richard Nixon resigned as President, charged that political favoritism played a major role in hiring practices of the Department of Housing and Urban Development during the Nixon administration. The study said HUD officials violated civil service regulations by keeping extensive political files on employees and job seekers. A patronage unit was set up in the department for the purpose of making sure persons with the right political connections got HUD posts.

A random review of four hundred files on job applicants showed "virtually all" were referrals from either the White House, Republican members of Congress, or other GOP political figures. HUD officials kept "political profiles" on many of its current employees, coded to relate political acceptability to the Nixon administration. Another report released some two months before, on October 19, 1974, accused the U.S. General Services Administration of exercising political job favoritism also. Such hiring practices were not unique to the Nixon administration alone. They have occurred at all levels of government.

A story is told that with the use of political jobs in jails, on election day a few jails are virtually unmanned because most of the guards reported for duty instead at the polls. There are many political jobs also at courts, sheriffs' departments, city hospitals and schools, the county street, water, parks, police, fire, and health departments, as well as city hall. Sometimes the quality of American life is hindered by political jobs because many people who are unqualified for the positions are given jobs. Thus the city's corporation council's office and district attorney's office have several openings, primarily for young lawyers. Because of inexperienced legal staffs, cities often lose many cases in court.

Zoning changes are another way the politician uses patronage. In cities they are usually made for the benefit of big business. For example, in 1974, the New Jersey State Commission of Investigation was told by two land developers that from 1968 through 1973 they had paid nearly $200,000 to Camden county officials. In return, they said they obtained zoning changes and other land concessions necessary for building condominiums and apartments. Three of the witnesses purportedly involved in graft, including the mayor of Lindenwood, refused to answer questions.[99]

In New York City the mayor appoints more than eighty city marshals for six-year terms to enforce the collection of money judgments by the Civil Courts. They get 55 percent on the first $10,000 and 3 percent on amounts in excess of $10,000 on the funds they collect.[100] For many years, sheriffs and marshals have become quite wealthy from their jobs.

Sheriffs and marshals have also been lucrative positions for a long time because of a fee system they have. For example, New York City marshals, who are paid to make personal deliveries of Civil Court orders, have been paying others or using the mails to serve warrants illegally and to deliver other court papers. In one case a Brooklyn marshal, with a reported income of $362,000 for 1973, was listed in the Department of Investigation records as having delivered garnishment papers that year to 12,722 people in the city, which appears almost impossible. In 1973, twelve of New York City's 83 marshals resigned under pressure, were fired for malfeasance, or failed to be reappointed after an investigation took place.[101]

Consultants are often paid huge fees for their studies. It is sometimes questionable if the public benefits from their work. However, there is no doubt that both the consultants and politicians benefit.

The Public Officers Law says it is a felony to accept or promise a reward in return for a vote. But even if it is not done in "direct" violation of the law, human nature compels one to vote where the money is. Most legislators receive campaign contributions and other gifts from interest groups. The interest group then expects the legislator to go along with their views.

When competitive bidding is required for government contracts, mayors and governors sometimes word the specifications of a bid so that their firm is selected. Advance notice on a bid may help a firm get a contract.

Politics is involved even in the courts. Judges are either appointed or elected. Patronage of the courts includes receiverships and refereeships in bankruptcy cases, trusteeships, guardianships, court-appointed lawyers to defendants who cannot afford to pay for one, and court employees. When a lawyer is appointed to a judgeship by a mayor, governor, or President it is usually for political reasons rather than because the lawyer is more qualified for the position than someone else. This is not to say that the appointed judges are not competent. It merely means that a more competent attorney may not be appointed to the bench if he doesn't have the proper connections.

When a judge is elected he usually campaigns for office the same as any other elected public servant. In some cities there are even primaries for judges. When a person is a judge he usually appreciates that he was chosen instead of someone else and is therefore obligated. Sometimes he extends his thanks by doing certain "small" things.

There is much patronage given from surrogate (or probate) courts across the nation. "Surrogates," as these judges are called, give out guardianships (to act as a counselor for a minor) to their friends and members of their party. The fee a lawyer receives is drawn from the estate and is based on the size of the estate rather than the amount of legal work involved. It is usually very lucrative.

Lawyers are required to end their political connections upon becoming judges. But how can a judge end his "friendship" with his friends who are politicians? Former Supreme Court Justice Abe Fortas drew criticism from the Senate for advising his friend President Johnson.

Court jobs include judges' clerks, bailiffs, secretaries, and recorders. A federal judge is appointed for life by the President and approved by the Senate. The President usually does not know personally all the judges he nominates. Names are suggested to the President by party leaders and one of the Senators from the nominee's state. When the Democrats are in power the judgeships usually go to fellow Democrats instead of Republicans, and vice versa. To get a prestigious judgeship a lawyer sometimes has to pay his party a large amount of money (usually from $10,000 to $50,000). Some judgeships are offered as an alternative to another office. Former Mayor of New York Vincent Impellitteri was offered a judgeship after he was denied the renomination for the mayoralty. After former New York City Council President Frank O'Connor lost the governor's race in 1966 to Nelson Rockefeller he was offered a federal judgeship to get him out of the political limelight. Also, there are 185 United States attorneys appointed by the attorney general, and there are more than seventy assistant United States attorneys in the Southern District of New York alone. So you can see that political patronage is quite plentiful in the courts.

In order to get along in politics you have to go along. It is recommended that you don't rock the boat if you want to succeed.

It is important for a Congressman to be on a committee that can help his district. Originally Congresswoman Shirley Chisholm was appointed to the Agriculture Committee, but her constituency wasn't interested in agriculture, so she was put on the Veteran Affairs Committee, where she could be more helpful to her constituency.[102]

Senator William Proxmire said that "one of the reasons I can attack the Pentagon is because there are no real defense installations in Wisconsin," his home state.[103] However, American Motors has large plants in Wisconsin, and Senator Proxmire helped them get tax advantages and government contracts. The General Services Administration purchased Ramblers for the Post Office and the FBI. This is typical, and every Congressman has his own self-interests so that his constituency can benefit.

Many legislators belong to law firms that have big corporate clients. So you can see that a conflict of interest can develop. It is interesting to note the *Martindale-Hubbell Law Directory*, which lists law firms and their clients. Sometimes the conflict of interest is quite noticeable, as in the case of the Florida and Washington, D.C., law firm of Senator George Smathers, which lists clients including Pan American World Airways, Western Union Telegraph Company, Standard Oil Company, Gulf Oil Corporation, and several other businesses including banks and insurance companies.[104] At the same time Senator Smathers is on the Finance, Small Business, Judiciary, and Joint Internal Revenue Taxation committees in the Senate.

The President appoints people to advisory boards, task forces, and Presidential commissions. Even though these positions are usually non-salaried they are sought after for prestige. There has been talk about the sale of ambassadorships, and although President Nixon contended that "ambassadorships cannot be purchased" from his administration, many ambassadors who were appointed by him gave large amounts of money to his election campaign.

Walter H. Annenberg, who was nominated ambassador to Great Britain on February 20, 1969, donated $254,000 to Nixon's reelection campaign in 1972. Shelby C. Davis, appointed ambassador to Switzerland on April 17, 1969, contributed $100,000 to President Nixon in 1972. Vincent Deroulet, son-in-law of Mrs. Joan Payson, owner of the New York Mets, who contributed $80,000 to Mr. Nixon in 1972, donated $53,000 to Nixon's reelection campaign in 1972, and was nominated ambassador to Jamaica on August 20, 1968, and resigned in July, 1973.

Ruth L. Farkas contributed $300,000 to Nixon's campaign in 1972 and 1973 and was nominated ambassador to Luxembourg on February 27, 1973. Kingdom Gould, Jr., contributed $100,000 to Nixon in 1972 and was nominated ambassador to Netherlands on August 24, 1973. John P. Humes, nominated ambassador to Austria on September 10, 1969, gave $100,000 to Nixon in 1971 and 1972. Arthur K. Watson, nominated ambassador to France on March 4, 1970, gave $44,000 in 1968 and $300,000 in 1971 to Nixon.

The first criminal charge ever preferred in connection with the selling of an ambassadorship was brought against Herbert W. Kalmbach in 1974. Mr. Kalmbach, who served as Mr. Nixon's personal lawyer and one of his principal fund raisers, pleaded guilty to the charge.

Kalmbach admitted having promised a diplomatic post to J. Fife Symington, a cousin of Senator Stuart Symington, Democrat of Missouri, in return for $100,000 in political contributions to Republican senatorial candidates in 1970 and to Nixon in 1972. Symington was ambassador to Trinidad and Tobago in the West Indies at the time of the transaction, but wanted a transfer to a prestigious European country. When the transfer was not forthcoming, Kalmbach offered to return the money, but Ambassador Symington declined to take it back.

Federal law prohibits bribery of government officials to obtain such posts. Despite this, big supporters have, and not only in the Nixon administration, occasionally been given ambassadorships. However, the fact that someone who is appointed an ambassador contributed a large sum to an election campaign means nothing by itself.

Mayors are affected too. The *New York Daily News* said, "Despite his pre-election and post-election promises, Mayor Abraham Beame has been slipping his own cronies and cronies' cronies into cushy provisional jobs almost as fast as former Mayor Lindsay's pets were booted out."[105] But it would be practically impossible for a mayor, governor, president, or any other elected official who has large amounts of patronage at his disposal, to ignore requests for jobs from supporters. Officeholders and politicians rationalize that as long as jobs have to be filled they might as well be filled by members of their political party. This principle applies to other forms of patronage also. If a road has to be fixed you might as well give the job to a friend (a fellow Democrat or Republican, depending on which party has power) who will appreciate it, as to someone you don't know, especially if they belong to the opposite party.

The governor of New York State has more than 1,500 patronage jobs at his disposal, carrying salaries totaling some $50 million a year. In addition, the party in power has other patronage at its disposal that runs into the millions. This includes insurance contracts, printing, construction, rental of private buildings for state offices, and the list goes on. The good governor is able to appoint qualified individuals who work for their high state salaries, while playing the political game of distributing patronage. It certainly is not an easy task.

Most of the governor's 1,500 appointees receive salaries of more than $20,000 a year. About thirty cabinet-level appointees of the governor each receive $47,800 annually. Hundreds of other positions range in salary from $20,000 to $45,000. He also appoints many with lower salaries. The state attorney general has the power to appoint over $13 million in jobs mainly for lawyers. Except for the governor himself, the attorney general has more high-salaried jobs to hand out than any other state official. The attorney general has more than 400 jobs at his disposal, with most salaries ranging from $20,000 to $46,600.

New York State spends more than $20 million a year for 18 boards, commissions, and authorities, most of whose members are political appointees who do little work in their state jobs. An overwhelming majority of these jobholders maintain full-time private occupations, usually law practices, while drawing state salaries, often in the $30,000 to $40,000 range. For example, eleven commissioners on the Workmen's Compensation Board are paid $32,575 a year apiece. This apparently full-time salary is paid for part-time work, no more than about three days a week.

The jobs go most often to former legislators, present and former party officials, and former state employees. Some of the other agencies with these jobs are the State Liquor Authority, State Commission of Investigation, the State Athletic Commission, the State Racing Commission, the State Tax Commission, and the Cable Television Commission.

The former chairman of the State Racing and Wagering Board, Emil Mosbacher, Jr., the yachtsman and a friend of former Governor Rockefeller, received a salary of $75,000 a year while he was its chairman. The board's other two members each receive $42,500 a year. Mr. Mosbacher resigned as chairman because he was criticized for his high salary and inexperience in gambling and racing. Former Governor Wilson immediately cut the salary of the chairman to $55,000 when he appointed Mosbacher's successor.

It is questionable whether many of these jobs are necessary at the high salaries. One reason (or excuse) why high salaries are needed is that if you pay people less you're inviting corruption.

In addition to salaries, most of these appointees have state cars at their disposal. The chairman of the State Power Authority has an airplane at his disposal also. Four members of the Power Authority receive $12,500 a year to meet once a month. The chairman has additional responsibilities and gets $25,000 a year. Another hidden cost is the large pensions most of these appointees receive. For pension purposes, a year's part-time work counts as a full year.

In addition to the paid positions, there are more than two hundred unpaid positions that are sought because of their prestige value. Some of these positions are to serve on the boards of visitors of various mental institutions and libraries, as well as the State Training School for Girls.

The state is also a friendly landlord for some officials. For example, the State University of New York provides 78 private homes to its officials and college presidents. The chancellor of the State University in Albany has a 23-room rent-free mansion, with a swimming pool. His salary is $57,650 a year, with $10,000 for expenses. Some state officials pay the state rent, but this is extremely nominal. For example, the president of the State University College at Purchase lives in a $135,000 home provided by taxpayers and pays only $94.94 a month rent.

★ 9 ★

Congress—
The Best Money Can Buy

Try to imagine a public official saying, "I'm sorry but I can't take a bribe or even do you a favor because I hold a position of public trust."

I once heard former Mayor Vincent Impelliteri say that the New York City police are the best in the world. Archie Robbins, a comedian yelled out, "Yes, the best money can buy." Robbins was referring to the recent scandal in the New York City police department when $73 million worth of heroin and cocaine was stolen from the department. It was assumed that the narcotics withdrawals were made by members of the police force who sold them to drug dealers at the going street rate. What the police did in many instances was to withdraw heroin (previously seized in arrests) from a storage depot on the grounds that it was needed as evidence. It was then replaced with an equal amount of sugar or flour.

But actually the United States Congress is the best money can buy. Big campaign contributions are given in return for an assurance of receiving special treatment. Campaign expenses have soared from $200 in 1846 by Abraham Lincoln to several hundred thousand dollars today. Usually only the richest candidates or the candidates who are able to raise enough money survive.

Since the 1950s unions have become important in elections. The AFL-CIO's political action arm, the Committee on Political Education (COPE), and the United Auto Workers' Good Government Fund (DRIVE) contributed more than $4 million to candidates in the 1970 election. These special committees were set up to collect members contributions because federal law prohibits using their own funds in political campaigns. The Seafarers International Union in 1968 contributed $1.4 million. Although these members' contributions are supposed to be voluntary there is pressure put on those workers who don't give their fair share. The American Medical Association's AMPAC gave $693,000 in 1970, and the National Association of Manufacturers' BIPAC gave $539,000 in 1970.

Professor William Domkoff in his *Fat Cats and Democrats* estimated that 55 percent of the Democratic Party contributions comes from corporate moneymen, 20-25 percent from labor, 10-15 percent from racketeers and gangsters in large cities, and about 15 percent from middle-class Americans. Domkoff says that the Republican contributors include more industrialists and bankers than the Democrats. Also the Republicans spend much more in campaigns than the Democrats do.[106]

Ninety percent of all the money raised for campaigns in the U.S. comes from the richest one percent of the population. In 1972 W. Clement Stone, an insurance magnate, gave over $1 million to Nixon's reelection campaign. He and his wife have contributed more than $7 million to Republican candidates since 1968. Stewart Mott, heir of the founder of General Motors, gave nearly three-quarters of a million dollars to the McGovern campaign in 1974, according to General Accounting Office figures. While these two men may never have asked anything in return for their contributions, it is unrealistic to say that an obligation does not exist to help the contributor who gave so much money if the opportunity comes around. In order to prevent such "strings" it is important to limit the amount of contributions and support public financing of campaigns. The $1 checkoff on your federal tax return ($2 for those filing jointly) is a step in the right direction. Checking the box will not increase your taxes or decrease your refund check. But if everyone checks the box, there would be at least $50 million for the 1976 Presidential election, perhaps enough to pay for it entirely from public funds.

Businessmen contribute because the Federal Corrupt Practices Act prohibits businesses from contributing. The seafarers union reportedly uses a goon squad to collect contributions from its members. Sterling Drug, Inc., asks its executives who earn more than $15,000 per year to give at least one-half of one percent of their salary. "We're asking for a voluntary contribution from you for a political fund to be allocated to those legislators whose election is important to our industry and to Sterling Drug, Inc.," says their letter.

Because there is a "limit" a person can give to a candidate's committee several committees with different names are usually established. A law passed in 1972, which requires candidates to file preelection disclosures, is not strictly enforced.

Few congressmen would admit that they can be "bought." The Ralph Nader Congress Project said this is like "a free-living woman who decides she might as well take money for what she enjoys, but insists she is not a prostitute." Contributors are guaranteed access to an elected official, if not anything else.

Lobbyists depend on access to the legislators. Lobbying is the direct persuasion of legislators. A lobbyist is anyone who works to influence decisions by public officials. This right to "petition the Government for a redress of grievances" is found in the first Amendment to the Constitution. Lobbyists got their name in the 1850s from hanging around the lobbies of government buildings looking for favors. There are currently more than five thousand full-time lobbyists in Washington. Most corporations have their representatives in Washington. Numerous other lobbyists are located across the nation in state capitals. Lobbyists provide the legislators with much information on various problems. Of course they are biased, but they are helpful to the legislator, especially when their "help" is followed up with a gift or contribution.

There is a sugar lobby, a tobacco lobby, a highway lobby, an oil lobby (the American Petroleum Institute), the Chamber of Commerce of the United States, the National Association of Manufacturers, the American Farm Bureau Federation, the automobile lobby, the United States Conference of Mayors, the National Rifle Association, and others. These lobbyists wine and dine the legislators at good restaurants, and give them tickets to athletic events and free junkets to faraway places, and of course you can't forget the liquor and cigars given to legislators. Interest groups also contribute to campaign funds.

Several Washington lawyers came to Washington in high posts with a Democratic or Republican administration and then used their contacts in government to develop a lucrative law practice with big corporate clients. Clark Clifford, a former secretary of defense, is one of the best known of this kind of lawyer.

Congressmen are people, and subject to the same temptations and flaws as other people. Yet they are granted immunity from arrest for statements made, or actions taken, in Congress, or while coming from or going to Congress. The privilege of congressional immunity has been abused for drunken driving, speeding, and other violations including felonies.

Legislators go on junkets with the official intention of learning about a situation firsthand but actually for a vacation, with sometimes the family along at government expense. In 1971, 53 senators and 221 representatives took foreign trips at public expense. Hong Kong and the Caribbean are favorite destinations. The United States Congress, in the midst of its probe of Watergate coverup attempts by the White House, quietly moved to cover up future public disclosure of such highly questionable activities by some of its own members. Congress made it impossible to determine the duration and total costs of its members and their committee staffs' official trips abroad.

Since 1961, federal law has required publication in the *Congressional Record* of reports on money spent traveling abroad by each member of Congress. In 1971 members of Congress and their aides spent more than $1.1 million on foreign travel, and in 1972 they spent more than $955,000. In October, 1973, Congress passed a bill eliminating the requirement for disclosure in the *Congressional Record*. The reason given by Representative Wayne L. Hays (Dem.—Ohio), chairman of the subcommittee that originated the action, was "We decided we weren't going to spend eight or nine thousand dollars to let you guys [reporters] do your stories on congressional travel." Hays

claimed congressmen passed the bill only to cut down the size of the
Record and not to cover up anything. In the same bill, Congress
voted itself a 50 percent increase in daily travel allowance—from $50
to $75 per day.

No action has been taken by Congress on about sixteen bills that
would prohibit travel outside the United States at government expense
of members who have been defeated, are retiring, or have resigned.
The bills are still in committee and will probably be there for a long
time.

In addition to Congress paying for travel expenses of its members,
many members of Congress travel as guests of government agencies,
such as the State and Defense departments. Members also travel often
without charge on ships of the Military Sea Transportation Service and
planes of the Military Airlift Command.

Representative Adam Clayton Powell Jr. (Dem.–N.Y., 1945-71)
was one of the most notorious junketeers. In 1962, the Harlem congressman traveled through Europe for six weeks with two female "assistants." Powell's itinerary included London, Paris, Rome, Vienna, Greece,
and Spain. On that trip, he took a six-day cruise on the Aegean Sea,
attended the Vienna film festival and several nightclubs. Powell tried
to rationalize the trip on grounds that they needed to study equal
employment opportunities for women in Common Market countries.

Senator Edward V. Long (Dem.–Mo., 1960-69) and Representative
Barrett O'Hara (Dem.–Ill., 1949-51, 1953-69) both traveled abroad at
government expense after Congress had adjourned in 1968. Both men
had been defeated in primaries, before they took their trips, and were
"lame ducks." Long and his personal secretary spent six weeks traveling
through nineteen countries. O'Hara and several staff members spent
about a month in Africa. While no congressman should be expected to
pay for necessary official trips out of their own pocket, congressmen
should not abuse this privilege.[107]

The congressman's right to free postage, called the "franking"
privilege, has been abused. Instead of a stamp a congressman signs
his name on the envelope. This is not supposed to be used for political
mail, but mail to constituents usually ends up this way, because a
representative is up for reelection every two years. Newsletters and
letters are sent to constituents by congressmen. Staff members are not
supposed to be used for political campaigns either, but this usually
happens. Ralph Nader's Congress Project said that "because the law
is so widely violated, violation becomes custom, and custom replaces
law."[108]

An 1872 law directs House and Senate officials to deduct from a
member's salary a day's pay for each day's absence, except in illness.
But even though there are numerous absences daily, this has been
done only twice. And there are two congressional employees who run

American flags up and down the Capitol flagpole so that members can give the flags away. More than a hundred flags are raised and immediately lowered daily.

Few men run for public office with the secret intent to profit by illegal means. It just happens to a few after they're in office. They need money to stay in office. Side benefits of being a congressman include cheap, tax-free meals in House and Senate restaurants, a tax deduction of $3,000 annually for living costs in Washington, free plants from the botanical garden, twelve free trips home per year, free travel abroad for official business, and plenty of other benefits.

A story told by one female Washington reporter concerns a senator who offered her a ride home from a party. On the way home he mentioned that his wife was out of town and he tried to make advances. She pulled away from him and said, "I thought you were offering me a ride home." He looked at her and said, "What do you think I'm running —a taxi service?" And there haven't been many arrests of prostitutes in Washington since a call girl was arrested who had in her possession a little black book containing names of many important men.

Congress itself has investigated ethics in government. One committee looked into the activities of the so-called "five-percenters." The five-percenter was a man who tried to obtain contracts for businesses on a contingent-fee basis. The committee found out that in many cases contracts were obtained by personal influence and gifts rather than by the quality of the goods or lowness of the prices.[109]

A congressional investigation into the activities of the Reconstruction Finance Corporation showed that the RFC had made many loans that it was extremely difficult to justify. In one case companies with several billion dollars of assets set up a corporation to conduct research into a possible new process. Although they could afford the $17 million they borrowed from the RFC, they didn't want to use their own money in case the project failed.[110] In a number of instances leading officials of the RFC would resign from that body shortly after the loan was granted and would accept positions with a salary increase with the successful borrower. One congressional committee investigating the Internal Revenue Service uncovered irregularities that caused the dismissal or resignation of many employees of the tax collection agency.[111]

It is understood, whether in Washington, Albany, or in any other capital where legislatures convene, that lobbyists get nothing for nothing. One Washington lobbyist said he paid $500 to a friend for a personal introduction to Gerald R. Ford, now President but then the House Minority Leader. He said it was "a good investment."[112]

Money can buy just about anything in Washington. Millions of dollars are paid out annually by individuals, groups, and businesses who want to get something done or not done or undone. Technically the money is usually given as a campaign contribution, but much of it doesn't wind up that way. The favor sought by the lobbyist may not necessarily be illegal or even improper, but presumably a member of Congress, a state legislator, or a governmental figure could get something done quicker than usual channels permit and could save money also.

In 1946 Congress passed the Legislative Reorganization Act, which regulated lobbyists halfheartedly. The act defines a lobbyist as one who indirectly or directly attempts to influence passage or defeat of any legislation before the Congress. Under the act lobbyists are required to register with the Clerk of the House of Representatives and the Secretary of the Senate and submit a quarterly report on their expenses and fees. But the reports are rarely accurate and comparatively low. For example, the lobbyist is not required to report campaign contributions made with his client's money. Most of the contributions are made this way. And only the lobbyist knows the number and amount of the payoffs, so the true amount can not be verified easily, if ever. Some lobbyists do not even bother to register.

According to the Federal Corrupt Practices Act of 1925, which dealt with campaign spending, candidates needed only to account for the campaign spending of which they had personal knowledge. Several committees of private citizens (i.e., Citizens for Smith, Attorneys for Smith, Professors for Smith, New Yorkers for Smith), with VIPs to head them, raised many donations. Some states required these committees to report on the money they raised and how they spent it, but most states did not. When the time came for a candidate to submit campaign reports, he could say he wasn't informed of the financial activities of all his committees. Also while the act put a $5,000 limit on an individual's contribution to a campaign committee, he could contribute $5,000 to several committees, because of the loose law. While corporations weren't supposed to make campaign contributions, their executives could and did contribute. The corporation could provide printing services, campaign buttons, stickers, pamphlets, personnel, and automobiles. Many contributions were made in cash and therefore not accountable unless a receipt had been signed. While unions could not contribute, they could form committees that did. Loans were often made to candidates. If a candidate won, who bothered to collect the loan? They knew they'd get their money back one way or another.

A member of the House must disclose annually to the Clerk any commercial affiliation that brings him an income of $1,000 a year or more, but he doesn't have to disclose how much more. A House member must also report stockholdings worth $5,000, or more but he doesn't have to disclose how much more. Senators make similar reports, but while representatives' reports are available to the public, the senators' reports are not publicly available. Congressmen must disclose the source of any honorarium for appearances and writings of $300 or more

Senators must report any gifts worth more than $50. Members of Congress are required to report any unsecured loans of $10,000 or more that have been outstanding for ninety days or more. But on the eighty-ninth day they can have the loan refinanced and thus do not have to report it.

In 1969 Nathan Voloshen, a powerful Washington lobbyist, and Martin Sweig, Speaker of the House John McCormack's administrative assistant, were investigated on charges of fraud and conspiracy involving government matters, government agencies, and government personnel. Voloshen had been using McCormack's office in the Capitol freely for bribes and payoffs. McCormack was not charged with any wrongdoing, but the propriety of Voloshen using the Speaker's office was questioned. Sweig was convicted on one count of perjury, and Voloshen pleaded guilty to charges of influence peddling and conspiracy. Voloshen was given a suspended sentence and fined. At Sweig's trial, McCormack pleaded ignorance of what was happening in his office. The Speaker said, "I am not an inquiring fellow." Voloshen was an acquaintance of Justice Mitchell D. Schweitzer, a judge on the "take." Voloshen's name was better known on Capitol Hill than the names of many Congressmen.

In 1955, when Bobby Baker was hired as the secretary of the Senate Majority Leader (then Lyndon Johnson), his salary was $9,000 a year, and his net worth was put as $11,000. Eight years later his salary was $19,600 a year and he was worth more than $2 million. He was involved in a vending company, a travel agency, a motel, and other businesses. As secretary he would coordinate the Democratic votes in the Senate and also raise money for Democratic candidates.

In 1963 Baker was sued by Ralph L. Hill, owner of the Capitol Vending Company. Baker was accused of using political influence to obtain contracts with defense plants for his vending machines. Hill brought the suit because Baker wanted $5,600 as a payoff to get Hill a contract to put his vending machines into factories doing business with the government. In January, 1971, Baker began serving a one- to three-year sentence at the federal prison at Lewisburg, Pennsylvania, as a result of a conviction on tax evasion, theft, and conspiracy to defraud the government. From 1963 to 1964 he was the focus of Senate hearings that exposed other deals. There were rumors around Washington that President Kennedy planned to drop Lyndon Johnson as Vice-President for the 1964 election because of Johnson's association with Baker. There was nothing improper about the association between Johnson and Baker, but because Johnson was at one time Baker's boss, Baker's troubles weren't very good for Johnson's image. Johnson, however, wasn't dropped from the ticket, because Kennedy was assassinated within two months after Baker's troubles began.

Lobbyists use money, and sometimes votes, to influence legislation.

Labor unions have plenty of money to offer senators and representatives but they also have plenty of votes. Cabinet members, ex-congressmen, former Presidential aides, former holders of high positions in government agencies, retired high-ranking military men, and others who have been around Washington use their previous knowledge and acquaintances to serve the special interest groups they represent as lobbyists. For example, Andrew J. Biemiller, who was a Democratic Congressman from Wisconsin from 1945 to 1949 later became director of legislation for the AFL-CIO.

Defense spending is the largest single item in the federal budget, and defense manufacturers find it beneficial to hire retired high-ranking military men and ex-cabinet members. Information in advance on future projects and size of bids is helpful to the manufacturers, and someone in the Pentagon is more likely to give that sought-after information to a retired high-ranking military man, who was a friend of his, than to someone he doesn't know.

In 1969 the Congressional Quarterly Service reported that as of 1960, the last year for which statitsics were made public, "more than 1,400 retired officers of the rank of major or higher were employed by defense contractors. The company employing the largest number was General Dynamics Corporation, then headed by former Secretary of the Army Frank Pace, which also received the largest defense orders in 1960. Despite a 1966 Executive Order prohibiting a retired officer from 'selling' or negotiating contracts with his former service, one industry source told Congressional Quarterly that 'at least 90 percent of the retired officers hired for top level positions by the defense contractors ignore that regulation.'" The order has turned out to be unenforceable.

Former Secretary of the Navy Dan Kimball was later president of the Aerojet General Corporation. Former Chief of Naval Operations Admiral Robert B. Carney later became chairman of the board of the Bath Iron Works and Shipbuilding Corporation. Both companies are defense contractors.

The chairman of the House Armed Services Committee is important because he has control of appropriations. While the late L. Mendel Rivers was chairman of that committee, a naval station, a shipyard, an air base, an army depot, a missile plant, and a mine warfare center were built in Charleston, South Carolina, part of his district.

When Ramsey Clark was appointed U.S. attorney general by President Johnson, his father, Justice Tom Clark, resigned from the U.S. Supreme Court to prevent a conflict of interest when the attorney general tried cases before the court. Such is not always the case. Thomas Hale Boggs, Jr., became a more effective lobbyist in Washington because his father was minority whip in the House and a late House majority leader. Boggs, Jr., is a lawyer with the Washington firm of

Patton, Blow, Verrill, Brand, and Boggs, registered lobbyists for the boating industry and other companies. With connections like Boggs, Jr., had, he couldn't help but be successful. Boggs, Sr., was also the ranking member of the Ways and Means Committee, the Joint Committee on Internal Revenue Taxation, the Joint Committee on Reduction of Federal Expenditures, and the Joint Economic Committee.

The First Amendment to the Constitution guarantees citizens the right to petition the government for redress of grievances, which is what lobbying is supposed to be about. If you have ever written a letter to your congressman expressing your opinion on any subject you have lobbied. The difference, however, between your letter and the way a professional lobbyist expresses his opinion is probably the backing of money by a lobbyist. However, even if what they do may be legally right, it is at times morally wrong and not in the best interest of the American people. There are many areas also, not entirely clear, because of many loopholes in current laws regulating lobbying, campaign contributions, and income of congressmen. (*Note:* Washington and Congress are specifically used as examples, but these situations, for the most part, hold true in most of the state legislatures.)

In the Ninety-first Congress seventy-six members of the House alone were lawyers. There is the "Tuesday-to-Thursday Club," in Washington, made up mostly of Eastern lawyer-congressmen who go home for long weekends to devote time in their law offices. There is also a "double-door policy" to circumvent the law that says lawyer-congressmen cannot be associated with firms doing business with the government. They print two sets of legal stationery, one of which is used for government-type cases and the other for non-government-related cases. Sometimes the congressman's name will appear on his law firm's stationery for its prestige value although he doesn't do any work.

The House Committee of Official Conduct in 1970 reported that at least forty-three members served concurrently as either directors or officers of financial institutions, usually banks or savings and loan associations in their home districts. At least fifty-two other House members did not hold such offices but did own stock in financial institutions. Of the ninety-five members involved, five were members of the House Banking and Currency Committee, which governs banking, and five others were on the House Ways and Means Committee, which controls tax relief affecting the financial industry and all tax policy. In what was a rare instance, Democrat Henry B. Gonzalez of Texas reported to the House Ethics Committee that a bank in his district offered him $14,000 in stock and a directorship, and he rejected both. It was rare, not because he was offered the stock and the directorship but because he admitted the offer.

The cost of political campaigns has skyrocketed in recent years. The 1964 political campaign cost $150 million, and the 1968 campaign cost jumped to $300 million. The increase in the number of primaries in recent years has caused campaign costs to increase greatly. Many candidates have had to discontinue a campaign at the primary level because of the inability to raise enough money to pay the high costs of campaigning. Until a candidate has the backing of his party, he has to look elsewhere for financial support. And even after millions are spent by a candidate, victory is not guaranteed. Senator George Aiken, Republican from Vermont, spent only $17.09 on his last reelection campaign. But this is a rare exception. Even in campaigns for minor local offices, for alderman for example, costs are often much higher.

Even if the payoff does not directly involve cash given to a congressman for his personal use, a "payoff" could include a campaign contribution, stock in a corporation (often in the name of a relative), giving a relative a good job in a company, sending the congressman on a trip (sometimes with his wife and children along), giving him a new car or other expensive gifts, giving his law firm a retainer, arranging a series of speaking engagements where the congressman would be nicely paid, or any number of other things.

A bill limiting campaign spending was passed by the Democratic-controlled Ninety-first Congress, but the bill was vetoed by President Nixon. Because Republicans have less trouble raising money than the Democrats, there was no point in giving the Democrats that kind of break.

The following are some reform measures that should be instituted to help discourage improper acts by public officials and those who run for election. Congressmen should divest themselves of all outside business interests, including stockholdings. Or else blind trust accounts should be set up. Dummy fund-raising committees for a candidate should be outlawed. The amount of money spent on campaigns should be further limited. Free television time should be made available to the major candidates as is done in England. Penalties for violations of campaign and lobbying laws should include jail sentences rather than just a fine and censure.

The Legislative Process

Ask not what your country can do for you, ask what you can do for your country.

PRESIDENT JOHN F. KENNEDY

Gifts of money and stock are occasionally used by lobbyists to persuade legislators to vote a certain way. Less than twenty-four hours after it had defeated a controversial quarter-horse harness track bill, the New York Assembly reversed itself on April 22, 1969, and approved the identical bill by a vote of seventy-nine to sixty-four, as eight assemblymen suddenly switched their votes from no and voted in the affirmative.

Then Assemblywoman Mary Anne Krupsak, now lieutenant governor, charged that stock in proposed quarter-horse tracks was offered to lawmakers in exchange for votes to legalize the sport. Ten months later, a lobbyist for a quarter-horse racing bill was charged in a perjury indictment with having made a series of attempts to bribe three assemblymen. The bill never saw the time of day in the Senate that year because of the bad publicity it attracted. According to rumors (the truth will never be known), the quarter-horse track lobbies spent at least $150,000 in their efforts on the bill.

There are 322 registered lobbyists, with at least another 300 unregistered lobbyists, in the New York state legislature. Many lobbyists don't bother to sign up because of the vague and unenforced laws that govern the lobbyists. There are lobbyists for industry, organized labor, trade groups, public school teachers, local governments, banks, insurance companies, railroads, organizations, and others. Present lobbyist laws, in most states, simply require the lobbyists to register but not to report how much money they spend and how. Many loopholes permit lobbyists to carry out their influence peddling more or less as they please. The public has a right to know how much money a lobbyist spends and where it goes, because money has been known to open the eyes and ears of many legislators. Legislators are supposed to represent all the people, and not only the special interest groups.

In 1974 the New York state legislature passed a bill that would have put teeth into state law regulating lobbyists, but Governor Wilson vetoed the bill. While the bill wasn't as tough as it should have been, it was better than no bill at all. As a result of Wilson's veto the lobbyists are as free as ever to spend their clients' money. Many felt that Wilson was gotten to by the lobbyists, and thus the reason for the veto.

Lobbyists serve a useful purpose to the legislators by providing them with information, some of which might not have been obtainable elsewhere. Lobbyists, in this respect, save the taxpayers some money, which might have been spent on research for certain bills. When the special interests "control" legislators, the general public interest is at a disadvantage.

In 1972 New York's two teacher unions spent nearly $750,000 in campaign contributions for candidates for the legislature. Many feel that when this kind of money is given out, you don't have to ask a favor in return. The legislators are obligated. In any case, a lobbyist will always find a receptive ear if he has donated an earlier campaign contribution to the legislator he wants to see. Lobbyists in Washington are not allowed on the floor of the House of Representatives or the Senate, but in New York State lobbyists are barred only from the Senate floor. By not barring lobbyists from the Assembly floor, it is possible for lobbyists to "influence" legislators even in the chamber.

It is estimated that about $20 million is spent annually on lobbying activities in New York State (the entire budget of the legislature is only $33 million). The amount includes the salaries and expenses paid to both registered and unregistered lobbyists, the wining and dining, the private parties, big public functions, the cost of bringing busloads of citizens to Albany to lobby for bills, campaign contributions, and the like.

According to records on file, and open to the public, in the secretary of state's office, 156 of the 322 registered lobbyists claimed they earned and spent more than $1.6 million on their activities. Other registered lobbyists didn't file any financial data, and very few of the lobbyists bothered to itemize their expenditures (one of those that did was Common Cause).

The biggest lobbyist in New York is the Albany law firm of De Graff, Foy, Conway and Holt-Harris (Holt-Harris is a Democratic traffic court justice in Albany), which earned more than $184,000 from 19 clients in 1973. The second largest lobbyist was former Republican Assembly Speaker Joseph Carlino, who earned more than $105,000 from eight clients. Former Assembly Majority Leader and State Republican Chairman Charles Schoeneck earned $67,714 representing 10 clients. An aide to former New York City Mayor Robert Wagner, Victor Condello, received $64,395 from 10 employers.

Among the larger groups who have lobbyists in New York State and the amount of money they reportedly spent in 1973 on such activities are: the State Civil Service Employees Association, $25,000; State Vending Association, $15,000; State Racing Association, $25,000; Transportation Workers of Greater New York, $20,000; Metropolitan New York Retail Merchants Association, $25,000; State Psychological Association, $25,000; Savings Banks Association, $8,333; State Wholesale Liquor Association, $13,750; Transportation Workers Union of

Greater New York Local 100, $20,000; Associated Industries of New York State, $25,405; and numerous others. Lobbyists often buy several tickets for partisan fund-raising and testimonial dinners, and usually give most of them away. The price per ticket, especially at Republican dinners, can run from $25 to $100 a ticket and higher. Sometimes a lobbying group, like the bankers, will buy several tables of tickets, with each table sitting 10. They are obligated to buy the tickets, many times at a cost of thousands of dollars, to promote goodwill. Some organizations, especially the unions, provide legislative candidates gratis with campaign buttons, brochures, and posters, which would ordinarily cost the candidates much money.

Legislators are often found wining and dining at the best nightspots and restaurants, with lobbyists picking up their checks. As one assemblyman put it, "A legislator can spend an entire session in Albany and never spend a dime to buy a meal." Hardly a day goes by when there isn't at least one breakfast, luncheon, dinner, or cocktail party sponsored by a lobbyist. The Empire State Chamber of Commerce meeting is the biggest function given by a lobbying group. It is held annually in the State Armory. More than 1,000 nonpaying legislators and their staffs attend the catered function, which costs in the thousands. Examples of the lobbyists expense accounts, in 1973, were: Consolidated Edison Co., $8,918; Sperry & Hutchinson Co., $6,276; State Bankers Association, $6,561; and the Chase Manhattan Bank, $6,881.

Lobbyists sometimes even arrange for prostitutes for legislators. One call girl in Albany estimated that she had "serviced" fifteen to twenty legislators in the last two years. The lobbyists sometimes ask call girls to appear at a party where legislators will be. A legislator can get lonely being as much as two hundred or so miles from his wife. One prostitute said most of her "Johns" come for "variety." Lobbyists will often spend much money to keep the legislators happy to help their cause. When State Senator Karen Burstein was first elected in 1972, she charged that female aides were nothing but sex kittens. That charge rocked a couple of marriages.

Lobbying in Massachusetts is done on about half the scale of New York. Nevertheless, much money is also spent. Insurance, labor, utilities, and banks are the biggest lobbies in Massachusetts. Among the larger groups who have lobbyists in this New England state and the approximate amount of money they reportedly spent in 1973 to protect their interests are: The John Hancock Mutual Life Insurance Company, $48,-000; the Massachusetts Port Authority, $39,962; Common Cause, one of the few to itemize their expenses, $30,415.74; Massachusetts Federation of Teachers of the AFL-CIO, $19,490; Associated Industries of Massachusetts, $20,000; the Charlestown Savings Bank, $15,154; Massachusetts Bankers Association, $10,000; Massachusetts Bar Association, $20,000; Massachusetts Blue Cross, Inc., $11,348; Massachusetts Blue

Shield, Inc., $11,700; Massachusetts Electric 'and Gas Association, $20,-000; AFL-CIO, $16,000; New England Telephone and Telegraph Company $19,500 (they got a rate increase that year); Massachusetts Mutual Life Insurance Company, $19,500; and the State Mutual Life Assurance Company of America, $20,000. Massachusetts has about 160 full-time and part-time lobbyists.

Five New York state assemblymen probably just thought they would have some fun during a visit to the Albany Medical Center Hospital in February, 1973. But their "fun" with a female technician during routine cardiovascular checkups led to newspaper headlines, a grand jury investigation, and an Assembly Ethics Committee report. The grand jury reported that two of the five acted in a "boisterous and obscene" manner. The legislators involved in this incident were never identified. Among other things, one asked the twenty-year-old technician if she was a virgin or had ever made love to an Italian, according to the grand jury report. The Assembly Ethics Committee did not do anything about the incident.

New York's Assembly established a public information office in 1973, but the way it was being run it was a waste of money because the people who worked there were not very knowledgeable about the legislature. A visit to the legislature, looking for information, may give one the impression that he is getting the runaround from person to person. But more often than not the runaround occurs because the employees are not very knowledgeable and/or are lazy rather than because they are not willing to give the information out.

A visitor to the legislature will also find that it is often difficult to find legislators in their legislative offices. This is not always because they are in the Assembly or Senate chamber or on other legislative business but because they are often busy looking after their own businesses. One morning before the end of the 1974 session, for example, one secretary said that the assemblyman was at his private law office and would not be at his legislative office until that afternoon.

Legislators are in Albany for only three or four days a week while the legislature is in session. The legislators rarely spend a normal eight-hour day in session. One exception was the last day in the 1974 session, May 16, when in an effort to finish their business before Friday they had a marathon 21-hour session. (There is no law requiring the lawmakers to complete their business by a certain date.) Actually the legislature is in session no more than about four hours a day. Is it too much to expect a full day's work from them?

Until the end of each session the legislature rarely does much. Most of the legislation is passed within the last few weeks, which is called logjamming. The legislators would not find it necessary to cram most of their work within the last few weeks if they worked at a continuous pace throughout the entire session. Many people feel that the legislature should be in session twelve months a year, but they usually have no longer than a five- or six-month session. Ironically at the end of each session they rush for adjournment. Our founding fathers expected that checks and balances, to prevent one branch of government from getting too powerful, would take place all the time. Anything short of a continuous basis appears to be unconstitutional. The fewer days that the legislature is in session, the less damage can be done. This is the reason why some state constitutions limit legislative sessions. Legislatures get around this by stopping the clock. The constitutionality of this procedure is questionable because the Minnesota Supreme Court has ruled it unconstitutional.

It is noteworthy to add that many of the employees at the legislature do very little work, if any, and during the day spend much time just conversing with their fellow employees over coffee or talk on the phone with friends. There is little doubt that a corporation like IBM, AT&T, or GM would go bankrupt if it were run like the legislature. It doesn't surprise many that from 1958 to 1974, the Rockefeller-Wilson years, the cost of government services showed an increase of 10.8 percent in New York State, while the average annual cost of groceries increased 4.9 percent. There are many jobs in the legislature that could be abolished, but in order to supply patronage they are not eliminated. A job in the legislature is often sought by party workers because of the good hours, vacations, fringe benefits, and good salaries. It is a rare occasion that jobs which could be used for patronage are eliminated, because the victor looks for all the spoils he can get.

Some people feel that the best way to obtain their goal of higher office is to use the legislature as a stepping-stone, and run for the assembly. It is not unusual for a former legislator to be appointed to a judgeship or a high-paying state job by the governor as payment for his help to the governor while he served in the legislature. In 1973 the legislature in New York approved a hundred new judgeships to be appointed by the governor to deal with the state's tough new drug law. This was highly criticized because the judgeships were costly and called unnecessary.

Nelson Rockefeller, while he was New York's governor, called New York's legislature "the most responsive in the nation," and he was right because the then Republican-controlled legislature was responsive to him. Because the majority leadership was the same party (Republican) as Governor Rockefeller and his successor, Malcolm Wilson, the two government branches had a close working relationship. For example, under the New York State Constitution, once the legislature has adjourned, it cannot call itself back into session; only the governor can, and then he has the final say on the matters to be considered. But if the legislature recesses, it can call itself back into session, for example, thirty days after the end of the spring session, to see if it cares to override any of the governor's vetoes. However, the relationship between the majority leadership, which controls the legislature, and the governor wouldn't permit a recess instead of an adjournment in order to have a veto session.

If most of the legislation can be crammed into the end of the session, then most bills passed in the session become "thirty-day bills" (those on the governor's desk when the session adjourns), and thus the legislature is dead for the year when he signs or vetoes them. In the 1972 session, 1,333 bills were sent to the governor. There were eight vetoes during the session, and 288 vetoes after the session ended for the year. One needed reform in the legislature is a mandatory legislative session, but until there is a change in the makeup of the legislature, such a change is not likely.

It pays to be a legislator. In 1974 the legislators in New York State gave themselves a 60 percent increase in salary despite the 5.5 percent to which ordinary citizens were limited at the time it was voted. The legislators' salaries were boosted from $15,000 to $23,500. They also get $40 per day for expenses while on official business in Albany and other areas outside of New York City. In New York City they get $50 for expenses. In addition, the legislators occasionally vote themselves "lulus," or extra pay for additional work. It is highly questionable whether they are entitled to this money. These lulus in the assembly usually go to committee chairmen, subcommittee chairmen, and ranking minority members of committees. The Assembly approved "lulus" for 76 of its 150 members, and the Senate approved 63 lulus for its 60 members, one for all and two for two members. The total cost of the lulus was $709,000. Thus the legislature annually costs taxpayers in New York State more than $33 million, and the price goes up every year. The printing bill alone for the legislature runs more than $2.5 million.

Legislators are given racetrack passes, gift calendars and diaries, honorary membership cards to various organizations (one of which is the Patrolmen's Benevolent Association), and invitations to social events. The Automobile Club of New York in 1974 gave free VIP memberships (worth $25) to 141 legislators from the New York metropolitan region.

More than one-third of New York's 210 legislators had banking ties in 1974. Also, 73 lawmakers owned bank stock, were bank directors or trustees, handled legal affairs for banks, or had collected campaign contributions from the banking industry. Ranking committee members are the most courted because they are in a better position to further the banks' cause. Banks are the most powerful lobby in New York State. The legislature may determine the amount of interest banks may charge, how much interest they must pay depositors, and other matters involving banks. It is no secret that a capitol friend is useful to have, and legislators most often welcome the friendship of the lobbyists.

Patronage in the legislature is plentiful, and in a time when many companies are not increasing their payrolls and even laying off many employees, the New York state legislature's payroll has increased. The biweekly payroll of the Assembly increased from $308,053 (1,175 employees) in 1973 to $379,360 (1,297 employees) in 1974. In the Senate the biweekly payroll increased from $295,000 (904 employees) in 1973 to $328,372 (1,024 employees) in 1974. Many of these jobs require little if any work and some of these jobs are no-show, where the job-holders just show up to pick up their checks once every two weeks.

★ 11 ★

Corruption

There is no kind of dishonesty into which otherwise good people more easily and frequently fall than that of defrauding the government.

BENJAMIN FRANKLIN

The Eleventh Commandment could very well be "Thou Shall Not Be Corrupt." People must have certain principles, ethics and morals. We must not yield to temptation. Nobody, neither rich nor poor, black nor white, is excluded.

Moses taught his people not to live by bread alone. He taught them to live by the Ten Commandments, a set of guidelines to live by. When Moses went up Mount Sinai to receive the Commandments his people corrupted themselves. They were impatient (they thought Moses would not return because he was gone more than forty days), and corrupted themselves in pursuit of their greed. However, those who lost faith and corrupted themselves were finally punished. This was almost six thousand years ago. You would think people would have learned their lesson. Karl Marx was right when he said history repeats itself, because there has been a trail of corruption since the birth of mankind.

Profiting from the government in this country goes back to the eighteenth century, when Robert Morris, "the financier of the revolution," sold flour to the French at a profit of 50 percent. Morris, a Philadelphia merchant, had received the first contract for the importation of arms, and he had been guaranteed a profit of 12,000 British pounds. In 1779 Thomas Paine accused Morris of using a position of public trust for private gain. Morris founded the Bank of North America in Philadelphia, and because of his financial juggling he served three years in prison.

The first time members of Congress profited on advance information was in 1790, just before Secretary of the Treasury Hamilton was to announce that he had a plan for redeeming at par value bonds that were issued during the war and had since depreciated. The almost worthless Continental and state bonds could be bought at 5 cents on the dollar or less, and nearly $70,000,000 (face value) was outstanding. Hamilton told some friends about his plan, and about 16 of the 26 senators and 29 out of the 64 members of the House, as well as some informed merchants, were able to "speculate" with the advance knowledge that they could easily make 10 to 20 times their investment in a short time. The "speculators" offered to take "worthless" paper off poor men's hands for as much as 5 cents on the dollar.[113]

Hamilton's opponent, Thomas Jefferson, was annoyed at this, but there wasn't much he could do because so many members of Congress profited on their inside information. Although this was the first time in this country something like this had happened, it wasn't by any means the last. Undoubtedly, it will continue long after you read this book.

Jefferson also accused Timothy Pickering, the secretary of war, of having been $500,000 short in his government accounts. This charge of corruption was difficult to prove because a mysterious fire destroyed some Treasury Department records.[114]

Insiders have made money on Wall Street by having advance knowledge of corporation earnings. Although it is illegal to profit by using such information it is done quite often. Sometimes corporation executives anticipating poor earnings and a stock decline will sell their stock at a higher price, and vice versa.

After the Civil War was a period of history known as the "age of exploitation." From the 1850s to the 1870s miners exploited our natural resources in search of gold and silver. Whenever anyone made a "strike" men from all over came to the site because of rumors. A few men found wealth but most were disappointed. Towns sprang up overnight. Storekeepers charged high prices, and claims holders "salted" worthless properties with nuggets in order to swindle gullible investors.

The Homestead Act, passed by Congress in 1862, gave land away free to those who went West. Wealthy speculators hired men to stake out claims because, while the land was given away free, each person's share was supposed to be limited.

In an effort to encourage railroads to expand, the Pacific Railroad Act of 1862 gave the Union Pacific and Central Pacific railroads five square miles of public land on each side of their right of way for each mile of track laid.

The Union Pacific railroad was built by the Credit Mobilier, a construction company that made exorbitant profits. When Congress threatened to investigate the railroad in 1868, Oakes Ames, a stockholder who was also a member of Congress, sold key congressmen and government officials more than three hundred shares of Credit Mobilier stock at a price far below its real value. Ames said these shares were placed "where they will do the most good." He added, "I have found there is no difficulty in inducing men to look after their own property." When these transactions were exposed, the House of Representatives merely censured Ames. The railroads also spent thousands of dollars for legal expenses that were really bribes.

Many scandals occurred during the Harding administration. Harding, a Republican, appointed some corrupt friends from his home state. They were known as the "Ohio Gang." Charles R. Forbes of the Veterans Bureau stole millions of dollars appropriated for the construction of hospitals. When exposed, he fled to Europe and resigned. Forbes later returned and was sentenced to two years in prison. Other Harding appointees were also exposed. Some were sent to jail and a couple committed suicide.

The worst of the Harding scandals involved Secretary of the Interior Albert B. Fall, a former senator. In 1921 Fall leased the Elk Hills oil reserve in California to Edward L. Doheny's Pan-American Petroleum Company, and the Teapot Dome oil reserve to Harry F. Sinclair's Mammoth Oil Company. In 1923 a Senate investigation disclosed that Fall received $100,000 from Doheny and $300,000 from Sinclair. As a result Fall was fined $100,000 and given a year in prison for accepting a bribe. The Supreme Court revoked the leases in 1927. Harding's attorney general, Harry M. Daugherty, was charged but not convicted of a fraud conspiracy to release seized assets from World War I.

Corruption also flourished in the Grant administration. The Whiskey Ring affair implicated Grant's private secretary, General Orville E. Babcock, and cost the government millions in tax revenue. Babcock and General John A. McDonald, supervisor of internal revenue, made arrangements with a group of distillers for the evasion of the tax on spirits. For these special and illegal arrangements, Babcock and McDonald became quite wealthy. Another ring, the Star Route gang, whose members included federal officials and members of Congress, was caught defrauding the government in connection with the carriage of mails. The mismanagement by Secretary of War William W. Belknap was exposed when he sold the store at Fort Sill.

Presidents Grant and Harding were not involved in the corrupt deals that took place during their administrations. They were gullible and their friends used their Presidential friendships to advance their own interests.

When Lincoln Steffens wrote *The Shame of the Cities* in 1904 he said, "The corruption of St. Louis came from the top"; the best citizens, the merchants and big financiers all profited from the corruption in the city.[115] Steffens said that it was common practice to bribe a legislator. If you wanted a bill passed, you had to pay. Also if you wanted a bill defeated, you had to pay. Men spent much money in order to get elected to the assembly. But it was worth it because after they took office they became quite rich through boodling. Building permits and city contracts were obtained through payoffs.

Graft took place in the police department, inspectional services, and with public contracts. The same happens today. Bookmakers and prostitutes stay in business by paying off the police. Also police are bribed so that they don't give out parking tickets. Building inspectors, fire inspectors, health, and electrical inspectors also get bribed for overlooking something.

Steffens observed how the streetcar lines and gas companies corrupted the governments of most of our large cities. The utilities have so much power that they are able to often regulate their supposed regulators.

Government subsidies to private groups are a source of corruption, whether it be a subsidy for mining companies, farmers, ship and airline companies, magazines and newspapers, or railroads. Is it right for the government to pay farmers millions of dollars not to plant crops when a great number of people go hungry in this country and all over the world? These subsidies are paid not only to poor farmers but to rich farmers also. The government even pays farmers not to distribute their crops. After Nixon received a contribution from the milk dealers the government permitted a three cents rise per quart in the price of milk.

About forty years before Hubert Humphrey became a reform mayor of Minneapolis (1945), that city had as its mayor a medical doctor ("Doc" Albert Ames). "Doc" Ames encouraged the police corruption that swept the city. After all, he received the biggest payoffs. The higher the office holder was, the more money you had to pay to bribe him.

In Minneapolis there were slot machines all over the city, gambling was open, prostitution continued as long as payoffs were made, bars were allowed to stay open after-hours if they paid for protection, and there was corruption in the police department. Police officers were burglarizing stores. All this continued in the open, and no attempt was made to keep anything covered up. Even if a few citizens spoke up against what was going on, they wouldn't be heard. A similar situation occurred in Albany as well as numerous other cities. Criminals came to Minneapolis from other cities because of the lawlessness. As if that wasn't enough, even the thieves in the Minneapolis jail were put on the streets again for the same purpose they were originally sent to jail.

Because there is so much to share in New York City, it is impossible to correctly estimate the amount of graft. Steffens said, "No Tammany man knows it all. Police friends of mine say that the Tammany leaders never knew how rich police corruption was till the Lexow committee exposed it, and that the politicians who had been content with small presents, contributions, and influence did not butt in for their share till they saw by the testimony of frightened police grafters that the department was worth from four to five million a year."[116]

The Buildings Department in New York City, as in other cities, controls much graft because there is always construction in the city. The Buildings Department is supposed to enforce strict building codes. In order to use cheaper substandard materials and not adhere to the strict codes, the architect and builders found it necessary to pay off the Buildings Department in order to save time and money.

Landlords of rent-controlled buildings find it beneficial to pay off officials of the Rent Control Boards. Suppose, for example, a family is paying $150 dollars a month rent for a rent-controlled apartment they obtained several years ago; the landlord cannot raise their rent unless that family moves. Therefore the landlord is apt to do whatever he can to get the family to move because he could raise the rent to $200 a month or more. The Rent Control Board helps the landlord by cooperating in his tactics. Why should the head of the Rent Control Board go against the landlord when the landlord is giving him money under the table to do otherwise?

The situation that occurred in the popular movie *Walking Tall* is not unique to Tennessee, where the movie, based on a true story, took place. The sheriff tried to clean up his town and found it wasn't easy. When he would manage to arrest criminals for gambling, prostitution, bootleg whiskey, and murder, the judge would let them off easy. The judge even tipped off those who would be raided. The criminals paid off the judges and legislators. They even tried to pay off the sheriff, but when he would not accept their bribes, they killed his wife and tried to kill him. It is a shameful story and one that could still be duplicated today. Bribery and crime are not unique to any one time or location.

It is no secret that the Mafia has bought certain judges, because in a few instances such practices have been exposed. When Michael Raymond, an admitted stock manipulator, testified before the Senate Permanent Investigations Subcommittee he said that Tommy Gamindorra, a lieutenant in the Joseph Colombo "family," told him that he didn't have to worry if he was ever arrested in Brooklyn because they (the Mafia) had judges on their payroll.

After he was accused of bribery, New York Supreme Court Justice Schweitzer retired from the bench in 1972. Raymond testified that he had paid $25,000 to Justice Schweitzer to give him a light sentence after he was indicted for grand larceny in a stock manipulation case in 1955. However, there undoubtedly have been instances that have not been revealed in the past and will not be revealed in the future. Judges are only human and subject to the same temptations as everyone else. Most judges are not corrupt or on the take. But unfortunately there are a few bad apples in every barrel.

Nathan Voloshen was accused of fixing criminal cases with judges and parole officials. One example occurred when a doctor gave Voloshen $300,000 to fix his income-tax evasion case before the doctor was given a suspended jail sentence and fined $15,000. Voloshen once offered *Life* magazine $50,000 to drop a story exposing him. The now-defunct magazine did not accept and ran the article.

Bribes have been paid for setting low bail, giving light prison sentences and fines, giving suspended sentences, fixing traffic tickets, accepting partial payment of fines on parking tickets, reducing the amount of taxes to be paid the government, reducing speeding and drunken driving to lesser offenses, and for being lenient. This does not, in any manner, mean that just because a judge gives a light sentence or was lenient he was being paid off. It simply means that these are some of the things that have been exposed.

Corrupt judges have been known to embezzle fines and various fees (such as marriage license fees) that should have been turned over to the government. Unauthorized loans have been made from estates. Payoffs have been made by bail bondsmen, litigants, and lawyers.

A county judge, Glenn J. Sharpe, of Bryan County, Oklahoma, was removed from office because he had improperly received over $13,000 for issuing waiver orders of blood tests, the three-day waiting period, and the state's age requirements for marriage from January 11, 1965, to July 26, 1967.

Judge Otto Kerner of the U.S. Court of Appeals had an outstanding reputation until 1973, when he was sentenced to three years in prison and fined $50,000 in a racetrack stock bribery scheme. Based on the recommendation of the Daley machine, President Truman appointed Kerner, a Democrat, U.S. attorney for the Northern District of Illinois in 1947. In 1954 he became a county judge and in 1960 he was elected governor of Illinois. He was reelected governor in 1964, and in 1967 he was appointed by President Johnson to head his National Advisory Commission on Civil Disorders, popularly known as the Kerner Commission, which investigated riots across the country. President Johnson appointed Kerner in 1968 to serve on the U.S. Court of Appeals.

On December 15, 1971, Judge Kerner and three former Illinois officials were indicted. The judge was charged with accepting bribes (stock) in exchange for seeing that certain racetrack owners received favorable treatment in the assignment of racing dates. Kerner was also accused of lying to a federal grand jury when he testified that he never discussed the awarding of racing dates with members of the Illinois Racing Commission. He was further charged with omitting $147,000 from his 1966 federal tax return, which was the amount he profited by from the stock. Under the maximum punishment, Judge Kerner could have been sentenced to prison for eighty-three years and fined $93,000. Although his sentence was significantly less, the disgrace of being indicted and found guilty was a heavy penalty to pay. It was suggested that Kerner's indictment was politically motivated because the U.S. attorney, James Thompson, was a Republican who was considered as a candidate for mayor of Chicago. In any event, the fact remains that Kerner was wrong. Kerner was paroled from prison, in 1975, after serving part of his sentence, because of poor health.

Thomas J. Mackell, the former Queens district attorney, was found guilty in 1974 of blocking the prosecution of a $4.4 million fast-money scheme in which hundreds of Queens residents and members of his staff had invested money. Mackell, a former detective and state senator, was the first district attorney in the city's history to be indicted, tried, and convicted on state charges for crimes committed while in office. His conviction was reversed by a state appeals court in 1975 on the ground of insufficient evidence.

THE WATERGATE SCANDAL

He that lies with the dogs, riseth with fleas.

The Watergate scandal, during the Presidential administration of Richard Nixon, was the biggest political scandal ever in United States history. The Nixon administration's problems came from its illegal and improper activities. Mr. Nixon's associates were not common criminals who had prison records. They were good family men who were religious, dedicated, and hard-working. The problem was that they were obsessed in their drive for power so much that they destroyed whatever power they had to begin with. They were probably not more corrupt than some of their predecessors. They did not steal any money. But because of their actions they did manage to damage the Presidency, and, at the time, the country suffered.

The heavy toll of Watergate included a President, a Vice-President, two attorneys general, a secretary of the treasury, a secretary of commerce, and several top White House aides and Nixon campaign officials. A total of more than fifty men were convicted or pleaded guilty. Terms in prison ranged from thirty days to twenty years, and fines ranged from $100 to $40,000. In addition, close to twenty corporations were fined from $500 to $35,000.

The Nixon men got mixed up in their aims and how to achieve them. They believed the end justifies the means, and weren't concerned about the effect of the means they used. They felt that anything was fair game. They failed to realize, however, that they weren't fighting a war—just trying to win an election. Even during wartime nations are limited in what they can and cannot do!

Criticism of Watergate, related activities, and the coverup even came from a few of Nixon's cabinet members. Nixon's attorney general, William B. Saxbe, a former U.S. senator from Ohio, said before President Nixon nominated him that Nixon's handling of Watergate was like "the man who plays piano in a whorehouse and says he doesn't know what's going on upstairs."

The Nixon managers realized, in early 1972, when Watergate was planned, that Nixon might not be reelected. Nixon's ratings in the Gallup Poll were low and the economy was not in good shape. There was a withdrawal of troops in progress, but Americans were still being killed and we were still actively involved in Vietnam. In addition, they were afraid of tactics like mugging, demonstrations, and kidnappings, which the McGovern people might have been planning. After all, a lot of radicals were believed to have supported McGovern and Nixon's men felt that anything was possible. The total picture was not as good as they had hoped it would be. This picture caused the Nixon men to panic. They knew that something had to be done if they were to win the election. They could neither strengthen the economy nor end the war in Vietnam within a short time. Being frustrated, they felt that their only alternative was to plan Watergate so that their position would be enhanced. We must remember that the Nixon men did not like dealing with uncertainties. They felt that Watergate was the answer to solve their frustration, fears, and suspicion. Looking back after the election, we can see that the bugging of the Democratic headquarters did not have a noticeable effect upon the election. Actually, it appears now that the effort to plan and carry out Watergate was a waste, to say the least.

The Nixon bund tried to maximize their power position by manipulating the Constitution to their advantage. They claimed privileges (executive privilege, impoundment of funds, executive orders and agreements) to extents greater than ever before. They thought they were above the law, could ignore subpoenas and court orders, could obstruct justice, destroy evidence, commit perjury, dismiss prosecutors (e.g., Cox), and bribe judges (e.g., offering the Ellsberg judge the directorship of the FBI). They attempted to use government agencies (the FBI, the CIA, and the Internal Revenue Service) to complete their partisan objectives.

U.S. Supreme Court Justice Louis D. Brandeis said in 1927, "Decency, security and liberty alike demand that government officials shall be subjected to the same rules of conduct that are commands to the citizen. In a government of laws, existence of the government will be imperiled if it fails to observe the law scrupulously. Our government is the potent, and omnipresent teacher. For good or for ill, it teaches the whole people by its example. Crime is contagious."

Justice Brandeis continued: "If the government becomes a law-breaker, it breeds contempt for law; it invites anarchy. To declare that in the administration of the criminal law the end justifies the means—to declare that the government may commit crimes in order to secure the conviction of a private citizen—would bring terrible retribution."[117]

The words spoken by the Justice are words to remember. If one understands them, he will realize the possible harm of the illegal acts that took place during the Nixon administration. We are a nation of laws, not men, and fortunately the law has prevailed over Watergate.

Not only did the Republicans suffer from Watergate, but in Nassau County, Long Island, New York, many important figures in Republican politics were indicted in 1973 and 1974. Congressman Angelo D.

Roncallo and four Oyster Bay town officials were indicted on charges of extorting political contributions from a Long Island contractor. Roncallo was later found innocent but was defeated in his reelection attempt in 1974.

Another case involved two other leading Nassau Republicans, District Attorney William Cahn and Assemblyman Joseph Margiotta, the powerful Nassau GOP chairman. The acting U.S. attorney for the Eastern District of New York investigated allegations that Margiotta ordered Cahn to sway a grand jury that had indicted three Republicans in an alleged parking meter kickback scandal but nothing resulted from that investigation.

The biggest blow to the Republicans in New York came when then Assembly Speaker Perry Duryea, then Assembly Majority Leader John Kingston, and Assemblyman Alfred Delhi (all Republicans) were indicted for participation in a vote-siphoning scheme. They were charged in December, 1973, with violations of the state's election law, in the creation and financing of what was called the Action Committee of the Liberal Party. The purpose of the operation, it was charged, was to draw votes away from Democratic candidates for the Assembly. The sections of the Election Law that applied to the case were declared unconstitutional by a State Supreme Court Justice. Therefore the charges were dropped against the three men. Acting U.S. Attorney Edward Boyd in Brooklyn had reportedly looked into possible mail fraud by the three Republicans in connection with the vote-siphoning scheme but nothing resulted from that investigation. Even though the charges were dropped, Duryea lost any hopes of being nominated for governor in 1974 instead of Governor Wilson, because of the publicity the case received.

On October 10, 1973, Vice-President Spiro T. Agnew resigned and pleaded no contest to a charge of cheating the government of $13,551.47 on his federal income-tax payment for 1967, his first year as governor of Maryland. The U.S. attorney general, Elliot L. Richardson, said the government's evidence against Agnew went beyond that, but to avoid a lengthy trial, a nominal plea was accepted. A plea of no contest, while not an admission of guilt, subjects a defendant to a conviction on the charge. Agnew's plea ended sixty-five days of insisting on his innocence and saying that he would not resign even if indicted. Agnew was fined $10,000 and given three years' probation. His resignation was the first time in the nation's history that the Vice-President resigned because of criminal charges.

The government stated that Agnew received payoffs while he served as executive of Baltimore County, governor of Maryland, and Vice-President. Agnew asked for and accepted cash payments totaling more than $100,000, according to the government. The payments were made in return for engineering contracts with the state of Maryland. Agnew was also disbarred. He had previously denounced as "damnable lies" allegations that he had taken money under the table.

Bribes and payoffs have been a "way of life" to do business. There have been some occasions when corruption was exposed and the violators were brought to justice. More often than not, however, corruption usually continues unnoticed. New Jersey has had its share of corruption. In one instance, Paul J. Sherwin, a former New Jersey secretary of state, was convicted in 1972 of trying to rig a $600,000 road contract in return for a $10,000 contribution to the New Jersey Republican Finance Committee. He was given a one- to two-year prison sentence.

Former U.S. Representative Bertram L. Podell of Brooklyn, New York, pleaded guilty in October, 1974, to conspiracy and conflict of interest in accepting $41,350 to help a Florida airline. He was sentenced to six months in prison. If the people who make the laws can't obey them, whom can we expect to?

Just three days after leaving office in January, 1975, the former Governor of Oklahoma, David Hall, was indicted for conspiring to bribe the Oklahoma secretary of state to use his influence, as chairman of the board administering state retirement funds, to invest $10 million in a company. Hall was found guilty.

Crime in city hall, not crime in the streets, has occasionally been a loud campaign cry. In 1973, municipal corruption was a campaign issue in six big cities in New York State. There have been many other instances when public officials have been in "hot water" because of wrongdoings by them. Undoubtedly, corruption will continue, and public scrutiny is needed to attempt to discourage it.

Campaigning

America has the best politicians money can buy.
WILL ROGERS

We have seen in preceding chapters that candidates are often selected by bosses behind closed doors and that nominating conventions are occasionally the "window dressing" of a democracy. We have also seen how powerful a political organization can be. Based on these circumstances, one may ask if it is worth it to campaign against the machine? What will your chances be? How will you conduct your campaign? How will you raise the necessary money for advertising, setting up a campaign office, placing posters and printing booklets? The answers to these and other questions about campaigning will now be discussed. However, one must have the drive and determination to carry out a successful campaign. It is not an easy task, but then again, it is a task that has to be done to make the government most effective. As Adam Smith, the famous economist, said, competition is the invisible hand to keep prices in line. In this case, competition is healthy to keep our elected officials in line. But the question remains—how to fight the machine?

First of all a political machine has hundreds of dedicated workers (from committeemen to ward leaders to government employees) at its disposal to help during the campaign and on election day. While it isn't right for a government employee to campaign while he is on the government payroll, such abuses occur frequently. Many legislators and congressmen campaign while the legislature and/or Congress is in session. During the 1974 campaign, for example, Congressman Hugh Carey and State Senator Mary Anne Krupsak both had very poor attendance records in the legislative branches to which they belonged. And even though their opponents tried to make their absenteeism a campaign issue, it didn't seem to bother the voters much, because they were both victorious. On the other side, while Malcolm Wilson was lieutenant governor he made approximately $500,000 from his law practice. By the way, the lieutenant governor's position is supposed to be a full-time one.

You should attempt to get the support of the ticket splitters as the committee to reelect Nixon did in the 1972 campaign. They encouraged Democrats, through convert John Connally, to vote for Nixon but not for other Republicans. This was a good campaign strategy, because many Democrats did not like McGovern. After all, the real purpose of a campaign is to get the "swing voter" and the "ticket splitter" to change his mind. Ticket splitting, as compared with voting the party line, is done by many voters, although not too long ago it was an exception. A Gallup Poll showed that 60 percent of the voters split their tickets in 1972.

A large volunteer, grassroots campaign force has to be organized to compensate for the numerous workers the machine has. The larger the force organized the better. Whereas it is easier for an organization candidate or an incumbent to attract volunteers, if you're a likable person and bring out the right issues, you should be able to organize an adequate staff. It's better to have a few dedicated workers than to have twice as many volunteers who aren't helpful. But remember, volunteers aren't paid, and whatever they do for you, you should be appreciative.

Once elected a candidate running for reelection has a great advantage as an incumbent. First, the incumbent is able to get more publicity in the news media than his opponent. More publicity helps to improve name recognition. While someone who is running for office for the first time has to call a press conference and hope that the press attends, in order to get publicity, an incumbent often has a captive press. Because of the high cost of political advertising, it is wise to have regular news conferences and send press releases to the media. A good relationship with the press is very important. Coffee and doughnuts or other refreshments after a news conference could prove to be a good investment. However, don't get them so drunk that they forget to write a story. While the refreshments might cost $10 or $15 or so, you could get several hundred dollars worth of advertising for free just from one news conference.

The best time to have a conference is sometime in the late morning, around eleven. The wire services should be notified, in addition to the local press, for a candidate for state or national office. Airport press conferences are the most difficult to plan because of planes occasionally being late. No one likes to wait around. The press conference should always begin on time. When calling a press conference, make sure you have something newsworthy to say so that the media will look forward to future conferences rather than to dread attending another boring one.

Posters and bumper stickers help to improve name recognition, and both are better than campaign pins. Pins are seldom worn after they are distributed. A person is more likely to put a bumper sticker on his car than wear a pin. Put posters in store windows. Many of these campaign items will complement your campaign nicely, but if you can't afford "luxuries" don't feel that your efforts will not be successful. Try to get printing and rent free or at a discount. Use less expensive campaign items (such as paper posters instead of cardboard ones). If you can afford it, give away pens, pencils, matches with your name, office, and slogan imprinted. The thought will be appreciated and it will help voters to remember you.

A candidate who is a hard campaigner will stand out. Attend public and private functions, ring doorbells, and be outgoing. Campaigning is not easy; it is a full-time job that begins early in the morning and ends late at night. It's not unusual for a candidate to have a schedule similar to the following: 7:30-8:30 A.M.: Greet workers at a local factory. 9:30 A.M.: At campaign office. 11:00 A.M.: Press conference. 12:30: Attend a luncheon and give a speech. 2:00 P.M.: Greet people on main streets. 6:00-7:00 P.M.: Ring doorbells. 7:00 to 12:00 P.M.: Attend dinners, clambakes, fairs, meetings, debates, visit bowling alleys. Campaigning requires many sacrifices from your family and your normal job. It is something that requires total effort on your part.

Don't take your election for granted. In the past, at the height of bossism, elections were often guaranteed, but such is rarely the case today. Don't feel you don't have to campaign. Howard Samuels, when he ran in the 1974 primary in New York State, made the fatal mistake of not trying as hard as he should have in the final days before the primary. A successful candidate takes nothing for granted.

Congressmen and senators send newsletters to voters at government expense, and while the letters may be viewed as campaign paraphernalia, they are sent out at no cost to the congressmen. This privilege is occasionally questioned, but it ends up just being another advantage of the incumbent.

Advertising by political candidates is big business today. Candidates recognize the value of television advertising, and therefore devote a substantial part of their campaign budget to it. The closer you get to election day, the more political television commercials you will see. Hugh Carey won the 1974 primary largely because of his television blitz prior to primary day. It was an expensive proposition for Carey, but without it, it is doubtful if he would have won.

Television stations, in their editorials and news commentaries, criticize the large amount of money spent on campaigns annually. In New York State, however, there is only one television station that gives commercials to candidates free of charge. It is WAST of Albany. In 1974, WAST gave candidates about $100,000 worth of free time. Unfortunately, more stations do not have a similar policy. A 30-second spot on local television costs: in the morning, about $60; in the afternoon, about $100; in the early evening, about $175; and in the prime time, about $600.

While television advertising is very expensive, extensive advertising can help turn an unknown person into a well-known candidate. Candidates also advertise a lot in newspapers. These rates are also high. For example, a full page in the *New York Times* costs about $8,000. Rates in smaller newspapers, although somewhat lower, are nevertheless costly. Candidates sometimes find it beneficial to rent billboards. Rates vary depending on location, but $100 a billboard per month is about what you would have to spend. The more billboards you rent, the better your name recognition.

Radio advertising is also expensive, but it is a good medium for reaching the public. It costs about $11 for a 30-second spot on the radio. Rates are sometimes higher, but this depends on the station and the time the spot is aired. In order for radio spots to be effective, it is necessary to have them played at least six times a day for at least three weeks before an election. The more times played the better. Some candidates make the mistake of running all their ads during the last week of the campaign. While the concentration of ads should be the greatest during the last week, ads should be placed, if financially possible, long before that on a regular basis.

Even for candidates for county office, it is not unusual to find $12,-000-plus allocated just for television. Candidates for statewide office find they have to spend several times that figure to get minimum coverage. Quite often candidates spend more to get elected than they would be paid once in office. Raising money is a big problem for many candidates. Ramsey Clark in his bid for the U.S. Senate in New York in 1974 was able to raise a large amount of money, more than $200,000. He said he would not accept contributions of more than $100. Instead of depending on a small number of large contributors, he raised his money by getting a large number of small contributions.

Campaigning is very expensive, but it is important to realize that money isn't the only factor in winning an election. Numerous candidates have lost elections even though they spent more money than their opponents during the campaign. The successful candidate takes nothing for granted. Even incumbents occasionally forget that they have to be reelected. That's when they run into trouble. It is important to be prepared and alert to the problems that the voters are concerned with, the issues. Once the basic campaign structure is organized, commercials are made, and the campaign is rolling, it is up to the candidate to present his case to the voters.

Political parties use various fund-raising devices to get money. Money has been an increasing factor in recent years in deciding who will win the election. While it is detrimental for a candidate to have to rely on large contributions, often a candidate must get large contributions if he is to continue his campaign at all. But in order to have an effective campaign much money is needed. We have seen what happened to the Republicans with Watergate. If the Republicans had not needed so much money to reelect Nixon Watergate might never have occurred. In any case it is important for both Democrats and Republicans to learn a lesson from Watergate. We must limit campaign spending and how much an individual can contribute to someone's campaign fund.

Dinners are held to raise money. These dinners, where the candidates appear, range anywhere from $25 to $5,000 a plate. There are fund-raising telethons, like the one held during the 1972 Democratic National Convention with party leaders and leading performers in attendance answering telephones. A direct mail program can go to millions of citizens, not only the wealthy. The Democrats have the Sponsors Club with more than 800 members; each contributes at least a thousand dollars. During the Kennedy and Johnson administrations it was known as the President's Club.

Income for the party comes from (1) dues to political clubs or organizations; (2) sale of tickets to dinners, clambakes, or dances (committeemen are expected to sell tickets); (3) fund-raising activities such as raffles and card parties; (4) renting the clubhouse hall for an evening; (5) contributions from businessmen, city employees, and people who benefited from the party through favors and jobs (it is impossible to say how much money is actually raised this way and from payoffs); (6) ads in party publications and programs (it may be bad for business if a businessman doesn't buy an ad; sometimes an ad will say "Compliments from a Friend").

Expenses of the party are (1) rent for clubhouse or party headquarters; (2) campaign expenses—vote buying, buttons, stickers, posters, billboards, television, radio and newspaper ads; (3) buying food baskets, fuel, and other items for the needy during the year; and (4) incidentals.

Even after long and expensive campaigns, many Americans don't bother to vote. More than 130 million were old enough to vote for President and other elective offices on November 7, 1972, but about fifty-five million people did not vote on Election Day. There was a time in this country when only white male property owners could vote. It wasn't until 1870 that blacks could vote. It wasn't until 1920 that women could vote. It wasn't until just a few years ago that the eighteen- to twenty-year-olds could vote. But now that so many people are able to vote, why is it that so many people don't take advantage of their Constitutional right to vote and elect our lawmakers and representatives?

A few people don't vote because they are in prison, are mentally incompetent, or have a number of other reasons. Some people have valid excuses, but most of the people who abstain from voting do not. Many people don't register because they fail to meet the residency requirements or are just plain lazy. Some eligible voters don't like the candidate their party nominates so instead of voting for the other party's candidate they don't vote at all. Some voters can't make up their minds so they don't vote. This is hardly a reasonable excuse, considering that we make many decisions every day of our life. Some voters don't vote because they say they are "busy," but if they really wanted to vote they probably could. Most polling places are open from at least nine in the morning until at least nine at night. And a few people forget to vote. Some people don't vote because they feel that their candidate will win by such a wide margin that it won't matter if they do not vote, or it could be that they feel their candidate doesn't have a chance, so why should they vote if their vote doesn't count? Some voters are absent from their polling places without having obtained an absentee ballot. College students, sick people, and people on vacation fall into this category.

Political scientists and others who have done research on voting behavior have said that most of the people who don't vote act this way because they feel that their vote doesn't count. Well, let me point out just how much your vote counts. In 1824 John Quincy Adams beat Andrew Jackson for President by only 45,000 votes. In 1844 James Polk beat Henry Clay for President by only about 138,000 votes. In 1880 James Garfield beat Winfield Hancock for President by only about 7,000 votes. More recently in 1960 John Fitzgerald Kennedy beat Richard Nixon for President by only about 119,000 votes. And in 1968 Richard Nixon beat Hubert Humphrey for President by only about 500,000 votes. For every vote in Nixon's plurality over Humphrey, 150 people did not vote. In 1962 the governorship of Minnesota was decided by just 91 votes. Races have sometimes been decided by a single vote.

People are becoming more involved in government and are becoming increasingly aware of the national issues, but yet so many people don't vote. In Presidential elections about 65 percent of the electorate usually votes. This usually falls in an off election by about 5 to 10 percent. Voter participation has not changed much over the years either.

History has shown that an individual's vote does count. Many people have fought for the right to vote. It is a right that many people have long waited for. It is a right that permits us to have, as President Abraham Lincoln said on November 19, 1863, in his Gettysburg Address, a "government of the people, by the people, and for the people."

It has been suggested that voting be made mandatory in this country as is done in Australia, Belgium, and Austria. Anyone who is eligible to vote in Australia but doesn't is sent a "please explain letter" from the Commonwealth Electoral office. If that office doesn't accept the explanation, the nonvoter is fined $10. The result is that better than 90 percent of the Australian electorate votes.

While most Americans have strong opinions on important issues, their views are based more on emotion than knowledge. Pollster Louis Harris said that while 89 percent can identify their own state governor no more than 59 percent can name one U.S. senator from their state, only 39 percent can name both U.S. senators from their state, and only 46 percent know the name of their own congressman.

You may ask if it is worthwhile to fight the machine or city hall. It is worthwhile as long as there is a chance for better government. And even though some reform candidates lose, many times reforms are instituted as a result of issues brought forth during a campaign. You may also wonder if you have a chance. Remember, many of the bosses of Tammany Hall, including Tweed, started out as reformers.

The writer wrote the following for his college newspaper; however, this lesson in campus politics, although written in a satirical vein, parallels politics of the past and present in American cities:

When most people in the college community think of politics they think of city, state and federal governments, political parties, machines, campaigns, elections, and other things that happen in the world of politics. They might think about the corrupt bosses of past and present. But not many people would think that college politics is just as dirty and corrupt as any well-known boss was (Tweed, Daley, Croker, *et al.*). The only difference is that Tweed and the other bosses often helped many people. Tweed gave poor people food, clothes, fuel, and jobs.

In case you're planning to run in the Student Senate elections soon it might be to your advantage if you are sly, shrewd, power-hungry, radical, two-faced (try not to show it), a procrastinator, and a liar (but don't let them know that).

Here are some instructions on how to run a campaign; they have been proven to work: Remember to be kind to potential voters because without them you can't possibly win. However, after being elected, when you don't need them anymore, you can stab them in the back as you might have done in the first place.

While campaigning, spread rumors and make promises even though you have no intention of keeping some of them. Create false issues. Say, "We want this and we want that," but after you are elected it doesn't matter what change for the better they will see. Tear down your opponents' campaign posters.

An effective method of publicity is to distribute circulars under every door in the dormitories, on every car's windshield, and on the walls and bulletin boards in all the buildings. Don't worry about the cost of paper because the college provides it for your use.

On the night before the election have a "pot" and beer party. This is as good as buying votes. On election day, have your "ton ton macoute" (goon squad) work at the polls and put pressure on the voters. Have them raid the dorms and make sure everyone votes.

If you need assurance of winning you can always see to it that the people counting the ballots make a "few" mistakes. Just have a worker of yours on the Election Committee (those who supervise the polls and count the ballots). In case you're worrying about the campaign and election rules—don't, because they are rarely enforced and even if someone makes an inquest, it's too late.

Remember, you too can be the boss of the next "Tweed Ring" at college.[118]

★ 13 ★

The Ethics of Politics

I usually accept bribes from both sides so that tainted money can never influence my decision.

SIR FRANCIS BACON

Thomas Jefferson said, "Give up money, give up fame, give up science, give up the earth itself and all it contains, rather than to do an immoral act." It is unfortunate that Nixon's aides, when they were planning Watergate, didn't remember what Thomas Jefferson said almost two hundred years ago.

An example of the ethics of politics can well be discussed by looking at the incidents surrounding Watergate. Throughout the Watergate hearings it was apparent that many aides to then President Nixon (from his close, top assistant to White House staff who rarely spoke with him) were guilty of wrongdoings and a lack of curiosity in asking what was the right thing to do. We wondered how the President could select such people to work for him—people who conceived and committed dirty tricks and did not let the President know what they were doing. Americans also wondered how some White House and campaign staff people would see something that didn't seem right and ethical but not do anything about the situation. They didn't ask questions for fear of the answers they would get. We also wondered how so many dirty tricks could be done right under the President's nose, yet he claimed he knew nothing about them.

It has been said that you judge somebody by the friends and associates he has. But is the President, or a political boss, responsible for the actions of his workers? After all, it is impossible for the President or any political boss to observe the actions of his workers all the time. Naturally a great amount of trust must be assumed between the boss and his workers. The President or political boss is responsible because he hired the workers. Under the system of chain of command those at the top must take responsibility for their subordinates. But even if the boss were viewed as not legally responsible for his subordinates' actions the public will thereafter scrutinize the boss. We have seen this happen with Watergate.

Why does an individual, or a group, resort to dirty tricks and other illegal and unethical acts like those disclosed in the Watergate hearings? Was it greed, loyalty, or a combination of both, or something else? The President's staff, just like people who have political jobs that aren't protected by civil service, knew that if President Nixon was not reelected they would be out of a good job within a matter of months.

191

In this respect there was greed involved. To the victor belongs the spoils, and the workers and everyone who contributed money to Nixon's campaign knew the consequences of losing the election. Loyalty was also involved. The Nixon men lied to grand juries and others. They were evasive in their answers. They didn't tell all they knew until they were faced with imprisonment themselves. After being with someone who has power and influence you begin to admire and respect that person. Naturally the closer you are, the more loyal you will be. Political bosses and Presidents earn the loyalty of many people because they generate what people want—wealth, power, and prestige. If it is not the person whom they respect, it is the position. Many people who do not vote for the President respect him after he is elected.

Abe Beame, shortly after he took office as mayor of New York City in January, 1974, had to name a new person to be deputy mayor three times within a few weeks because at the last moment it was found that two of the prospective deputy mayors had problems with their income taxes. It's hard to get good help all over today!

Gene Boyce, an assistant minority counsel for the Senate Watergate Committee, said that Alexander Butterfield, a former deputy assistant to the President who first told the Watergate Committee that conversations in the White House were recorded, "seemed torn between loyalty to the President and honesty with us." Butterfield said, "This is something the President doesn't want revealed, but I don't have any other choice. I thought he was one of the finest public servants I'd ever met."

Before Watergate people thought conspiracy, burglary, perjury, secret meeting, mugging, kidnapping, call girls, blackmail, big expensive yachts, illegal wiretapping and eavesdropping, and espionage all lumped together could happen only in the movies. Boy, were they wrong! There had been espionage between nations and industrial espionage (stealing corporate secrets) for years. With the campaign of 1972 we saw a new dimension of espionage—political espionage.

Herbert L. Porter said during the Watergate hearings that he didn't do anything to say that what they were doing wasn't right because "of the fear of group pressure that would ensue, of not being a team player." Where were his independent values? But Porter was not the only person who feared not being a team player. Porter said his loyalty to President Nixon caused him to abdicate his own conscience and disapproval. Porter said "I first met Mr. Nixon when I was eight years old in 1946, when he ran for Congress in my home district. I wore Nixon buttons when I was eight and when I was ten and when I was twelve and when I was sixteen. My family worked for him in campaigns. I felt as if I had known this man all my life—not personally, perhaps, but in spirit. I felt a deep sense of loyalty to him."

Chairman Ervin questioned Maurice Stans, CREEP treasurer, about a $50,000 cash contribution given to a group of Maryland Republicans who were holding a banquet honoring then Vice-President Agnew. Stans said, "They wanted to make it look more successful than it apparently was." Stans admitted that the money had been sent in cash so that it could be mixed with other receipts. Ervin said, "They wanted to practice deception on the general public, as to the amount of honor that was paid to the Vice-President."

Jeb Stuart Magruder realized that when the breakin of Democratic headquarters was approved "it was illegal and that it was inappropriate." Magruder said, "Although I was aware that they were illegal we had become somewhat inured to using some activities that would help us in accomplishing what we thought was a cause, a legitimate cause." The Nixon staff thought that the end would justify the means. Magruder said at the time that he saw "ethical, legitimate people" breaking the law. At the hearings he said it was "an absolutely incorrect" decision to approve the breakin and that "two wrongs do not make a right."

Magruder was sentenced to ten months in prison for his participation in Watergate. After Magruder was sentenced he said, "I was ambitious, but I was not without morals or ethics or ideals. There was in me the same blend of ambition and altruism that I saw in many of my peers. Somewhere between my ambition and my ideals I lost my ethical compass. I found myself on a path that had not been intended for me by my parents or my principles or by my ethical instincts. It has led me to this courtroom."

L. Patrick Gray III, former director of the FBI, said that he destroyed some documents when told to do so by the President's top assistant, John Ehrlichman. Mr. Gray sadly said, "I believed that I was acting faithfully, loyally, properly and legally pursuant to instructions given me by top assistants to the President of the United States. I have come to believe, however, what I should have realized then, that my acceptance of the documents in the first place, and then keeping them out of the normal FBI files, was a grievous misjudgment." Mr. Gray did, at the time, what any other loyal American would do; he trusted the President of the United States and his top assistants. Looking back, how naive could one be? Would you have done different?

James McCord, one of the original Watergate defendants, testified that a very important reason for his participation in the Watergate operation was "the fact that the Attorney General himself, Mr. John Mitchell, at his office had considered and approved the plan, according to Mr. Liddy."[119] Mr. Baldwin, another defendant, was told that if at any time he had trouble establishing his authority for being in a certain place or for having a weapon, he was to mention John Mitchell. Baldwin further testified: "I felt that I was in no position to question John Mitchell," because if the Attorney General approved what they were doing it must be legal. He found he was wrong.

John J. Caulfield said before the Senate Committee that "it was a great honor for me to serve as a member of the President's staff. I had come from a rather humble background, a police officer. I did receive this great opportunity to serve on the President's staff. I felt very strongly about the President. I was very loyal to his people that I worked for, I place a high value upon loyalty. Now, out of the blue, I am injected into this scandal." Caulfield, at the request of John Dean, was the person who made an offer of executive clemency to James McCord.

Bernard L. Barker, one of those arrested in the Watergate complex, said he was looking for "documents that would prove that the Democratic Party and Senator McGovern were receiving contributions from organizations that were leftist organizations and inclined to violence in the United States, and also from the Castro government." The Republicans tried to link the Communists with the McGovern campaign. McGovern was so much to the left that it seemed possible at the time, especially to Nixon's reelection committee. A number of people who were involved in Watergate claimed they were bugging the Democrats for national security reasons, and they didn't think they were violating the law.

Charles Colson, special counsel to the President, said before the 1972 election that "I would walk over my grandmother if necessary" to get President Nixon reelected. The transcript of one of Nixon's conversations shows that the President, after noting that Democrats suspected the White House of responsibility for the Watergate breakin remarked, "They think I have people capable of it. And they are correct in that Colson would do anything." Colson pleaded guilty in June, 1974, to a charge that he attempted to obstruct justice and influence the trial of Dr. Daniel Ellsberg for releasing the Pentagon Papers in 1971. Because of Government interference, Dr. Ellsberg's trial was thrown out of court by the federal judge who handled the case. Colson admitted to trying to disseminate derogatory information about Ellsberg and his attorney.

The title of David Halberstam's book *The Best and the Brightest* is paradoxical because he shows that the men who made the policies on Vietnam were not, with some rare exceptions, "the best" or "the brightest." Halberstam took the view that victory for the United States in Vietnam was impossible, even from the beginning. That regardless of what we did Hanoi was certain to win, and that we turned what was basically a civil war in the south into an international conflict. He points out that our mistakes in Vietnam stem from some of our failures in China, and Vietnam was inherited in part from the McCarthy era, of a red under every bed. But while Communists are no longer completely unified, Communist rulers, like Brezhnev and Mao, still have the same aim—the conquest of power by any and all means. We have seen, in Vietnam, Americans deceived by Presidents, a waste of billions of dollars that could have, without a doubt, been put to better use in this country, and the death of more American soldiers than we lost in World War II.

In Vietnam, as in Watergate, we have seen the tragic degradation of this country's moral and ethical standards. Vietnam and Watergate could have been avoided. I don't think we can accept the Tolstoyan theory of history, that men are but chips on the great waves of events. The one good thing that happened as a result of Vietnam and Watergate is that we have had a chance to examine what we did wrong. This self-examination helps keep us in perspective and on a course. We have seen our mistakes and one hopes that we will learn from them. Unfortunately, in many cases we do not. Marx said history repeats itself. And how right he was.

Halberstam said the Kennedy-Johnson Secretary of Defense Robert Strange McNamara would "lie, dissemble, not just to the public . . . but inside, in high-level meetings . . . always to serve the Office of the President. Bob knew what was good for the cause, but sometimes at the expense of his colleagues . . . He loved power and sought it intensely, and he could be a ferocious infighter where the question of power was concerned. Nothing could stand between him and the President of the United States."[120]

McNamara did not stand alone. There were many like him before and while he was there, and after he left and at this very moment. Too many of the men in power in Washington loved power far too much for their own or their nation's good. Power corrupts. They manipulated their power in a Machiavellian fashion, with ruthlessness, lying, deceit, and an exaggerated sense of loyalty to the President.

Aristotle and Montesquieu felt that "men entrusted with power tend to abuse it."[121] It need not be that way, and it is easy to be a Monday morning quarterback, to look back and say you would have done things differently if it was up to you to make the decision. Only God knows what the future will bring us. For us only time will tell the story.

Notes

1. William L. Riordon, *Plunkitt of Tammany Hall* (New York: E. P. Dutton & Co., Inc., 1963), p. 17.

2. *Barnes vs. Roosevelt,* Supreme Court Appellate Division, vol. I, p. 76.

3. Thomas E. Dewey, *Twenty Against the Underworld* (Garden City, New York: Doubleday & Company, Inc., 1974).

4. A Report by the New York State Commission of Investigation (May 1964), p. 97.

5. *Delinquent Real Estate Taxes in Albany County,* a Report by the New York State Commission of Investigation (March 1961).

6. *Ibid.*

7. *Ibid.,* p. 24.

8. *Ibid.,* p. 29.

9. *Ibid.,* p. 37.

10. *Times Union* (Albany, New York), December 15, 1972, p. 3.

11. *An Investigation of Purchasing Practices and Procedures in Albany County,* a Report by the New York State Commission of Investigation (May 1964).

12. *Fifteenth Annual Report of the Temporary Commission of*

13. *Times Union,* December 17, 1972, p. B2.

14. Walter Goodman, *A Percentage of the Take* (New York: Far-*Investigation of the State of New York,* April 1973. rar, Straus and Giroux, 1971), p. 132.

15. *Fifteenth Annual Report.*

16. *Ibid.*

17. *Ibid.*

18. Edward S. Silver, Statement of Acting Chairman on behalf of the Temporary New York State Commission of Investigation, at the conclusion of the public hearings concerning its investigation of alleged police corruption, and other related matters in the City of Albany, October 1973.

19. *Ibid.* Hereafter this report will be referred to as the Silver Statement.

20. *Sixteenth Annual Report of the Temporary Commission of Investigation of the State of New York,* September 1974, pp. 299-301.

21. *Ibid.,* p. 319.

22. *Ibid.*, pp. 264-265.

23. *Ibid.*, p. 266.

24. The Silver Statement.

25. *Sixteenth Annual Report*, p. 168.

26. *Ibid.*, p. 382.

27. *Times Union*, June 6, 1973.

28. *Sixteenth Annual Report*, p. 175.

29. *Ibid.*, p. 176.

30. *Ibid.*, p. 180.

31. *Ibid.*, p. 181.

32. *Ibid.*, p. 182.

33. *Ibid.*, p. 183.

34. Lyndon Baines Johnson, *The Vantage Point* (New York: Popular Library, 1971), p. 100.

35. *The Knickerbocker News* (Albany, New York), October 19, 1966, p. 18A.

36. *Ibid.*, October 11, 1966, p. B1.

37. *Times Union*, July 4, 1974, p. 3.

38. *New York Daily News*, June, 1974.

39. *Times Union*, June 13, 1974, p. 11.

40. *Knickerbocker News*, October 16, 1974, p. 11A.

41. A. Connable and E. Silverfarb, *Tigers of Tammany* (New York: Holt, Rinehart and Winston, 1967), p. 25.

42. Gustavus Myers, *The History of Tammany Hall* (New York: Burt Franklin, 1917), p. 36.

43. U.S. House of Representatives Report No. 41 on Election Frauds in New York, 1868, pp. 12, 13, 20.

44. *Ibid.*, pp. 28, 40, 41.

45. *Ibid.*, pp. 626-627.

46. *Ibid.*, Report of Majority, pp. 40-45.

47. Jerome Mushkat, *Tammany: The Evolution of a Political Machine 1789-1865* (Syracuse, New York: Syracuse University Press, 1971), p. 366.

48. M. R. Werner, *Tammany Hall* (New York: Doubleday, Doran & Company, Inc., 1928), p. 194.

49. Connable and Silverfarb, *Tigers of Tammany*, p. 166.

50. Werner, *Tammany Hall*, p. 162.

51. Connable and Silverfarb, *Tigers of Tammany*, p. 156.

52. Report of the Special Committee of the Board of Aldermen Appointed to Investigate the Tweed "Ring" Frauds, Together with the Testimony Elicited During the Investigation. Board of Aldermen, January 4, 1878. Document No. 8, pp. 212-219.

53. *New York Times*, April 13, 1878.

54. Connable and Silverfarb, *Tigers of Tammany*, p. 178.

55. *New York Times*, June 2, 1886.

56. Connable and Silverfarb, *Tigers of Tammany*, p. 210.

57. Werner, *Tammany Hall*, p. 344.

58. Report and Proceedings of the Senate Committee Appointed to Investigate the Police Department of the City of New York, 1895, 5 volumes, vol. I, pp. 446-448. Hereafter this report will be referred to as the Lexow Investigation.

59. Lexow Investigation, vol. V, pp. 5378-5379.

60. Myers, *The History of Tammany Hall*, p. 292.

61. Lincoln Steffens, *The Shame of the Cities* (New York: Mc-Clure, Phillips & Co., 1904), p. 298.

62. Proceedings of the Court for Trial of Impeachments, The People of the State of New York Against William Sulzer, as Governor.

63. Werner, *Tammany Hall*, p. 517.

64. Riordon, *Plunkitt of Tammany Hall*, p. 5.

65. *Ibid.*, p. 11.

66. Connable and Silverfarb, *Tigers of Tammany*, p. 273.

67. *New York Times*, April 21, 1934, p. 2.

68. Warren Moscow, *The Life and Times of Carmine De Sapio and the Rise and Fall of Tammany Hall—The Last of the Big Time Bosses* (New York: Stein and Day Publishers, 1971), p. 12.

69. Goodman, *A Percentage of the Take*, p. 216.

70. *New York Times*, July 7, 1974, p. E5.

71. *Ibid.*, October 1, 1971.

72. *Ibid.*

73. *Ibid.*, June 1, 1970.

74. Mike Royko, *Boss* (New York: New American Library, 1971), p. 191.

75. *Ibid.*, p. 196.

76. *Ibid.*, p. 36.

77. *Chicago Tribune*, September 1, 1925.

78. Royko, *Boss*, p. 76.

79. *Ibid.*, p. 80.

80. T. Harry Williams, *Huey Long* (New York: Alfred A. Knopf, Inc., 1969), p. 6.

81. *Ibid.*, p. 18.

82. *Ibid.*, p. 535.

83. *Ibid.*, p. 735.

84. *New York Times*, September 11, 1935.

85. Merle Miller, *Plain Speaking* (New York: G. P. Putnam's Sons, 1974), p. 133.

86. *New York Times*, July 18, 1928.

87. Case Committee Report, *New Jersey State Senate Journal*, 1929, p. 1104.

88. Dayton D. McKean, *The Boss: The Hague Machine in Action* (New York: Russell & Russell, 1940), p. 78-81.

89. Elmer L. Irey and William J. Slocum, *The Tax Dodgers* (New York: Greenberg Publishing, 1948), pp. 247-248.

90. Alec Barbook, *God Save the Commonwealth* (Amherst, Massachusetts: University of Massachusetts Press, 1973), p. 23.

91. Joseph Dinneen, *The Purple Shamrock* (New York: Norton and Co., 1949), p. 45.

92. James Michael Curley, *I'd Do It Again* (Englewood Cliffs, New Jersey: Prentice-Hall, Inc., 1957), p. 36.

93. Dinneen, *The Purple Shamrock,* p. 184.

94. Martin and Susan Tolchin, *To The Victor* (New York: Vintage Books, 1971).

95. Riordon, *Plunkitt of Tammany Hall.*

96. Tolchin, *To The Victor,* p. 116.

97. *Ibid.,* p. 119.

98. *Ibid.*

99. *New York Times,* December 8, 1974, p. E7.

100. Tolchin, *To The Victor.*

101. *New York Sunday News,* May 12, 1974, p. C5.

102. Tolchin, *To The Victor.*

103. *Ibid.*

104. *Martindale-Hubbell Law Directory.*

105. *New York Daily News,* December 5, 1974, "The Old Pol Game."

106. William Domkoff, *Fat Cats and Democrats.*

107. *Congressional Quarterly,* Washington, D.C., May 18, 1974, pp. 1289-1292.

108. Mark J. Green, James M. Fallows, and David R. Zwick, *Who Runs Congress?,* Ralph Nader Congress Project (New York: Grossman Publishers, 1971).

109. See *Influence in Government Procurement,* Hearings before the Investigations Subcommittee on the Committee on Expenditures in the Executive Department, U.S. Senate, 1949. See also Senate Report 1232, 81st Congress, 2nd Session, 1950.

110. See Study of *Reconstruction Finance Corporation,* Hearings and Reports, U.S. Senate, 1950-1951, 3 vols. See especially *Favoritism and Influence,* Senate Report 76, 82nd Congress, 1st Session.

111. See *Internal Revenue Investigation,* Hearings before a Subcommittee of the Committee on Ways and Means, U.S. House of Representatives, 82nd Congress, 1st Session.

112. Robert N. Winter-Berger, *The Washington Payoff* (New York: Dell Publishing Co., Inc., 1972), p. 12.

113. David Loth, *Public Plunder—A History of Graft in America* (New York: Carrick & Evans, Inc., 1938), p. 79.

114. *Ibid.,* p. 81.

115. Steffens, *The Shame of the Cities,* p. 30.

116. *Ibid.*, p. 294.

117. *Olmstead vs. the United States*, 1927.

118. *The Westerner*, Western New England College, Springfield, Massachusetts, March 21, 1973.

119. Testimony of James McCord, vol. 1, p. 128, the Ervin Committee.

120. David Halberstam, *The Best and the Brightest* (Greenwich, Connecticut: Fawcett Publications, Inc., 1972).

121. See Locke, *The Second Treatise on Civil Government*, section 141.

Index

201